THE
EVERYTHING
®

CIVIL WAR
BOOK

Everything you need to know about
the war that divided the nation

Donald Vaughan

D0520168

Adams Media Corporation
Avon, Massachusetts

Copyright ©2000, Adams Media Corporation.
All rights reserved. This book, or parts thereof, may not be reproduced in
any form without permission from the publisher; exceptions are made for
brief excerpts used in published reviews.

An Everything® Series Book.
Everything® is a registered trademark of Adams Media Corporation.

Published by Adams Media Corporation
57 Littlefield Street, Avon, MA 02322. U.S.A.
www.adamsmedia.com

ISBN: 1-58062-366-2

Printed in the United States of America.

J I H G F E D C B

Library of Congress Cataloging-in-Publication Data
available upon request from the publisher.

This publication is designed to provide accurate and authoritative information
with regard to the subject matter covered. It is sold with the understanding that
the publisher is not engaged in rendering legal, accounting, or other professional
advice. If legal advice or other expert assistance is required, the services of a
competent professional person should be sought.
— From a *Declaration of Principles* jointly adopted by a Committee of the
American Bar Association and a Committee of Publishers and Associations

Cover illustrations by Barry Littmann
Interior illustrations by Kurt Dolber

This book is available at quantity discounts for bulk purchases.
For information, call 1-800-872-5627.

Contents

CHAPTER 1
Causes of the Civil War / 1

CHAPTER 2
On the Eve of War / 25

CHAPTER 3
Political Leaders of the North and South / 51

CHAPTER 4
Military Leaders of the North and South / 83

CHAPTER 5
The Major Battles of the Civil War / 119

CONTENTS

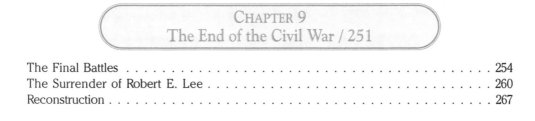

CHAPTER 9
The End of the Civil War / 251

APPENDICES

INDEX / 287

A Different Kind of War

Few events in the history of the United States have captured the hearts and minds of the American people quite like the Civil War. The four-year conflict threatened to render a republic still in its infancy and pushed to the breaking point the strength and endurance of its people. In the end, as the smoke of the final battle cleared over the countryside, the North was the decided victor. But the cost of that victory was tremendous. The once proud South lay in ruins, its lofty goals of self-government slowly beaten down by a war of battle and attrition that cost it almost everything it had in terms of manpower, industry, and commerce. And while the North didn't suffer quite as much in terms of physical destruction, it too paid a high price in lives lost and families torn asunder. Observed Confederate General Robert E. Lee during the battle of Fredericksburg: "It is well that war is so terrible, or we should grow too fond of it." At the close of the Civil War, there was no remaining fondness for war on either side.

The Civil War was unique in many ways. It was the first "modern" war in terms of weaponry (the breechloader and the magazine rifle were both introduced during the conflict), and it was the first major war to make full use of the telegraph (developed in 1837) to relay information to and from battlefields. In addition, it was the first to use a railway system—more than 30,000 miles worth, all but about 9,000 miles of it in the North—for troop and supply deployment.

Most importantly for historians today, the Civil War was also one of the first major military events to be widely chronicled by both sides as it happened. Newspaper and magazine journalists from the North and South, as well as overseas, covered every aspect of the conflict from beginning to end, often with vivid, at-the-scene descriptions of major battles. Photographers, most notably

Mathew Brady, and sketch artists from the major magazines also brought the war to life, with both brutal and touching images of its carnage and participants. A picture, they say, is worth a thousand words, and the work of Brady and others who covered the war from the front lines speaks volumes.

The war was barely over before participants and observers raced to publish their thoughts and interpretations on the previous four years. They all, it seemed, from Jefferson Davis and Ulysses S. Grant to the battle-hardened private, were eager to tell the world what they saw, felt, and experienced as the war raged around them. Many soldiers wrote long letters home or detailed their day-to-day activities in diaries that managed to survive the ravages of time. The result is a remarkable record of how the war began, how its battles were planned and fought, how the governments of the North and South struggled to survive and carry on, and how the conflict affected the weary hearts and minds of the entire nation. Written in these time-worn pages are tales of remarkable bravery and craven cowardice in the face of overwhelming odds, of stunning military victories and devastating defeats, of heart-wrenching acts of kindness and revolting acts of butchery and violence. Every emotion from exultation to paralyzing fear was chronicled in the simple words of the men and women who experienced them, amazing annals that today help put a very human face on a war that to many is now nothing more than a long list of boring facts and figures.

Over the years, there has been a strong tendency to idealize the Civil War. As each generation grows farther and farther from the conflict, its brutality and bloodshed is often glossed over with a *Gone with the Wind* type romanticism. But the Civil War was far from romantic. For most participants, it was a horrifying nightmare of bloodshed and innocence lost. Men—many in their teens—died by the thousands in a single battle, and they often died horribly, body parts blown away at close range by metal balls the size of a man's thumb. The lucky ones died instantly. Those who weren't so lucky lay bleeding on the battlefield until their life ebbed away or,

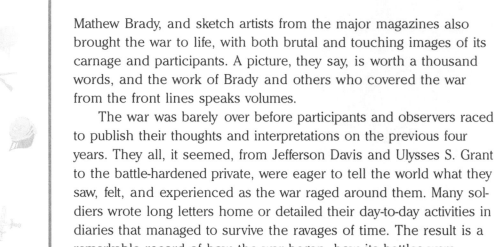

sometimes worse, were carried off to field hospitals where amputation (often without anesthesia) was the treatment of choice for most battle injuries.

Imagine for a moment that you're a soldier in the thick of battle at Fredericksburg or Gettysburg or Chickamauga. It doesn't matter what side you're on, the feeling of dread and hopelessness is the same. Visualize the scream of enemy artillery, of mortars exploding around you, of bullets whizzing loudly past your head. Men who just months ago might have been your neighbors are shooting at you. They're so close that you can see the panic and fear in their mud-stained faces, the same panic and fear that is no doubt reflected in your own. You shoot and reload, shoot and reload, praying to God that you get them before they get you. Without warning, your best friend is shot in the head by a dreaded Minie ball. It happens so quickly that he doesn't even have time to cry out, his lifeless body  simply falls at your feet. But you don't have time to mourn the loss of your friend's life—you're too busy fighting to preserve your own. Such was the Civil War for hundreds of thousands of men.

This book is an overview of that conflict. The next nine chapters contain everything you need to know about the Civil War—how it started, the men who fought it, the battles that cost so many lives. You'll learn about the two warring sides, their weapons, uniforms, camp life, and more. And you'll learn how the nation began the lengthy healing process once the war came to an end.

This book doesn't attempt to interpret or analyze the Civil War. Instead, it offers a simple but comprehensive chronicle of the conflict from start to finish, derived from the diaries, books, and recollections of the men and women who experienced it. It's in their memories that this book is dedicated.

1

Causes
of the
Civil War

It's impossible to narrow the cause of the Civil War to a single issue or act. Most people today, if asked, would probably say slavery. But while it's true that slavery was one of the most important contributing factors to the conflict, it was not the singular cause. In truth, the war was the result of myriad cultural and political issues that perniciously set the North and the South against each other for decades before the first shots of the war were fired.

To understand why the Civil War occurred, it is important to know what the United States was like in the mid-1800s. Unlike the 50 states we have today, the United States in the years preceding the Civil War was more like two separate countries living together as one. The North and the South were more disparate than they were alike, and these differences became increasingly vivid until, like a bickering married couple on the verge of divorce, they simply couldn't bear to live together anymore.

A short 10 years before the war began, the vast majority of Americans in both the North and the South lived in rural areas

rather than cities. Agriculture remained the biggest contributor to the nation's economy, and in this way, the two regions were very much alike. But between 1850 and 1860, the nation's burgeoning cities—particularly in the North—received a massive influx of immigrants. The number of farm dwellers increased by 25 percent during this period, while urban populations rose by a remarkable 75 percent. New York City, for example, reached a population of nearly 800,000 by 1860, making it the greatest city in the Western hemisphere.

Many of these new city dwellers were country folk looking for a new way of life, but a greater number were immigrants from overseas, primarily Ireland and Germany, hoping to strike it rich in the Land of Opportunity. As a result of this influx, the nation's population increased by 35 percent to nearly 31 million. But the South didn't benefit from this population spurt. By 1850, only a third of

Americans lived in the South, compared to half at the beginning of the century. And of the nation's 10 largest cities, only New Orleans was located in the lower Southern region.

Indeed, the years before the war's onset saw some dramatic and fundamental changes in the nation's face. The North quickly took advantage of the amazing new products resulting from the industrial revolution, such as Cyrus McCormick's mechanical reaper, and great factories sprang up almost overnight as huge deposits of iron, coal, copper, and other important manufacturing basics were discovered and made available. It would be this industrial power, this ability to produce weapons and other goods, that would give the North a decided edge as the Civil War progressed.

The economy of the South, in comparison, remained based primarily on agriculture, with England and the Northern states being its biggest customers. (In 1852, a mere tenth of the goods manufactured in America came from Southern factories and mills.) Cotton, in particular, was a huge cash crop that brought large amounts of money to the region, though tobacco, rice, indigo, and other products were also widely grown. By 1860, the South was producing nearly three-fourths of the raw cotton used throughout the world—an estimated 1 billion pounds a year. But because the South lacked the manufacturing capability of the North, the region was forced to buy back the goods created from the products it grew, placing it at an economic disadvantage that angered many Southerners. This inequity played a large role in widening the division between the North and the South.

EXPANSION AND STATES' RIGHTS

As the United States thrived and flourished during the early nineteenth century, the demand for expansion grew increasingly loud. The Western regions cried to be settled, and a growing number of Americans felt the nation's borders were ordained by God to extend from the Atlantic Ocean to the Pacific, a philosophy known as Manifest Destiny. If regions owned by other countries could be purchased, so be it. If not, they were more than likely to be taken by force. The Mexican War (1846–48), for

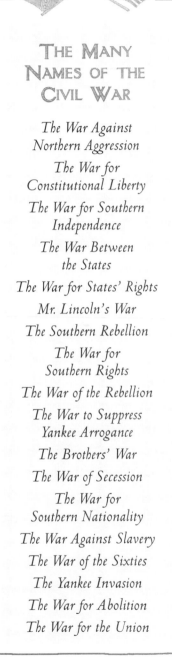

THE MANY NAMES OF THE CIVIL WAR

The War Against Northern Aggression

The War for Constitutional Liberty

The War for Southern Independence

The War Between the States

The War for States' Rights

Mr. Lincoln's War

The Southern Rebellion

The War for Southern Rights

The War of the Rebellion

The War to Suppress Yankee Arrogance

The Brothers' War

The War of Secession

The War for Southern Nationality

The War Against Slavery

The War of the Sixties

The Yankee Invasion

The War for Abolition

The War for the Union

example, was little more than a trumped-up conflict designed to wrest large tracks of Western territory from Mexico when that country refused to sell the desired lands. The United States provoked Mexico again and again until Mexico finally responded, and war was immediately declared. Though small in number, American forces were better equipped than their Mexican counterparts, and after several relatively one-sided battles, the war ended on September 14, 1847, with the American occupation of Mexico City. On February 2, 1848, the Treaty of Guadalupe Hidalgo turned over to the United States 525,000 square miles of territory that would eventually become California, Nevada, Utah, most of Arizona and New Mexico, and parts of Colorado and Wyoming. It was the largest addition to the United States since the Louisiana Purchase in 1803.

The acquisition of this Western territory, as well as other tracts acquired earlier, created a growing rift between the North and the South in regard to the issue of slavery and, at the same time, states' rights. The South, naturally, wanted the new territories to allow slavery (years of planting land-depleting crops such as tobacco and cotton forced many Southern plantation owners to desperately seek new farmland), but the North did not. The Northwest Ordinance, enacted in 1787, stated that all territories north of the Ohio River were to be free and that those south were to be slave, and up to 1819, the two regions were equally divided, with 11 states each. However, pending growth required new action.

The first solution was the 1820 Missouri Compromise, legislation that was specifically designed to keep both sides happy. The issue came to a head in 1819, when Missouri requested admittance to the United States as a slave state—an act that went against the Northwest Ordinance, since most of the territory lay north of the Ohio River. Worse, the addition of a new slave state would disrupt the balance previously enjoyed between the North and the South. Luckily, Maine asked to be admitted as a free state at almost the same time as Missouri, thus maintaining parity.

But it quickly became evident that the addition of new states would result in constant conflict. To settle the issue of Missouri's

CIVIL WAR FACTOID

The first combat fatality of the war was a man named Elmer Ellsworth, who was shot on May 24, 1861, while removing a Confederate flag from the roof of a hotel in Alexandria, Virginia. Ellsworth was a close friend of Abraham Lincoln.

THE TRAGEDY OF HUMAN CARGO

Slavery is a most barbaric institution, and the import of slaves to the United States from West Africa was barbarism in its rawest form. Commonly known as the Triangle Trade, it involved exchanging rum, cotton, and other goods with Arab traders for West African slaves, selling the slaves to plantation owners in the West Indies, and returning to America with profits from the sale of goods, such as sugar and molasses, as well as slaves who had been "broken in" on the Caribbean islands. This seasoning process involved placing new slaves with old hands, who taught them what to do and made them more docile and subservient, a process that doubled their value. The number of Africans who were snatched from their homeland as part of the Triangle Trade is impossible to determine, though the number of slaves brought to the United States is estimated at between 10 and 12 million. Many slaves were prisoners of war, others were criminals or debtors, and some were simply villagers sold by their money-hungry tribal kings and chieftains.

The voyage from Africa to the West Indies was the most harrowing and brutal portion of the trip. Slaves, having first been fattened up like cattle, were placed in a ship's hold almost like cordwood, with little room to sit up, much less stand. They were painfully shackled together, poorly fed (many slaves refused to eat the strange food they were given), given impure water to drink, and lacked any type of sanitary facilities. This lack of basic sanitation, combined with the vomiting that often resulted from fear and seasickness, created an almost overpowering stench in a slave ship's cargo hold and helped promote a wide range of diseases.

The voyage from Africa to the West Indies could take from 6 to 10 weeks, and many slaves died during the trip, their bodies simply tossed overboard to feed the sharks. If a ship's provisions ran low, the slaves were the last to be fed and the first to be discarded if necessary. Many slaves, when given the opportunity, threw themselves into the ocean rather than face a life of bondage in an unknown land.

The importation of slaves to the United States was banned by federal law in 1808, but the institution was able to continue right along as the slaves who were already here reproduced and kept the cycle going generation by generation, much to the delight of Southern plantation owners. The first United States census in 1790 counted 697,897 slaves. Twenty years later, despite a two-year ban on slave importation, the figure had grown by an astounding 70 percent.

William Lloyd Garrison

Born in 1805, Garrison grew up in a poor but religious family in Newburyport, Massachusetts. He attended school until the age of 13, then became an apprentice at the *Newburyport Herald*. Within four years, he was writing hard-hitting essays for the paper's editorial page. In 1827, Garrison moved to Boston to write for a temperance newspaper called the *National Philanthropist*. There, he met abolitionist Benjamin Lundy, who brought him over to the cause. However, Garrison quickly broke with Lundy and his followers over the issue of slave colonization (Garrison believed in equal rights for all, not in shipping freed slaves back to Africa) and started his own radical branch of the abolitionist movement.

Garrison is probably best known as the publisher of the leading abolitionist newspaper of its time, the Boston-based *Liberator*, which he began publishing in 1831. Though its circulation never exceeded three thousand, the newspaper was a leading voice in the New England abolitionist movement and carried wide influence. Garrison often described slavery as a criminal act, and his fervor and commitment brought many New Englanders into the abolitionist fold.

statehood and keep things peaceful for a while, members of Congress, led by noted orator and statesman Henry Clay of Virginia, hammered out the Missouri Compromise, which admitted Missouri as a slave state and Maine as a free state and nullified the Northwest Ordinance by redrawing the boundaries of slavery from north of the Ohio River to north of the 36° 30' parallel.

However, the territory acquired as a result of the Mexican War would require another compromise 30 years later. The Compromise of 1850, brokered again by Henry Clay, with tremendous input from Daniel Webster of Massachusetts, did little to affect the institution of slavery in the United States, aside from officially prohibiting it in the District of Columbia. It admitted California into the union as a free state but allowed newly acquired territories to decide for themselves whether slavery should be permitted. Clay and Webster, who both opposed slavery but felt the issue shouldn't be allowed to tear the nation apart, struggled to make the Compromise acceptable to both the North and the South. However, neither side was particularly happy over the legislation. Some Southern politicians, such as John C. Calhoun of South Carolina, felt the Compromise didn't go far enough in securing the future of slavery, and they raised the specter of secession if things weren't eventually changed. The North, on the other hand, was appalled by a provision within the bill that required Northerners to return escaped slaves to their owners. But despite these objections, the Compromise was passed by the House and the Senate and, for a decade, helped keep the peace between the two regions.

The Missouri Compromise and the Compromise of 1850 both dealt in part with an issue of particular sensitivity to the South—states' rights. The federal government's right to decide important issues within a

John C. Calhoun

If any single individual can be credited with instigating the Civil War, it's John Caldwell Calhoun, one of the South's most vocal states' rights and slavery advocates. Calhoun was born near Abbeville District in South Carolina in 1782. He received his education in the North, attending Yale University and receiving his law degree in Litchfield, Connecticut. He entered politics at 26, serving two years as a member of the South Carolina legislature. In 1810, he was elected to the U.S. House of Representatives as a War Democrat and received much publicity for his endorsement of United States participation in the War of 1812. Calhoun was appointed secretary of war by James Monroe in 1817 and became vice president under John Quincy Adams in 1825. However, Calhoun's feelings toward the federal government began to change during his second term as vice president, this time under Andrew Jackson.

At issue was a protective tariff on imported goods that Calhoun felt exploited South Carolina. It was while fighting the tariff that Calhoun (who resigned the vice presidency to return to the Senate) developed his infamous "doctrine of nullification," which held that state conventions could nullify any national law by declaring it unconstitutional. When Congress passed a second protective tariff in 1832, South Carolina embraced Calhoun's theory and nullified the new import tax. The resulting constitutional crisis included a threat by South Carolina to secede from the Union and counter threats from President Jackson to employ federal troops to prevent such an action. South Carolina eventually backed down, but the conflict bolstered the issue of states' rights, which Calhoun saw as an effective way of protecting the South from Northern encroachment.

Calhoun remained an influential power in the Senate until 1850. His last speech—read by a colleague because Calhoun was too ill—argued against the Compromise of 1850, which Calhoun felt did not sufficiently protect the institution of slavery. Calhoun also noted that continued interference by the North on the issue would no doubt force the Southern states from the Union. Calhoun died from tuberculosis on May 31, 1850, just a few weeks after his final speech and a full decade before the civil war he had forewarned.

THE UNDERGROUND RAILROAD

Despite its name, the Underground Railroad was not a real railroad but a loose system of safe havens (typically the homes or businesses of free slaves and white abolitionists) that helped slaves escape to freedom in the North.

Runaway slaves usually traveled the Underground Railroad by night, walking or riding from one safe-house, or "station," to another until they were able to cross the border into a free state. The most frequently traveled routes ran through Ohio, Indiana, and western Pennsylvania. Many slaves continued on until they were safely in Canada, which refused to deport escaped slaves.

(continued)

state was something with which many people, especially those in the South, vehemently disagreed, and the shifting balance of power between the federal government and individual states would remain a hot-button issue that would contribute strongly to the beginning of the Civil War.

The Tenth Amendment to the United States Constitution states that "the powers not delegated to the United States by the Constitution, nor prohibited by it to the States, are reserved to the states respectively, or to the people." To most citizens of the South, this amendment clearly prevented the federal government from inter-fering in a state's individual affairs—such as the institution of slavery. If changes were to be made, only the population of a given state could make them. The South felt the federal government was over-stepping its bounds every time it attempted to abolish or otherwise deal with the issue of slavery in that region or in territories seeking statehood and balked loudly whenever challenges were made. In short, the proud Southern states didn't like being told what to do and begged simply to be left alone.

An example of how strongly the Southern states felt about Northern intrusion can be found in South Carolina's 1832 "nullifi-cation," or suspension, of a heavy tariff placed on imports four years earlier at the insistence of Northern merchants who wanted to protect their goods and profits by increasing the price of European imports. John C. Calhoun, one of the South's most vocal advocates of states' rights (and slavery), called the tariff unconstitutional and laid the groundwork to have it nullified. When a South Carolina state convention issued an ordinance to do just that, it nearly brought the nation to the brink of war. President Andrew Jackson threatened to send federal troops to the port of Charleston to enforce the tariff, and the governor of South Carolina threatened to meet them with an armed militia. At the last minute, war was averted with the Compromise Tariff of 1833 (also brokered in part by Henry Clay), which gradually reduced tariffs until 1842. As a result, the South Carolina convention voted to repeal the Ordinance of Nullification, and war was averted, at least for a while.

THE ISSUE OF SLAVERY

Without question, the issue of slavery was one of the most volatile in the smoldering enmity between the North and the South. In the decade prior to the onset of hostilities, the voice of abolition grew steadily louder in the North, forcing the South into an increasingly stoic and uncompromising defensive position. The more the North insisted that slavery was morally wrong and should be abolished, the more the South resisted. But it would take the 1860 presidential election of Abraham Lincoln—and the South's perception that his administration was going to push for the abolition of slavery nationwide—to cause 11 Southern states to eventually secede.

Though the imprisonment of another human being for forced labor is unimaginable today, the institution of slavery has a long history in this country. Slaves were used for labor in the original 13 colonies (the first shipment of Africans were brought to this country in August 1619, arriving at Jamestown, Virginia, on a Dutch ship; they were sold as indentured servants, though their plight was little different from that of outright slaves), and some of the United States' most revered figures, including George Washington and Thomas Jefferson, were slave owners. (Washington freed his slaves in his will; Jefferson, his finances shaky, had to rely on his creditors to grant his five favorite slaves their freedom.) By the time of the Revolutionary War, slavery was legal in all 13 colonies, though those in the Northern regions were beginning to realize that the institution simply wasn't profitable. The five northern colonies eventually banned slavery outright, but it continued to flourish in the South, where slaves were used to work plantations and large farms.

Between 1510 and 1870, more than nine million Africans were captured and taken from their homeland for a life of slavery around the world. Nearly half of them were bought to the United States, primarily the Southern region, where the climate encouraged agriculture on a large scale. Outlawed in all Northern states by 1846, slavery quickly became the backbone of the Southern agricultural economy. The growing global demand for cotton, in particular, gave the institution new life at a time when many people in both the

THE UNDERGROUND RAILROAD
(continued from previous page)

Abolitionists participating in the Underground Railroad were subject to harassment and even prison. But as the issue of slavery became increasingly important, more and more abolitionists volunteered their time and homes. Free blacks, women's antislavery societies, and various abolitionist organizations provided food, clothing, and money to runaway slaves over the course of their escape, which could take days and even weeks.

THE FUGITIVE SLAVE ACT

The Fugitive Slave Act required federal marshals and deputies to aid in the capture and return of escaped slaves throughout the United States. It was included in the legislation as a way of appeasing the South, but it served only to inflame the angry passions of abolitionists in the North. Antislavery and anti-Southern sentiment skyrocketed in the Northern states as a result of the Fugitive Slave Act, and moderate abolitionists joined their more militant brothers in protesting what they saw as federally subsidized kidnapping.

The Act provided for the appointment of commissioners to administer the cases of captured runaways. These commissioners were paid on a case by case basis—$10 for each fugitive slave sent back to the South and $5 for each accused black person who was set free. As might be expected, this bizarre bounty system quickly became rife with corruption, and the number of convicted runaways far exceeded the number of blacks who were exonerated. In many cases, blacks were returned to the South based only on affidavits from Southern courts or the vague statements of white witnesses.

Abolitionists feared that the new law would lead to terrible abuses against Negroes living in the North, and they were right. There are reports of Southern bounty hunters arresting and sometimes kidnapping blacks who had lived in the North as free people for more than 20 years, or claiming children born in freedom to escaped slaves as "property" of their parents' original owners. As a result, efforts on the part of abolitionists to protect blacks living in the North increased dramatically, though many blacks, believing that there were virtually no laws to protect them, fled to Canada.

North and the South were starting to believe that it would disappear by itself if left alone.

Growing and harvesting cotton was hard, backbreaking labor, even with the use of Eli Whitney's cotton gin, and black slaves were commonly used to do the work that white farmers and plantation owners thought was beneath them. So important had cotton become as a cash crop that of the 2.5 million slaves engaged as agricultural workers in 1850, 75 percent worked at cotton production. So it's easy to see how the South, which had become so dependent on the labor force of slavery, was reluctant to give it up. By the time the first shots of the Civil War were fired, more than four million slaves lived in the South—approximately one-third of its population.

THE LIFE OF A SLAVE

Contrary to the relatively happy picture of plantation slaves painted by books such as *Gone with the Wind*, the life of a slave in the South was exhausting, degrading, and filled with violence. Slaves had no rights, they were not allowed to legally marry or own property, and slave families were often divided up and sold piecemeal to different owners at whim. Those employed as farmhands faced backbreaking labor and grueling hours. Typically, farmhands were to be in the fields at daybreak and were forced to work almost nonstop until the sun went down, with only 15 minutes at noon for a quick, seldom satisfying lunch. Most farmhands worked six days a week, with Sunday off if they were lucky. During what little free time they had, slaves took care of their own quarters, tended a small garden, or worked on neighboring plantations for a little spending money.

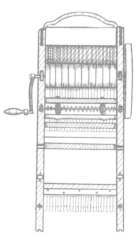

The conditions in which most slaves lived were deplorable. They slept in cramped, drafty quarters, often packed six to twelve in a single shack. The food they were given was usually of poor nutritional value, and medical care was often unheard of. As a result, it is estimated that fewer than four in 100 slaves lived past the age of 60. Slaves commonly died of diseases such as malaria, yellow fever, cholera, and typhoid, and those that weren't taken by illness were often afflicted with worms, dysentery, and painful, rotting teeth.

Slaves were expected to obey their masters without question and to always show great humility by lowering their gaze and speaking softly whenever they were in the company of whites. Anything that remotely resembled dissent was met with harsh, often brutal punishment, including vicious beatings with whips, chains, and fists—usually in front of other slaves to teach them a lesson as well. Slaves that tried to escape were sometimes hobbled with a spike through the ankle or placed in iron fetters. Slave collars were also commonly employed to teach troublesome servants a lesson. Some had bells on them that told all of their every move; a more punishing version had lengthy prongs sticking out on four sides that prevented its wearer from lying down. Minor offenses such as drunkenness or simple disobedience were often punished by a day in wooden stocks, which clamped tightly around the slave's neck and wrists.

Since slaves seldom benefited from their labor, most worked as slowly and poorly as they could get away with without being punished, contributing to the inherent inefficiency of the system as a whole. But as the years wore on, a life in bondage drove many slaves to despair. They had little to live for—nothing to look forward to except hard labor until the day they died—and many took their own lives. As a final outrage, dead slaves were often buried at night because their families and friends had to work all day. In the eyes of many slave owners, a slave's death wasn't sufficient cause to lose even an hour of work time.

Plantation and farm owners worked hard to keep their slaves subservient, but rebellion was more common than many people realize. As noted, many slaves revolted by working slowly, poorly, and inefficiently, or by quietly sabotaging tools and farm equipment. But there were violent and armed insurrections as well, as might be expected when an entire body of people is kept shackled in forced labor. The 1831 Nat Turner Rebellion is one of the most famous slave uprisings, but it certainly wasn't the first. In 1708, a Native American slave and a Negro woman in New York killed their owner and his

The Nat Turner Rebellion

In the annals of slave rebellion, the story of Nat Turner is one of the most dramatic in terms of intent, violence, and bloodshed. Raised by his African-born mother on a Virginia plantation owned by Samuel Turner, Nat Turner was taught to read by his owner's son. His father escaped when Turner was young and never returned, and Turner himself managed to escape at one point, only to return four weeks later of his own volition.

Turner became extremely religious over the years and began preaching the gospel to his fellow slaves, who came to call him The Prophet. In 1825, Turner reported having visions of the Second Coming of Christ, and other visions that encouraged him to kill his enemies with their own weapons. In 1831, a solar eclipse was interpreted as a sign from God that Turner should kill his oppressors and lead his people to freedom.

In August 1831, Turner and seven other slaves killed the entire Travis family (who had acquired Turner from Samuel Turner) with hatchets and axes, fulfilling God's "command" that he slay his enemies with their own tools. Turner and his followers then began terrorizing the area, picking up recruits from other area plantations until their numbers totaled more than 60. Their goal was the county seat of Jerusalem, Virginia, where they planned to take the armory, though they apparently hadn't thought past that.

Turner and his followers attacked area farms and plantations for two days, but the rebellion quickly became disorganized, with many members getting drunk on stolen liquor. Word of the rebellion spread rapidly through the area, and Turner's followers were met by an armed militia outside Jerusalem. Many were killed or captured in the ensuing battle. Turner and approximately 20 followers managed to escape the melee but were attacked again a short time later. Turner escaped again, this time with four followers, and hid in the woods for nearly six weeks before he was finally captured.

On November 11, 1831, Turner and 16 followers were executed by hanging for the bloody uprising, but their deaths wouldn't be the last. Slaves throughout the region were terrorized and attacked by federal troops, and more than two hundred slaves were killed as payback and as a warning to others that any attempt at insurrection would be met with harsh punishment. Another bit of fallout resulting from Nat Turner's rebellion was legislation that prevented slaves from learning to read or write. An ignorant slave, the thinking went, was a docile slave.

family of six. And in 1712 and 1741, two more New York slave riots resulted in the death of 13 whites and 50 blacks.

Probably the most violent mass slave uprising was the Stono Rebellion, which occurred on September 9, 1739, in Stono, South Carolina. In that incident, a slave named Jemmy led approximately 20 other slaves in an attack on a store that resulted in the death of two white shopkeepers. Taking what weapons they could find, including guns and powder, the small group quickly grew to nearly 100 slaves. With St. Augustine, Florida—and supposed freedom—their destination, the gang went on a killing spree that resulted in the deaths of more than 30 whites. An armed militia eventually cornered the group in a field, slaughtering 44 of them. According to written accounts of the incident, many of the murdered slaves were decapitated, and their heads placed on fence posts as a gruesome warning to others who might be considering a similar plot. However, two other violent slave revolts occurred in South Carolina that same year, resulting in even more brutal laws for the control of slaves.

THE MANY VOICES OF ABOLITION

The call for the end of slavery could be heard as far back as Colonial days, but the abolitionist movement didn't become a serious force in the North until the 1830s. Driven primarily by religious fundamentalism, early abolitionists felt that slavery was a moral abomination in the eyes of God and that the sooner it was abolished, the better. Not surprisingly, Southerners felt otherwise and viewed the growing abolitionist movement as just another Northern force trying to encroach on their lifestyle and economy.

The first official abolitionist organization, the American Anti-Slavery Society, was founded in December 1833 and included William Lloyd Garrison, the publisher of the abolitionist newspaper *The Liberator*, and industrialists Arthur and Lewis Tappan.

John Brown

John Brown was a vociferous opponent of slavery. Unfortunately, he was also more than willing to use violence and bloodshed to further the cause he so fervently believed in. As a result, Brown is best remembered today as the radical abolitionist who fomented a slave rebellion and tried to capture the armory at Harpers Ferry, Virginia.

Brown was born in Torrington, Connecticut, in 1800 to poor Calvinist parents. Though he received little schooling as a child, Brown would grow up to be a powerful and charismatic speaker who drew the attention of many prominent abolitionists, including Frederick Douglass

Brown found his true calling as a radical abolitionist. In 1855, he joined five of his sons in the Kansas Territory to aid Free-Soilers in their fight against proslavery factions. His most notorious contribution to the battle was the 1856 slaughter of proslavery settler James Doyle; Doyle's two sons, William and Drury; Allen Wilkinson, a member of the proslavery territorial legislature, and Bill Sherman, another proslavery settler. Brown and his sons were never arrested for the killings, which came to be known as the Pottawatomie Massacre.

Brown later conceived a plan to lead a slave insurrection in the South and start a republic of free blacks in Virginia's Appalachian Mountains. The scheme was doomed from the beginning, but Brown was able to persuade a number of prominent abolitionists to back it. On October 16, 1859, he and 22 followers rode into Harpers Ferry. They planned to take the federal arsenal and armory there and use the weapons to arm slaves in a rebellion they hoped would spread throughout the South.

The group was able to take the poorly guarded arsenal and armory with relative ease, and Brown immediately sent two black followers into the countryside to recruit area slaves for his grand rebellion. But Brown's plans quickly turned to shambles. The thousands of slaves Brown had expected never showed up. Instead, the residents of Harpers Ferry surrounded the arsenal and armory, trapping Brown and his men inside. The angry mob then began firing on them, killing two of Brown's sons. By the following afternoon, Brown had barricaded what remained of his group, along with their hostages, in the fire engine house next to the armory. A company of marines, led by Lieutenant Colonel Robert E. Lee, soon arrived to put down the insurrection.

On the morning of October 18, Lee sent in cavalry officer Lieutenant Jeb Stuart to demand Brown's surrender, but Brown refused. Stuart then signaled for the marines to charge, and in the ensuing melee, two of the raiders were killed with bayonets. Within minutes the uprising was over and Brown and four remaining followers were captured.

Brown and his followers were charged with murder, treason, and inciting insurrection and sentenced to death by hanging. Brown was executed on December 2, 1859.

Harriet Beecher Stowe

Harriet Beecher Stowe wrote several well-received novels and nonfiction texts in her lifetime, but most people today remember her only for her first literary effort, *Uncle Tom's Cabin*. The vehemently antislavery book would inflame the passions of slaveholders and abolitionists alike and make Stowe an international celebrity as well as one of the most hated women in the South.

The reaction to *Uncle Tom's Cabin* was nothing short of remarkable. The book literally flew off the shelves, selling 10,000 copies the first week and an incredible 300,000 copies by the end of the year. Within five years, more than 500,000 copies of *Uncle Tom's Cabin* were sold in the United States, and the book was translated into 20 languages. The royalties from the book made Stowe a relatively wealthy woman (she had also done well with her previous publishing efforts) but she also found herself vilified in the South, where the book was found inflammatory and extremely unflattering. One slave owner was so enraged by Stowe and *Uncle Tom's Cabin* that he sent her a slave's ear in a box.

The organization viewed early reforms of the institution, such as banning slavery from new states, as too limited and called for its complete eradication. Members also wanted full political rights for freed blacks. The abolitionist movement spread quickly, and soon there were more than a thousand chapters of the American Anti-Slavery Society throughout the Northern states, boasting a membership of nearly a quarter of a million people. The word was spread through newspapers, lectures, pamphlets, and huge petition drives.

Some abolitionists, especially those in the most militant fringes of the movement, found that the society's philosophy didn't appeal to them. Many abolitionists faced violent reaction in both the North and the South, and it wasn't uncommon for abolitionist-newspaper printing presses to be seized and newspaper offices to be ransacked. Sometimes the violence went even further. In 1837, Reverend Elijah Lovejoy, the editor of an antislavery newspaper in Illinois, was killed by an angry proslavery mob enraged by his advocacy.

The Fugitive Slave Law of 1850 and the publication of Harriet Beecher Stowe's *Uncle Tom's Cabin* in 1852 gave the abolitionist movement renewed strength in the North as more and more whites came to realize the inherent evil, violence, and degradation of slavery. For a nation based on freedom, to hold an entire group of people in bondage went against the laws of both God and the Constitution, they cried, but again the South refused to listen.

A number of prominent blacks aided the abolitionist movement with tales of brutality against slaves and the risks slaves faced in trying to escape. Frederick Douglass, in particular, lent a strong, intelligent voice to

The Dred Scott Decision

Dred Scott was a slave who thought he should be free. His case went all the way to the Supreme Court, where the majority decision would keep him in bondage and further split the United States on the issue of slavery.

Scott was the property of John Emerson, an army doctor from Missouri. Emerson traveled frequently as part of his job, and between 1834 and 1838, he took Scott with him to army posts throughout the United States and the Western territories, including Illinois and the Minnesota Territory, where slavery had been outlawed by the Missouri Compromise. Scott returned to Missouri with Emerson in 1838, and after Emerson's death in 1843, he sued in the Missouri courts for his freedom and that of his family, with the argument that his stay in a free state and free territory had made him a free man. The Missouri courts ruled against Scott, but Scott's fight was just beginning.

Over the next several years, the case went through numerous lower courts, all but one ruling against Scott. The case was appealed to the Supreme Court in 1854, but due to a backlog of cases, it wasn't heard until 1856. Scott's position was argued by Montgomery Blair, who would later become postmaster general under Abraham Lincoln. The chief justice was 80-year-old Roger Taney, who had freed his own slaves in 1818 but still believed in the institution of slavery. Despite Blair's best efforts, the court ruled against Dred Scott, dashing his hopes for freedom.

☆ ☆ ☆

Dred Scott Ruling by the Supreme Court

When the Dred Scott ruling by the Supreme Court became public, Southern slave owners celebrated, confident that the issue had finally been laid to rest. In fact, so confident were many Southerners that slavery was now fully and officially endorsed by the United States government that bills to reopen the African slave trade were presented in Congress. In the North, people were stunned, disgusted, and outraged. Many saw the decision as a call to arms and began their abolitionist activities with renewed vigor; others who had tried to remain neutral on the subject of slavery found themselves compelled to join the abolitionist cause. In that way, the Dred Scott decision actually helped bring about the end of slavery. It also helped Abraham Lincoln become the first Republican president by widening the divisions over slavery within the Democratic Party.

Frederick Douglass

Few people fought harder for the rights of African Americans or were more active in the abolitionist movement than Frederick Douglass. A powerful speaker and writer, he edited and published the influential abolitionist newspaper *The North Star* for nearly 17 years and helped spread the word on the evils of slavery in numerous speeches throughout the North.

Douglass was born Frederick August Washington Bailey in 1817. His mother, Harriet Bailey, was a slave, his father an unknown white man. Sent to Baltimore at age eight to work as a house servant, Douglass was educated by the mistress of the house, who taught him to read and write. He made his way to New Bedford, Massachusetts, where he found work as a ship caulker and changed his last name to Douglass to avoid those who might try to return him to his owner.

At age 24, Douglass attended a meeting of the Massachusetts Anti-Slavery Society, where he spoke for the first time about his life as a slave and his escape. William Lloyd Garrison, the leader of the society, was taken with Douglass's speaking skills and immedi-ately hired him as a full-time abolitionist lecturer. Often Douglass would begin his speeches with these provocative words: "I appear this evening as a thief and a robber. I stole this head, these limbs, this body from my master, and ran off with them."

As the nation grew closer to civil war, Douglass strived to make slavery one of the key issues. And after war was declared, he worked hard to encourage blacks to join the Union Army, believing that participation in the war effort would go a long way toward abolition and full citizenship.

After the war was over, Douglass continued to work for the cause of civil rights, clashing with President Andrew Johnson over his reconstruction policies, which Douglass felt didn't provide sufficient relief to long-suffering Southern blacks.

President Ulysses S. Grant appointed Douglass to a number of government positions, including marshal of the District of Columbia and consul general to Haiti. Douglass died in his home in Cedar Hills, Washington D.C., in 1895, at the age of 78.

the abolitionist cause and worked hard to spread the word of freedom. Other prominent abolitionists included the following:

- ✪ Theodore Parker was a Boston minister who encouraged his parishioners to help runaway slaves any way they could. Practicing what he preached, Parker helped hide dozens of runaway slaves from federal agents who had been sent to recapture them and bring them back to their owners.

- ✪ Sojourner Truth (real name: Isabella Baumfree) was an illiterate slave who fled her New York owner in the 1820s and spent most of the rest of her life lecturing on the horrors of slavery. Truth explained to Harriet Beecher Stowe that she chose her new name because God intended her to "travel up an' down de land, showin' de people der sins, an' bein' a sign unto dem."

- ✪ Charles Calistus Burleigh was an attorney who, at age 24, became a lecturer for the Middlesex Anti-Slavery Society in Massachusetts. A gifted speaker, Burleigh countered the common fear that freed blacks would undercut the wages of whites in the North with the argument that blacks would stop fleeing to the North once they were free in the South, that freed blacks would increase the market for Northern manufacturing, and that an educated black with earning power would work harder than any slave and contribute greatly to society.

- ✪ Charles Lenox Remond was the first black man to speak at public meetings on behalf of abolition. Born a free man in Salem, Massachusetts, Remond became an agent of the Massachusetts chapter of the American Anti-Slavery Society, and in 1840, he represented the organization at the first World Anti-Slavery Convention in London. Remond was not content with simple emancipation. He demanded that blacks also be rewarded in relation to their contributions to society, a concept that, not surprisingly, received little support in the South.

Frederick Douglass

Harriet Tubman

✪ Harriet Tubman was a small yet scrappy Maryland slave who ran away from her master in 1849 and spent the better part of her life helping other slaves reach freedom through the Underground Railroad. A force to be reckoned with despite her small stature, Tubman, who was given the nickname Moses for helping more than three hundred slaves escape bondage, was known to pull a gun on frightened slaves who tried to back out once they were on the run (she also carried laudanum to quiet crying babies that might give them away). Tubman, who had a flair for disguise, was never apprehended during her forays into the South, nor were any of the slaves she helped to escape. Slave owners in the South came to loathe Tubman for her emancipation activities, and a hefty reward was offered for her capture.

Interestingly, the South had its share of abolitionist activity too. In the late 1820s, Southern abolitionist groups actually outnumbered Northern groups, with many important Southerners freeing their slaves and assisting colonization efforts. And in 1832, the Virginia legislature debated a proposal for gradual, compensatory emancipation that would have become effective in 1861. Obviously, the legislation didn't succeed, and the Southern abolitionist movement slowly died. Over the years, the South first adopted a defensive attitude toward slavery, then attempted to show that slavery, far from being evil, was actually good for the economy and for the slaves themselves. Of course, the more the South tried to defend slavery, the louder the cry for its destruction by Northern abolitionists.

BLEEDING KANSAS

The North and the South managed an uneasy but peaceful coexistence on the issue of slavery for a long time, but as the nineteenth century progressed and the nation began to expand westward, slavery became an increasingly sensitive topic, with Northern abolitionists pushing harder and harder for slavery's elimination.

The issue reached the boiling point in 1854, when part of the land acquired in the Louisiana Purchase was divided into two territories, Kansas and Nebraska, along the 40th parallel. The Kansas-Nebraska Act, written by Illinois Senator Stephen Douglas, a railroad tycoon who had a vested financial interest in opening up the territory, all but voided the Missouri Compromise of 1820 and introduced the concept of popular sovereignty—the right of a people organizing as a state to decide by popular vote whether to allow slavery.

Kansas was the first to test the concept, voting overwhelmingly to become a free state. Proslavery advocates, however, refused to accept the popular vote and poured into the territory from nearby slave states such as Missouri in an attempt to shift the balance. In the North, these proslavery troublemakers were known as border ruffians, and they gave freesoil settlers no end of grief. Violence and bloodshed became common as proslavery and antislavery factions battled throughout the Kansas wilderness, earning the region the nickname "Bleeding Kansas." More than two hundred people died in the vicious guerrilla warfare. In one of the most horrifying acts of mayhem, radical abolitionist John Brown, four of his sons, and two comrades shot and hacked to death with broadswords five proslavery settlers near Pottawatomie Creek on May 24, 1856, in retaliation for a raid by proslavery forces in the town of Lawrence.

It could be said that the fighting that occurred in the Kansas territory was the first of the Civil War because it strongly reflected the issues and sentiments that would eventually lead to Southern secession.

> ### CIVIL WAR FACTOID
>
> John C. Calhoun was a talented statesman and gifted orator, but he wasn't much of a romantic. He was said to have once sent his wife-to-be a love poem consisting of 12 lines, each beginning with "Whereas," except for the last line, which began "Therefore."

SECESSION

Though the Southern states had threatened to secede from the Union over various issues (particularly slavery and states' rights) for many, many years, it caught the world by surprise when they actually did so. The straw that broke the Southern camel's back was the election of Abraham Lincoln, a Republican and avowed opponent of slavery who was supported by many vocal abolitionists. Fearful that the North, which was richer, more populous, and industrial, would even more insistently impose its will against them, the Southern states felt they had no recourse but to pull away from the Union and form their own nation. They had the right to do so, many felt, because sovereign states had formed the Union, and thus any state that felt oppressed by the federal government could justly withdraw rather than submit to laws it deemed harmful.

CIVIL WAR
FACTOID

Abraham Lincoln was the
first American president to
wear a beard. The look set a
precedent, and of the next
nine men to hold the high
office, only William McKinley
was clean shaven.

Of course, the federal government felt otherwise, deeming secession a treasonous act. But President James Buchanan (1791–1868), considered by most historians an average statesman at best, was loathe to do anything about it, preferring instead to run out the final days of his term as quietly as possible and then turn things over to the newly elected Lincoln. Buchanan did say that he felt the Southern states had no legal right to secede, but he also claimed that he lacked the authority to stop them and was less than anxious to start a war over the issue while he was still in the White House. One of his last acts as president was to call for a national referendum—a time-killer guaranteed to stave off the whole mess until Lincoln could take office—on whether force should be used to preserve the Union. To his credit, Buchanan did refuse to turn over Fort Sumter, located in Charleston Harbor, to a rebellious South Carolina, though he managed to foul up even that endeavor by failing to reinforce the compound with men and supplies and leaving its commanding officer with less than clear orders on how to proceed.

It's interesting to note that as the presidential election of 1860 grew nearer, the warning bell of Southern secession rang louder and louder. Southern newspapers increasingly advocated withdrawal from the Union as it became clear that Lincoln was the front-runner, but most Northern leaders failed to heed these omens, having heard them so often in the past. Lincoln refused to issue any kind of statement that might appease the frightened South during his campaign, though his opponent, Stephen Douglas, took the threats seriously. When Republicans overwhelmingly won October state elections in Pennsylvania, Ohio, and Indiana, Douglas realized that Lincoln's presidential victory was a foregone conclusion, so he immediately traveled to the South in a desperate attempt to prevent the destruction of the nation. The majority of Northerners, on the other hand, chose to view the bitter divisiveness through rose-tinted glasses. The common belief was that the South was simply beating its chest and would fall back in line once the presidential election was over. Sadly, it was not to be.

South Carolina was the first state to secede, passing the Ordinance of Secession by unanimous vote during a state convention in Charleston on December 20, 1860. The convention drew a huge crowd and was attended by delegates from throughout the state as well as the governor of Florida, representatives of Mississippi and Alabama, and four former U.S. senators. The ordinance, which in essence lit the fuse that would ignite the Civil War, simply stated: "We, the people of the State of South Carolina, in Convention assembled, do declare and ordain that the union now subsisting between South Carolina and other States under the name 'The United States of America' is hereby dissolved." As the delegates left St. Andrew's Hall, Charleston literally burst forth in celebration. Crowds cheered, church bells rang out, and cannons were fired in jubilee. To most South Carolinians, it was the beginning of a new and wonderful era. Four years later, South Carolina would face the terrible wrath of William T. Sherman and his men, many of whom would take great joy in leveling large portions of the state they blamed for causing the Civil War.

Six other states quickly followed South Carolina's lead: Mississippi, on January 9, 1861; Florida, on January 10; Alabama, on January 11; Georgia, on January 19; Louisiana, on January 26; and Texas, on February 1. Following the fall of Fort Sumter on April 14, 1861, four more states left the Union to join the Confederacy: Virginia, on April 17; Arkansas, on May 6; North Carolina, on May 20; and Tennessee, on June 8. Together, these 11 states would make up the Confederate States of America.

Reaction to Southern secession was mixed on both sides. The overwhelming percentage of Southerners favored the move because they were tired of what they saw as growing interference in their culture, lifestyle, and economy from Northern politicians, industry, and bankers. But there were dissenting voices as well. Many Southerners felt that secession was too strong and volatile an act and that the differences between the two regions could be amicably worked out without resorting to the destruction of the Union.

In the North, opinion ran the gamut. Many felt that Southern secession was a good thing and that the Union should simply let the rebellious states go. But the majority agreed that secession was treason, that it very well might destroy the republic, and that force should be used if necessary to bring the Southern states back into the Union. President Abraham Lincoln wasn't eager to pit American against American in a civil war, but he also realized that eventually something would have to be done. The South would force his hand with the taking of Fort Sumter.

CIVIL WAR FIRSTS

The Civil War can claim a lot of firsts—some good, some not. They include the first railroad artillery, submarine, periscope for trench warfare, land mine fields, naval torpedoes, antiaircraft fire, telescopic sights for rifles, repeating rifles, fixed ammunition, organized medical and nursing corps, workable machine gun, income tax, withholding tax, tobacco tax, American conscription, Medal of Honor, photography of battle, bugle call "Taps," African American U.S. Army officer (Major M. R. Delany), U.S. Navy admiral, widescale use of anesthetics for the wounded, and American presidential assassination.

On the Eve
of War

THE MASON-DIXON LINE

The Mason-Dixon line is named for Charles Mason and Jeremiah Dixon, the British astronomers who surveyed it between 1763 and 1767. Today, the boundary is generally regarded as the demarcation point between the Northern states and the Southern states of the Civil War.

The line, which runs along the northernmost border of Maryland and Pennsylvania and also includes the northern border of Delaware, was surveyed and established to settle a boundary fight between Maryland and Pennsylvania. However, the dispute lingered long after the Mason-Dixon line was created, with many Maryland residents

(continued)

Immediately prior to the secession of the 11 Southern states that would make up the Confederate States of America, the United States of America was comprised of 34 states and eight organized territories. Two states—Nevada and West Virginia—would be admitted to the Union during the war, and several others would be admitted shortly after. West Virginia was a particularly unexpected surprise. Though technically in the South, 50 western counties decided to break away at the onset of the war because they were home to more Union sympathizers than Confederates. The Union welcomed the region warmly, happy to have yet another ally.

The North and the South, as noted earlier, were decidedly different in a great many ways, but the secession of the Southern states crystallized the rift between the two regions by literally dividing the nation in half. A handful of Southern states with at least some Union loyalties, such as Kentucky and Delaware, helped separate the North from the Deep South, but otherwise, the two regions literally rubbed shoulders. When Virginia left the Union on April 17, 1861, it meant that Confederate forces were practically on the White House doorstep. In fact, once the war began in earnest, Lincoln could see from the second floor of the White House fluttering Confederate flags over Arlington Heights, Virginia, and, at night, light from Confederate campfires south of the Potomac River. As a result, the protection of the District of Columbia—the very seat of Union government—became a priority.

Even after secession occurred, neither side was particularly anxious to go to battle. Both regions had relatively small armies and neither was really prepared for any type of lengthy engagement. In the beginning, Southern leaders said they simply wanted to be left alone, though they did add that the expansion of the borders of the Confederate States of America was a long-range goal. In the North, the biggest issue was preservation of the Union, which meant bringing the Southern states back into the fold—through military force if necessary. The common thinking was that individual states may have had certain inalienable rights, but those rights did not extend to the dissolution of the Union. The future of the nation depended on putting an end to Southern secession.

THE UNION

The United States of America found itself a much smaller nation on June 8, 1861. That's the date that Tennessee—the last state to secede—broke Union ranks and joined its Southern sisters. On that date, the Union consisted of only 23 states and eight territories, including the Indian Territory between Texas and Kansas.

Even without the Southern states, the Union, led by President Abraham Lincoln, made up nearly three-fourths of the area known as the United States of America. Its chances of victory in the event of war were also considerable, at least on paper. According to the census of 1860, the population of the Northern states was nearly 22 million. Of that number, an estimated 4 million were men old enough to fight in combat if called. Even more impressive, the North had nearly 100,000 factories employing more than a million workers, and nearly 20,000 miles of railroad—more than the rest of the world combined—and 96 percent of the nation's railroad equipment. On the economic front, Union banks held 81 percent of the nation's bank deposits and nearly $56 million in gold. All of this strongly suggested that the South would be at a severe disadvantage should war break out. However, history would show that the South was more tenacious (and pugnacious) than originally believed and would frequently triumph against overwhelming odds. The North may have held the advantage in every conceivable way, but the Civil War was far from an easy triumph.

THE MASON-DIXON LINE

(continued from previous page)

insisting that certain lands in Pennsylvania still belonged to them.

Some historians speculate that the Mason-Dixon line inspired the South's nickname of "Dixie," though others believe the popular moniker was derived from the ten-dollar note issued by Louisiana, which was steeped in French culture and influence. As a result, the word ten was written as the French dix, and for a while, the ten-dollar notes were commonly known as "dixies."

THE UNION STATES

California
Connecticut
Illinois
Indiana
Iowa
Kansas
Maine
Massachusetts
Michigan
Minnesota
Nevada (added as a free
    state in 1864)
New Hampshire
New Jersey
New York
Ohio
Oregon
Pennsylvania
Rhode Island
Vermont
West Virginia (added as a
    free state in 1863)
Wisconsin

UNION POLITICS

American politics has always been an odd creature, with a wide variety of political parties and affiliations springing up throughout the nation's history. But the Civil War saw more than its share of political combat, particularly in the North.

Heated debate and partisan rancor over the Kansas-Nebraska Act of 1854 plunged Union politics into turmoil. Out of the carnage rose a new political organization known as the Republican Party, made up primarily of abolitionists, Whigs, Free-Soilers, and leaders of industry and banking. The party's key platform was a more central economic policy that benefited the North more than the South, but angering the South even more was the Republican Party's ambition to eliminate slavery. The Southern states immediately saw the party as a serious threat to everything they held dear, and their fear escalated with the election of Abraham Lincoln, the first Republican to hold the high office.

Lincoln was not the first Republican presidential candidate. That honor goes to John Fremont, famous for his exploration and conquest of California, who ran on the Republican ticket in 1856 and lost to James Buchanan. But even though Fremont lost the election, the Republicans did quite well at the polls. Four years later, the Democratic Party, which had held the White House for nearly four decades, was so splintered over the issue of slavery that the door was open for a Republican victory.

However, as with most things political, the Republican Party itself was torn asunder over the course of the war, dividing itself into three distinct splinters. Conservative Republicans favored the gradual emancipation of slaves and kindness toward the South following the war. Moderate Republicans urged faster emancipation and some punitive economic and political sanctions. And radical Republicans sought immediate emancipation and harsh punishment against the South. Many radical Republicans saw the Civil War as a great opportunity to change everything they perceived as wrong with the South and hoped to make it more "Northern" during the coming Reconstruction by setting up Northern-run schools, hospitals, and even state and local governments. All three factions would test Lincoln's resolve as the war ran its course.

Like the Republican Party, the Democratic Party had also split into opposing factions—the Peace Democrats and the War Democrats. The Peace Democrats (also known as Copperheads, because they were believed to be deadly to the Union), considered the war unconstitutional and supported the Southern cause. Their position was that the Republican Party caused the Civil War by forcing the South to secede and did so only to strengthen its own power base and force racial equality, a phrase intended to frighten racists who might otherwise support the Union cause. Peace Democrats could be found in every Northern state, but the largest concentration was located in the Midwest, where fear of emancipation was strongest and anti-Republican sentiment ran deep.

On the other side were the War Democrats, who believed strongly in the Union cause and supported the Lincoln administration on most issues. Most War Democrats had no strong feelings regarding the institution of slavery in the South and felt no compunction about restoring the Union without emancipation if necessary. It's interesting to note that Lincoln delayed passage of the Emancipation Proclamation in an attempt to remain on friendly terms with the War Democrats and maintain unity in regard to the war effort.

Northern politics were fickle, and the ranks of the Peace Democrats and the War Democrats fluctuated wildly according to how the Union fared over the course of the war. During those periods when the North lost more battles than it won and public sentiment edged toward cutting Union losses and bargaining for peace, the number of Peace Democrats rose. But when the North began winning strategic victories and it appeared that the South was lost, the War Democrats became the party to join.

THE CONFEDERATE STATES OF AMERICA

The 11 Confederate states may have appeared small and weak in comparison to the far more industrial Union states, but what they lacked in size and population they more than made up with sheer guts and willpower. Together, the states had a total population

THE CONFEDERATE STATES

Alabama
Arkansas
Florida
Georgia
Louisiana
Mississippi
North Carolina
South Carolina
Tennessee
Texas
Virginia

THE BIRTH OF WEST VIRGINIA

West Virginia was added to the Union over the course of the Civil War. Like the United States itself, Virginia was actually two very different regions living as one. The eastern portion of the state was home to the plantation-owning, slaveholding aristocracy and the center of state government, and it benefited the most from the fiscal policies and public improvements that came from the state officials in Richmond. The citizens of the mountainous region west of the Alleghenies felt constantly slighted and ignored by their brothers to the east. There were more farming, mining, and manufacturing concerns than plantations, and slavery was not particularly widespread.

In the spring of 1861, residents of Virginia's

(continued)

of about 9 million people—a figure that included 4 million slaves, who certainly could not be expected to fight on the South's behalf should war break out. Because its economy was almost entirely based on agriculture—primarily cotton—the South had only 20,000 factories employing an estimated 100,000 workers. And, as noted earlier, the South's railroad system was inconsequential compared to the North's, with less than 9,000 miles of track—much of which would be destroyed during the war's waning days as a result of William T. Sherman's march through Georgia and into the Carolinas.

All of these factors would severely hamper the South's war efforts in almost every way. Its lack of industry, for example, would prevent it from manufacturing much needed war goods, particularly firearms, ammunition, and large artillery, and its emphasis on cotton over food crops would help little in feeding its military personnel. In fact, one of the most important contributing factors in the Confederacy's final surrender was the literal starvation of its troops in the last months of the war.

HOW THE CONFEDERATE STATES OF AMERICA GOT STARTED

As the Southern states began to secede, their leaders in Congress resigned their positions and headed home, both eager and anxious. Their home states had done a mighty and wondrous thing, but the chore of government was only just beginning.

During the first week of February 1861, delegates from six of the original seceded nations (the delegates from Texas were still in transit) met in Montgomery, Alabama, to discuss the formation of a new republic and the form of government to lead it. Montgomery was an odd choice for a provisional capital; though now a thriving, bustling city, in 1861 it was little more than a tiny backwater town with unpaved streets and a population of just eight thousand. But it would quickly become both famous and infamous as the birthplace of the Confederate States of America. The capital of the Confederacy would be moved in May 1861 to Richmond, Virginia.

On February 8, the convention announced the establishment of the Confederate States of America and made itself the provisional Congress. With that, the delegates faced a bizarre paradox—establishing a centralized government for a collection of states that had pulled away from the Union because of their distaste for federal authority. It was a difficult job, but the delegates worked quickly. Their first act was to unanimously select Jefferson Davis as the Confederacy's provisional president and Alexander Hamilton Stephens of Georgia as its vice president. (The two men would be formally elected, having run unopposed, in November 1861 and inaugurated on George Washington's birthday—February 22, 1862.)

The next five weeks were spent developing a form of government that would appeal to as many Southern voices as possible in the hope of swaying the remaining uncommitted slave states. The resulting constitution, approved on March 11, sounded quite a bit like the one the states had just abandoned but with some very important differences. Cabinet members were allowed to participate in legislative debates, the president was limited to a single six-year term and given power to disapprove specific appropriations in any bill he signed (in essence, a line item veto), and the "sovereign and independent character" of each state was made quite clear in that the new constitution prevented the federal government from levying protective tariffs, making internal improvements, or overruling state court decisions. The individual states were also free to create their own armies and could enter into separate agreements with each other if they so desired. And while it remained illegal to import slaves from outside the nation, the central government was constitutionally prohibited from passing any laws denying the right to own slaves. Thus, it was hoped that the leadership of the Confederate States of America would avoid the issues and problems that had forced them to secede from the Union in the first place.

Jefferson Davis seemed to be a good choice for president in that he was generally regarded as a moderate on most issues, a fact that made him appealing to a variety of diverse voices. William Lowndes Yancey, a vocal champion of secession, introduced Davis to the cheering throngs, following his selection as

THE BIRTH OF WEST VIRGINIA
(continued from previous page)

western counties expressed their opposition to secession in a statewide referendum, but they were outvoted by factions in the east. Anxious to remain with the Union, regional leaders gathered for a convention in Wheeling, and by June 20, they had formed a pro-Union state that was quickly and enthusiastically embraced by the Lincoln administration. Senators and representatives were elected to take Virginia's vacated seats in the U.S. Congress as plans were made to create an entirely new state.

A constitutional convention was organized the following January, and four months later, West Virginia formally requested statehood. West Virginia officially joined the Union on June 20, 1863.

provisional president, with the words, "The man and the hour have met. Prosperity, honor, and victory await his administration." Davis's inauguration was cause to celebrate, and the event turned into a huge party with thunderous applause, clanging church bells, cannon fire, and countless renditions of "Dixie," which quickly became the new nation's unofficial anthem. Actress Maggie Smith demonstrated what the South thought of the North by dancing on an American flag, an act that outraged Northern Unionists.

With the ratification of a constitution and Davis's inauguration as president, the Confederate States of America became a reality. But when analyzed in legal and historical context, the new nation seems clearly born from the will of a few rather than the many. While secession and the formation of a new republic may have been what the majority of Southerners wanted, neither issue was put to a popular vote in the Southern states. Their withdrawal from the Union was decided at state conventions by a total of 854 men selected by their legislatures. And of that number, 157 voted against secession. In fact, Tennessee left the Union by an act of its governor, following the public defeat of a secession proposal.

Nonetheless, the act was done and the South's destiny set. The region had proved that its talk of secession was not merely a bluff, leaving a stunned North to decide how to react. Bringing the South back into the Union by whatever means necessary would be one of Abraham Lincoln's first and most important acts as president and would set the course of his administration, and indeed the entire nation, for the next four years.

UGLY ECONOMICS

Slavery, the backbone of the Southern agricultural economy, was also one of the region's greatest hindrances in its fight with the North. While the North flourished amid the Industrial Revolution, the South did everything it could to hold industry at bay, maintaining what was essentially an archaic and ultimately doomed way of life. As a result, when fighting commenced in earnest, the Confederacy found itself at an immediate and substantial disadvantage in terms of manufacturing power sufficient to maintain an effective war effort.

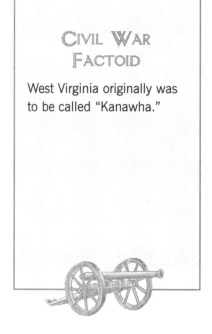

CIVIL WAR FACTOID

West Virginia originally was to be called "Kanawha."

Proslavery Voices in the Union

Slavery was not the most important issue at the very onset of hostilities between the Union and the Confederacy. Certainly, the institution played an integral role in widening the rift between the two regions, but as the North and the South began to amass their individual war machines, the real issue was Southern independence. The Confederacy was fighting for its very existence, while the North's biggest war aim was the preservation of the Union.

Indeed, the issue of slavery was not universally condemned in the North, as many people believe. A good share of Northerners didn't really care if the institution continued in the South or not, with many hoping, both secretly and publicly, that it would. In many cases, Northern advocacy for Southern slavery stemmed from fears that an influx of newly freed Southern blacks would flood the North, take jobs from whites, and drive down wages. It was racism in its most basic form, and it spread rapidly, especially among European immigrants who held the most difficult and lowest paying industrial jobs.

The issue of slavery forced Abraham Lincoln to walk a thin tightrope as war became imminent. Though morally opposed to slavery himself, Lincoln needed the congressional support of Northern Democrats, most of whom had little objection to the continuation of slavery in the South, so both he and Congress went out of their way to stress that they wanted to preserve the Union without interfering with the unique institutions of any state. In other words, if the Union could be restored with Southern slavery still in place, so be it. It was hoped that this tact would also help appease the slaveholding border states of Maryland, Kentucky, and Missouri, which wavered dangerously on which side to support. If they decided to join the Confederacy, the Union cause would be almost hopeless.

Though he greatly opposed slavery, Lincoln's greatest concern as president was keeping the nation together at any cost, and he was willing to compromise greatly to do it. Only later in the conflict would the elimination of slavery in the South become a primary aim of the Union's war effort.

The reason was simple: Slavery had enabled the South to establish and enjoy an antiquated gentry lifestyle. While the slaves worked the land, their owners were free to indulge their affluent tastes. It was a genteel way of life, but it essentially froze the South in time. As the North forged ahead in terms of industry and growth, the South remained pretty much the way it had been during Thomas Jefferson's time. A dependence on slavery had prevented the region from developing a class of skilled workers, and this would cost the South greatly in its struggle to maintain its independence.

History has shown that the Civil War, unlike earlier military conflicts, was very much an industrial war. Success went to the army with the most guns and cannons and the ability to keep its fighting forces armed and supplied. The Union had the upper hand, and Confederate leaders knew it. The Confederacy had plenty of men willing to fight, but it lacked all of the basic resources to help them do it well. Strategy plays an integral role in the success of any military campaign, but strategy means little if you don't have guns, bullets, and other supplies. As the war raged on far longer than either side had anticipated, this frustrating limitation would play a deciding role in its ultimate outcome. Slavery made the South, and it would help bring it down in a way no one had ever foreseen.

Though the war helped spark industry and growth in the North, the Union still suffered economically, at least in the beginning. More than $300 million owed Northern businessmen was lost when the Southern states seceded from the Union, continuing an economic depression that had begun in 1857. War expenditures reached an astounding $2 million a day during the latter years of the conflict, inflation skyrocketed, and war profiteers flourished. But as the war effort continued, the economy picked up fairly quickly. The government was spending a huge amount of money to keep its war machine marching, and Northern industry and businesses benefited greatly. Farmers in the Midwest also thrived as a result of the war. Though they had lost Southern plantation owners as clients for their produce, particularly corn, government demand more than made up for it.

But while the North did well economically as a result of the war, profits were tainted with the blood of its fighting men. To the thousands of Northern families who lost loved ones on the battlefield, it was hardly a fair trade.

THE TERRITORIES

Arizona
Colorado
New Mexico
Utah
Nebraska
Washington
Indian Territory

THE BORDER STATES

Not all slave-owning states immediately leaped on the secession bandwagon. Four border states in the upper portion of the region—Maryland, Kentucky, Missouri, and Delaware—were cautious in determining how to proceed after the first Southern states withdrew from the Union.

Even though slavery was legal in all four of the border states, the proportion of slaves and slave owners was less than half of that in the states that had already pulled away from the Union. Their sentiments on the issue weren't as strong as those in the Deep South, where slavery was much more an ingrained part of the lifestyle, and state leaders debated long and hard on which side to join in the coming conflict. Delaware was the first to act, quickly rejecting a Southern request to join the new Confederacy.

The Confederacy had a lot to gain by way of population, industry, and defense in getting the border states to join. Between them, the states would have added 45 percent to the white population (meaning more able-bodied soldiers), as well as more industrial output and military supplies. Their location, especially that of Kentucky and Maryland, would also have had tremendous strategic value should the Union Army invade. Maryland, in particular, was vitally important because it would have enclosed Washington, D.C., on three sides, putting a tremendous squeeze on the political power center of the North. But despite the pleas of Confederate leaders and more than a few battles, all four of the border states, though proslavery, eventually remained in the Union.

At first, it seemed that Maryland might do otherwise. A strong pro-Confederacy attitude developed there shortly after the fall of Fort Sumter when, on April 19, 1861, a Massachusetts regiment passing through on its way to Washington, D.C., shot several civilians after being attacked by an angry mob in Baltimore.

What became known as the Baltimore Riot started when the crowd tried to prevent the soldiers from reaching Washington by blocking transports that were to take them through Baltimore. The soldiers were eventually forced to get off the transports and march through the city, with the angry crowd in pursuit. Shouting epithets, the mob became increasingly bold and started throwing bricks and rocks at the frightened soldiers. Some of the soldiers panicked and

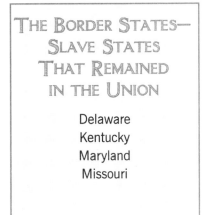

THE BORDER STATES—
SLAVE STATES
THAT REMAINED
IN THE UNION

Delaware
Kentucky
Maryland
Missouri

fired blindly into the teaming mass of humanity, causing tremendous confusion and mayhem. Terrified, the soldiers raced to the railway station as police struggled to hold the now enraged crowd at bay. The soldiers managed to escape, leaving much of their equipment as well as their marching band behind, but the cost was high—four soldiers and 12 civilians dead, scores injured, and thousands of dollars in property damage. Many consider the Baltimore Riot to be the first bloodshed of the Civil War.

Maryland officials were outraged at the carnage and demanded that no more Federal troops be sent through the state. And just to make sure their message was clear, the mayor and police chief of Baltimore approved the destruction of key rail bridges to prevent Union troops from entering the metropolis. At the same time, secessionist sympathizers tore down telegraph wires to Washington, cutting off communication to the nation's capital for a couple of anxious days.

On May 13, Federal troops—including members of the Massachusetts regiment that had been attacked the previous month—occupied Baltimore and declared martial law. Several prominent citizens, including the chief of police and a number of city commissioners, were arrested for their alleged role in the riot, and suspected secessionists (including the grandson of Francis Scott Key and several state legislators) were held without formal charges ever being brought against them. Federal forces would present an occupying presence in Baltimore for the duration of the war. Meanwhile, Governor Thomas Hicks and the state legislature voted against secession, declaring Maryland neutral in the rift between the North and the South, an obviously difficult position to maintain. When state elections were held in November 1861, the Union Party won a stunning victory, and Maryland remained pro-Union for the rest of the war, though there were continuous grumblings from pro-Confederacy factions.

Missouri also had a hard time deciding where its allegiance lay. On one side was Governor Claiborne Fox Jackson, a former "border ruffian" who advocated secession; on the other was pro-Union Congressman Francis P. Blair, who happened to be the brother of Lincoln's postmaster,

MASON DIXON

Montgomery Blair. Many of the residents of Missouri were slave owners, but the overall makeup of the population was decidedly different from that of the states in the Deep South. A large number of German immigrants had settled throughout Missouri, with the greatest concentration around St. Louis, and they had little interest in or regard for most Southern traditions—especially slavery.

When a convention of Missouri legislators rejected a proposal to secede, Governor Jackson appealed to newly elected Confederate President Jefferson Davis for help in capturing the Federal arsenal in St. Louis, which happened to be the largest facility of its type in all of the slave states. The firepower in the arsenal was sufficient to arm enough secessionist Missourians to forcefully take the state out of the Union. However, the plan failed when Union Captain Nathaniel Lyon easily defeated the governor's militia with the assistance of area German Americans. The Confederate prisoners were paraded through the streets of St. Louis, sparking a riot that resulted in the deaths of two soldiers and 28 civilians.

Still determined to join the Confederacy, Governor Jackson appointed Mexican War veteran Sterling Price as commander of secessionist troops. It appeared that war was imminent, but again, Lyon's forces saved the day, driving Price out of Jefferson City and Boonville. Governor Jackson countered by moving the capital of Missouri from Jefferson City to Neosho, creating his own government and declaring Missouri a Confederate state. Union forces immediately established their own government in Jefferson City and managed to control the state from then on with a heavy presence of Federal troops and Union control of the Mississippi River.

Kentucky, the birth state of both Abraham Lincoln and Jefferson Davis, was even more divided on the issue of which side to join in the conflict between the North and the South. Bordered by three free states and three slave states, its sympathies were fairly evenly split between the Union and the Confederacy. Like Maryland, the state legislature voted to remain neutral, an act that was considered very close to secession, since neutrality was based on the doctrine of state sovereignty, or independence from the decisions of a central government.

Lincoln was torn over what to do about Kentucky. Because it was neutral, a lot of goods were being forwarded through it to the

CIVIL WAR
FACTOID

Despite technically being a Union state, Missouri troops fought on both sides of the war, with more than 100,000 fighting for the Union and nearly 40,000 taking up arms on behalf of the Confederacy. Over the course of the conflict, about 75,000 Kentuckians fought for the Union, and 25,000 fought for the Confederacy.

THE CONFEDERACY AT A GLANCE

Population at the start of the war was 9 million (5.5 million whites, 3.5 million slaves), with nearly 1,140,000 men of combat age. An estimated 850,000 joined the Confederate Army and Navy.

Economy:
- 20,000 factories, employing nearly 100,000 workers
- 9,000 miles of railroad
- $47 million in bank deposits
- $37 million in gold

seceded states, which certainly didn't help the Union cause. But Lincoln decided to treat Kentucky with a gentle hand rather than force the issue, and in the end his plan paid off when state elections in June and August 1861 saw tremendous Unionist victories. The state's official stance of neutrality came to an end when Confederate troops under Major General Leonidas Polk invaded Kentucky from Tennessee to take the strategically important city of Columbus. Polk was chased by Brigadier General Ulysses S. Grant, who occupied Paducah. The two sides battled in Kentucky for nearly a year until the state came under firm Union control in 1862 and remained so for the duration of the war.

Even though the Confederacy would have benefited from the strategic location of the border states, it wasn't shedding many tears over its loss. Instead, it concentrated on what it had rather than what it didn't have, bolstering its borders on land and sea, gathering supplies, enlisting soldiers, and generally gearing up for a war that seemed inevitable. Now that the new nation had been formed, it was time to protect itself.

MAKING ARMIES AND OFFICERS

Today's Army is constantly at the ready. When orders to move out are given, forces leap into action with lightning speed. But things were considerably different at the onset of the Civil War. The North's army was fairly small, consisting of just 16,000 men, and the newborn Confederacy had no ready army at all. As the inevitability of war became clear, both sides set about bolstering their military might, forming armies made up primarily of volunteer state militia and selecting officers to lead them. It would prove a Herculean task.

Following the bombardment of Fort Sumter, Abraham Lincoln, believing the conflict would be over fairly quickly, called on the states to provide 75,000 militia at the government's service for a 90-day enlistment. The call brought a rush of eager young recruits anxious for a little excitement. It also forced the remaining Southern states—Virginia, North Carolina, Tennessee, and Arkansas—to leave the Union and join the Confederacy. Though their sympathies were with the South, all four states had hoped until the very last moment that

the situation could be settled without the risk of bloodshed. That hope was dashed with Lincoln's call to arms.

The state militias that made up the Northern Army at the beginning of the conflict were an interesting but often motley group. Very few of them had received any type of combat training, and most of their drill instruction had been solely for show. In other words, they were civilians playing soldier who had been asked to become the real thing.

The typical militia regiment was made up of companies from neighboring towns, and many of the groups had never even met, much less trained together. This proved to be a serious hindrance, because warfare in the mid-1800s required soldiers to engage in highly intricate movements as they went from marching formation to fighting formation. Coordination was essential and could be instilled only through numerous and lengthy drills, something the majority of militiamen had never done. On the battlefield, they would prove to be next to useless.

In addition, the Union and Confederate armies at the onset of the war lacked any type of cohesion when it came to national uniforms. Members of the various state militias often dressed in gaudy, impractical uniforms of their own design, which caused untold confusion on the battlefront. Their units also had individual names such as the Frontier Guard, Rough-and-Ready Grays, and Susquehanna Blues. To make the confusion worse, some of the Grays were from Northern states and some of the Blues were Southern, which made telling the difference between enemy and friendly forces more than a little difficult. The official blue uniforms of the North and gray uniforms of the South wouldn't come until later in the war.

The individual companies were often led by men with little or no military experience or background. Instead, they were chosen as leaders by popular vote or because they were of higher social status than the others. Field experience would quickly eliminate leaders who were unfit, but in the beginning, the armies of both the North and the South were composed primarily of amateurs leading amateurs.

Which is not to say that there weren't plenty of career soldiers on both sides, though the North had a difficult time deciding how best to use them. Lieutenant General Winfield Scott commanded the

THE UNION AT A GLANCE

The population at the start of the war was 22 million, with 4 million men of combat age. An estimated 2 million men joined the Union Army and Navy.

Economy:
- 100,000 factories employing more than 1 million workers
- 20,000 miles of railroad and 96 percent of all of the nation's railroad equipment
- The majority of coalmines and canals, which were vital for industrial growth.
- $189 million in bank deposits
- $56 million in gold

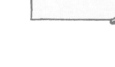

DIXIE

"Dixie" was the anthem of the Confederacy. This song echoed the pride of the South. However, it wasn't written by a Southerner; its composer was Daniel Decatur Emmett, a New Yorker and one of the originators of the blackface minstrel show. The song's actual title is "Dixie's Land," and it was composed in 1859.

Even though "Dixie" quickly became the unofficial anthem of the new Confederate republic, the song enjoyed tremendous popularity on both sides of the conflict. Confederate soldiers sang it around campfires, and proud Southerners sang it in the streets and at rallies and parties. Northern troops sang it as they marched toward the first major battle of the war, and "Dixie" was played by military bands in both Richmond and Washington following Robert E. Lee's surrender to Ulysses S. Grant at the war's end. The song was also played at the inaugurations of both Jefferson Davis and Abraham Lincoln.

Following are the lyrics to "Dixie":

I wish I was in de land ob cotton,
Ole time dar am not forgotten;
Look away, look away, look away, Dixie Land.
In Dixie Land whar I was born in,
Early on one frosty mornin',
Look away, look away, look away, Dixie Land.

Chorus:
Den I wish I was in Dixie! Hooray! Hooray!
In Dixie Land, I'll take my stand,
To lib and die in Dixie.
Away, away, away down south in Dixie
Away, away, away down south in Dixie.

Battle Hymn of the Republic

A wide variety of sentimental ballads and rallying battle tunes became popular over the course of the Civil War, but for the North, none spoke more eloquently about its mission than "The Battle Hymn of the Republic."

The song has an intriguing history. The music—popularized by a marching song titled "John Brown's Body"—was actually a Southern camp-meeting hymn first heard in Charleston in the 1850s. The stirring lyrics were created by Julia Ward Howe, a noted poet whose husband, Samuel Gridley Howe, was an ardent abolitionist and a financial supporter of John Brown. Samuel Howe was also publisher of *The Abolitionist*, a popular Boston antislavery newspaper.

But while Howe may have written the poem, the song was made popular by a Union Army chaplain named Charles Caldwell McCabe, who was captured by Confederate forces and placed in Libby Prison in Richmond, Virginia. During his incarceration, McCabe taught the song to his fellow prisoners and later sang the song during fund-raisers for the chaplains corps. In a now-famous incident, shortly after the Battle of Gettysburg, McCabe sang "The Battle Hymn of the Republic" before an audience that included President Lincoln. The president was so moved by the rendition that he rose to his feet and asked to hear it again. Soon after, "The Battle Hymn of the Republic" became the Union's unofficial anthem.

Following is Howe's poem, inspired by the Book of Isaiah. It first appeared in the February 1862 edition of *The Atlantic Monthly*:

Mine eyes have seen the glory of the coming of the Lord;
He is trampling out the vintage where the grapes of wrath are stored;
He has loosed the fateful lightning of his terrible swift sword;
His truth is marching on.

I have seen Him in the watch fires of a hundred circling camps;
They have builded Him an altar in the evening dews and damps;
I have read his righteous sentence in the dim and flaring lamps;
His day is marching on.

I have read a fiery gospel, writ in burnished rows of steel;
"As ye deal with my contemners, so with you my grace shall deal";
Let the hero, born of woman, crush the serpent with his heel,
Since God is marching on.

He has sounded forth the trumpet that shall never call retreat;
He is sifting out the hearts of men before his judgement seat;
Oh, be swift, my soul, to answer Him! Be jubilant, my feet!
Our God is marching on.

In the beauty of the lilies Christ was born across the sea;
With a glory in His bosom that transfigures you and me;
As he died to make men holy, let us die to make men free,
While God is marching on.

Union Army at the beginning of the war. Though battle experienced and an able strategist, he was now 75 years old and in poor health. After a few Union defeats and growing public dissatisfaction, Scott was retired and replaced by George B. McClellan. Lincoln would spend a lot of time shuffling his officers around.

The Confederacy was a little better off in terms of officer material because a great many of the Union's best military minds, most of them West Pointers, had defected to the South. As a result, Jefferson Davis, himself a West Point graduate with a lot of field experience, planned to use trained soldiers for his general officers as often as he could. One of his first appointees was Robert E. Lee, who had rejected command of the Union's principle army after Virginia seceded; Davis made him a full general in the Confederate Army.

Other bold Confederate officers included Pierre Gustave Toutant Beauregard, appointed to command the chief Confederate Army in Virginia, General Albert Sidney Johnston, and General Joseph E. Johnston. Both Beauregard and Joseph E. Johnston would find their military skills hampered by a rancorous relationship with Jefferson Davis.

UNION AND CONFEDERATE CABINET OFFICERS

During the early days of the Civil War, the Union and the Confederacy were governed by an intriguing collection of men. Following are the early cabinet members for both governments:

Union

- Secretary of State William Henry Seward. As a senator from New York, he fought vigorously to prevent the spread of slavery in the territories but softened his stance somewhat in later years. He believed that the many compromises that had held the nation together would eventually fail, and in 1858, he warned that the bitter fighting over slavery would result in an "irrepressible conflict" between the North and the South. Seward had hoped to be a presidential contender in the 1860 election but lost the Republican nomination to Abraham Lincoln. He was appointed secretary of state in a conciliatory gesture by Lincoln, a position Seward at first rejected. Once in, however, Seward worked hard to make his presence felt in every aspect of the administration. In 1861, Seward proposed a diversionary war with a foreign power, such as England or France, as a way of reuniting the nation; Lincoln quickly rejected the idea. Seward was attacked and seriously wounded on April 14, 1865, by an accomplice of John Wilkes Booth, but he recovered and was able to return to his job under Andrew Johnson. Seward died in 1872.

✪ Secretary of the Treasury Salmon P. Chase. One of the most radical and controversial members of Lincoln's cabinet, Chase served three years before conflict with Lincoln forced his resignation. Chase came to prominence in Ohio as an abolitionist lawyer who specialized in defending runaway slaves and entered the Senate in 1848. He later served two terms as governor of Ohio and became a prominent member of the newly formed Republican Party. Like Seward, Chase hoped to be the Republican candidate in the 1860 presidential election but accepted Lincoln's invitation to join his cabinet. Though he had little experience in finance, Chase was able to contain a mounting budget deficit and effectively finance the Union's war effort. He was also instrumental in restructuring the nation's banking system and helped push through the Legal Tender Act of 1862, which introduced a national paper currency that became known as "greenbacks." With his eye still on the presidency, Chase began a surreptitious move toward the 1864 Republican presidential nomination, but word leaked out, causing him tremendous embarrassment. He offered his resignation to Lincoln, who accepted a few months later. In December

1864, Lincoln nominated Chase as chief justice of the Supreme Court. Chase made one more failed bid for the presidency in 1868, then continued to serve on the Supreme Court until his death in 1873.

- Secretary of the Navy Gideon Welles. Welles, a noted Connecticut journalist and politician, was chosen by Lincoln as secretary of the Navy so that New England would have a voice in the cabinet. And though he had no prior naval experience, he proved quite adept at the job, preparing the strategy for and overseeing the execution of the Union blockade of Southern ports and promoting the construction of ironclad ships. So well did Welles do his job that he held the post until 1869. In retirement, he wrote numerous articles and books on the Civil War, including a three-volume autobiography that provided an intimate account of the Lincoln administration.

- Secretary of War Simon Cameron. Cameron achieved his cabinet position as a result of a convention agreement that Lincoln knew nothing about and proved so corrupt and generally inept that Lincoln shipped him off to be minister to Russia within a year of his appointment. Cameron was replaced by Edwin M. Stanton, a vocal unionist who had served as attorney general under James Buchanan.

- Postmaster General Montgomery Blair. Blair came from a family well known in national politics since the era of Andrew Jackson. He was the only member of Lincoln's cabinet to advise sending needed provisions to Fort Sumter and threatened to resign, just two weeks after taking office, if Lincoln did not act on the issue. Blair proved to be a responsible and effective postmaster general and instituted a number of important postal reforms during his four years in office.

Confederate

- Secretary of State Robert Toombs. A rich and powerful Georgia plantation owner, Toombs resigned his United States Senate seat following the election of Abraham Lincoln and returned to his home state to assist its secession. Toombs hoped to be the first president of the Confederacy and was very disappointed when he was passed over in favor of Jefferson Davis. Davis offered Toombs the position of secretary of state, but Toombs quickly became bored (since the Confederacy had not been recognized by any foreign powers, there was little for the secretary of state to do) and remained in the position only five months before resigning to become commander of a Georgia brigade on the Virginia front—despite the fact that he had no military training. While secretary of state, Toombs urged restraint at Fort Sumter but became an advocate of all-out war once the first shots had been fired. Toombs narrowly escaped arrest at the end of the war by fleeing to Cuba and Europe, but he returned to Georgia in 1867.

✪ Secretary of the Navy Stephen R. Mallory. Mallory is unique among the early Confederate cabinet members in that he held his position throughout the entire war. Prior to secession, Mallory was a senator from Florida and served as Naval Affairs Committee chairman, a position that would make him well suited as secretary of the Navy for the Confederacy. When he first took office, the Confederate Navy consisted of just 10 ships mounting 15 guns and no organizational framework. But Mallory loved ships and the ocean and managed to create an imposing naval force despite limited resources and scant support from his government. Realizing the South could never compete with the sheer strength of the Union Navy, Mallory encouraged innovation and strongly supported the development of ironclad ships, torpedoes, and even submarines. Shortly after the surrender of the Confederacy, Mallory was arrested by federal forces and imprisoned at Fort Lafayette for 10 months. He finally received a full pardon from President Andrew Johnson and returned to his law practice in Pensacola, Florida.

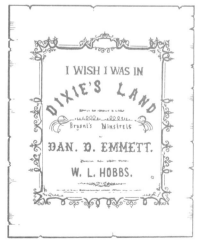

I WISH I WAS IN
DIXIE'S LAND
Bryant's Minstrels
DAN. D. EMMETT.
W. L. HOBBS.

- ✪ Attorney General Judah P. Benjamin. Benjamin was one of the most prominent and influential Jewish-American statesmen of the nineteenth century. He was also a brilliant legal mind, attending Yale University at age 14. He became a successful attorney in New Orleans and owned a sizable plantation with several slaves. In 1852, Benjamin was elected to the U.S. Senate and remained in office until Louisiana seceded from the Union. He was appointed attorney general by Jefferson Davis, with whom Benjamin had been good friends, but the position didn't give him much to do, and Davis named him secretary of war in 1861. Benjamin was transferred to the State Department a year later and was influential in securing for the Confederacy some much-needed foreign loans. At the end of the war, Benjamin avoided arrest by fleeing to the Bahamas and then to England, where he settled and resumed his law practice.

- ✪ Secretary of War Leroy P. Walker. An Alabama native, Walker was offered the position of secretary of war primarily to give his home state a voice in the Confederate cabinet. However, he quickly proved himself inept at the job and resigned after just seven months. Walker was replaced by Judah P. Benjamin, but four others would also hold the difficult post over the course of the Civil War.

- ✪ Secretary of the Treasury C. G. Memminger. Memminger was born in Germany and, after the death of his parents, spent his childhood in an orphanage in Charleston, South Carolina. But he refused to let his humble beginnings hold him back, and Memminger quickly achieved prominence in prewar South Carolina. As the Confederacy's first secretary of the treasury, Memminger instituted a financial policy, based on paper money, that did little to help the new republic, and as inflation rose, Confederate money became nearly worthless. Often a scapegoat for programs instituted by Congress, Memminger resigned as secretary of the treasury in June 1864.

EUROPEAN REACTION TO SOUTHERN SECESSION

When the Southern states left the Union to form their own nation, it was hoped that the Confederacy would quickly be recognized as an independent republic by the major foreign powers—England, France, and Russia. Such recognition would add strength to its legal claim of independence, as well as provide much needed financial and weapons support for the war with the North. However, the issue was not an easy one to settle. England and France had defeated Russia in the Crimean War, giving them the greatest control over Central and Eastern Europe, and both would have been ecstatic at the fall of the United States government. Russia, on the other hand, needed the United States as an ally to help control its European enemies.

Shortly after the fall of Fort Sumter, England's Queen Victoria declared her nation neutral in the conflict but acknowledged the Confederacy as a belligerent nation, which meant it could buy arms from neutral nations and capture merchant and military vessels. Confederate leaders had hoped for more concrete recognition, but accepted the status in the hope that full recognition would come later. The Lincoln administration, on the other hand, viewed England's neutrality as a hostile act and expressed its displeasure.

The Union had expected from the beginning that England would disavow the Confederacy, specifically over the issue of slavery, which most Britons considered a loathsome institution. (The first Confederate commissioners to England reported in May 1861 that "the public mind here is entirely opposed to the Government of the Confederate States of America on the question of slavery . . . The sincerity and universality of this feeling embarrass the government in dealing with the question of our recognition.") But while the British government acknowledged its disgust over the Confederacy's continued use of slaves, it ultimately decided on a position of neutrality primarily for financial reasons—British textile manufacturers were dependent on Southern cotton.

CIVIL WAR FACTOID

The delegates of the Confederate provisional congress constructed and ratified their new nation's constitution in a matter of weeks. It took the U.S. Continental Congress two years from draft to ratification (1787–89) to achieve a similar feat. Of course, the U.S. Continental Congress was starting from scratch, whereas the Confederate provisional congress at least had a template from which to work.

THE TRENT AFFAIR

The *Trent* Affair began when a Confederate blockade runner slipped out of Charleston Harbor on the night of October 11, 1861. Its mission was to transport James Mason, the Confederacy's envoy to England, and associate John Slidell to London and Paris to discuss the issue of Confederate recognition.

Arriving in Havana, Cuba, the two men transferred to the *Trent*, a British mail steamer that was bound for England. The next day the *Trent* was intercepted by the Union ship *San Jacinto*. Two shots were fired across the bow of the *Trent* and the ship was boarded—in clear violation of international law. Charles Wilkes, the captain of the *San Jacinto*, demanded Mason and Slidell's surrender. The *Trent* sailed to Boston, where Mason and Slidell were arrested and jailed. The *Trent* then continued on to England.

Union officials had no qualms over Captain Wilkes's

(continued)

Much to the Union's anger, England's neutral position meant that it could still aid the Confederacy in a number of ways. One of the most damaging to the Union war effort was British production of Confederate blockade runners and warships, particularly in Liverpool, where Southern sympathies ran high. Technically speaking, the construction of these ships violated Britain's Foreign Enlistment Act, which forbade the construction and arming of warships in British territory for a belligerent power, but the South (and its British sympathizers) found a number of helpful loopholes.

In one instance, a commerce raider ordered by Confederate agent James Bulloch was able to make it out of England after Bulloch provided forged papers showing that the ship was owned by a merchant of Palermo. To circumvent the Foreign Enlistment Act, the ship was put to sea unarmed, its heavy guns following on another vessel. The ship, later named the *Florida*, was sent to the Bahamas, fitted with its guns, and turned against Union merchant vessels. It destroyed 38 American ships before being captured by the Union Navy in October 1864. A second warship, the *Alabama*, also made it out of England following a lot of legal wrangling, espionage, and outright lies (the ship went on a "test run" and simply never returned). The *Alabama* destroyed or captured 64 American merchant vessels before being sunk by the *USS Kearsarge* in June 1864.

Particularly adept at garnering Southern sympathy among the British was Henry Hotze, a Swiss-born Alabamian and talented propagandist who worked ceaselessly to sway British opinion regarding the Confederacy. Hotze sweet-talked his way into the British social elite and wrote pro-Confederate editorials for a number of British newspapers. Hotze also quickly realized the value of being all things to all people. He told liberals that the South was fighting for its right to self-determination, and he told conservatives that the South's ruling class was defending its liberties against a greedy Union government. British businessmen were courted with the promise that the Confederacy would open its ports to free trade without protective tariffs.

THE SOUTHERN COTTON EMBARGO

One aspect of the Union's attack on the Confederacy was a naval blockade of Southern ports, designed to help strangle the South by preventing goods from coming in or going out. The blockade was only partially effective, considering the small number of ships in the Union Navy and the vast expanse of Southern shoreline, but it did strike an important blow against the Confederacy by preventing foreign businesses from legally doing trade with Southern states. As a result, a major goal of Confederate diplomacy in the first years of the war was to convince England to declare the blockade illegal so that the Royal Navy could come in and protect British trade with Southern merchants.

In 1861, the Confederacy hoped to force England's hand through an unofficial policy that became known as "cotton diplomacy." Knowing that England imported nearly three-fourths of its cotton from the South, Confederate farmers began withholding cotton supplies from British textile manufacturers. Their goal was to use economic extortion to compel England (and to a lesser degree, France) to recognize the new Confederate republic as an independent nation. It made sense in theory: No cotton meant no textile production, thus bringing the entire industry and thus the government to its knees. The concept dated back to 1858, when James Hammond of South Carolina made a speech suggesting that the withholding of cotton would cause England to topple "and carry the whole civilized world with her, save the South."

There was just one flaw with the plan: England and France both had more cotton than they knew what to do with. A bumper crop just prior to the war pushed prices down and allowed the two nations to stockpile almost two years' worth. In fact, as late as 1862, England was able to ship some of its cotton back to mills in New England. In addition, England had found ample new sources of cotton in Egypt and India, which had become part of the British Empire. British leaders contemplated the situation for a while and finally decided that the loss of Southern cotton was less of a problem than the loss of the more lucrative Northern industrial markets, especially during wartime. When all was said and done, "cotton diplomacy" netted the Confederacy almost nothing.

THE TRENT AFFAIR
(continued from previous page)

behavior and commended him on his "patriotic conduct" in capturing the Confederate diplomats. The British, however, were genuinely outraged. With rhetoric reaching a fever pitch on both sides, British Prime Minister Lord Palmerston issued an ultimatum that the Union couldn't ignore: release Mason and Slidell or face war. England still sent an imposing eight thousand soldiers to Canada as a show of force. Worse for the Union, the incident only increased sympathy for the Confederacy.

Lincoln, realizing that the Union needed England more than England needed the Union, quickly backed down on the issue. By late December, he acknowledged that Mason and Slidell had been arrested illegally and agreed to release them. On January 1, 1862, the two men were turned over to British officials and allowed to continue to England.

3

Political Leaders of the North and South

LINCOLN ARRIVES IN WASHINGTON

Abraham Lincoln's arrival in Washington for his first inauguration was anything but celebratory. He was forced to sneak into the city because of threats on his life.

On the train journey that took Lincoln and his family from Illinois to Washington, Lincoln stopped in Philadelphia and met with a private detective named Allan Pinkerton. Pinkerton reported that his agents had uncovered an assassination plot against Lincoln by Confederate sympathizers. Pinkerton advised Lincoln to arrive in Washington a day earlier than planned, but Lincoln refused because of social commitments. Later that day, Lincoln received confirmation of the assassination

(continued)

The Civil War presented the greatest challenge faced by an American president up to that time and possibly ever. It could be argued that World War I and World War II were equally daunting in scope, logistics, and manpower, but those conflicts pitted American servicemen against the military might of foreign powers, not against each other.

The fact that Americans were forced to do battle with each other is one of the most tragic features of the Civil War, and just one of many factors that made the conflict unique in the course of American history. The Civil War truly was a war that pitched brother against brother and friend against friend, and this horrible aspect took an agonizing toll on the two men in charge—U.S. President Abraham Lincoln and Confederate President Jefferson Davis. Both men realized that they literally were fighting for the existence of their respective republics, but both also loathed the fact that victory meant taking the lives of a great many of their countrymen.

In the 135 years since the end of the Civil War, Abraham Lincoln has been analyzed, eulogized, mythicized, and deified. His assassination created an American Christ figure unparalleled until the assassination of John Kennedy 98 years later, and debate still rages among historians regarding the man and his presidency. But while Abraham Lincoln certainly had his faults and made many missteps as president, the 20/20 hindsight of history has shown that the United States could not have had a better leader during the nation's greatest crisis. Above all else, Lincoln was a man of kindness, compassion, intelligence, and integrity, and he did what he considered necessary to keep the Union whole.

In contrast, Jefferson Davis has been condemned over the years as a traitor and is often placed on the same page with Benedict Arnold in the pantheon of American villains. But this is an unfair comparison. Davis was a proud American but always a Southerner first, and when it became apparent that compromise could no longer keep the North and the South together, he had no choice but to follow his conscience and advocate secession. He wasn't so much anti-American as he was more pro-South (as were a great many people at that time). President of the Confederacy wasn't a job Davis particularly wanted, but he did his very best to serve the new republic. Unfortunately, he faced odds so overwhelming that failure, no matter who held the office, was almost assured.

It's interesting to note, by the way, that Lincoln and Davis shared more similarities than differences. Both men were born in Kentucky. Both men were relatively unpopular leaders, especially during those times when their side experienced devastating losses on the battlefield. Both men had to deal with conflicting political sentiment within their administrations and the public at large. Both men experienced serious problems with their military leaders. And, on a personal level, both men suffered extreme hardship and the loss of dear friends and loved ones over the course of the war.

At the end of the Civil War, Abraham Lincoln was declared a hero and Jefferson Davis a scoundrel. Yet both men were merely following their hearts and doing what they considered best for their countries, as any good leader would.

ABRAHAM LINCOLN: A SHORT BIOGRAPHY

Few American presidents have had to face the turbulence and turmoil that met Abraham Lincoln at his inauguration and followed him throughout the duration of his presidency. He had barely settled into the White House when the roiling cauldron of dissent between the North and the South came to a head, forcing him to make the most difficult decision any president has had to face—that is, declaring war against his fellow countrymen. Lincoln did so with a heavy heart, his intent only to preserve the Union as he felt the Constitution required. Lincoln did not find glory in war, only horror and death. He did all he could to end the conflict quickly, and when the dust settled over the final battlefield, he had planned to greet the defeated South with kindness rather than animosity and immediately set about to mend the physical and emotional carnage the war had wrought. Ultimately, however, the war would cost Lincoln his life and the nation one of the finest leaders it ever had.

LINCOLN ARRIVES IN WASHINGTON
(continued from previous page)

plan from General Winfield Scott.

After completing the next day's festivities, Lincoln secretly returned to Philadelphia. Disguised in a brown hat and overcoat, he slipped into the last sleeper car on the Baltimore-bound train and was passed off as the invalid brother of one of Pinkerton's female detectives. Guarding Lincoln on the trip was Pinkerton and Ward Hill Lamon, a close friend of Lincoln's from Springfield.

Lincoln's train safely reached Baltimore around 3:15 A.M. and Lincoln's coach was quickly hooked to a train going to Washington. He arrived in the nation's capital at dawn on February 23, and his family arrived in a separate train later that day.

LINCOLN'S CHILDHOOD YEARS

Abraham Lincoln was born on February 12, 1809, to Thomas and Nancy Lincoln on the family farm near Hogdenville, Kentucky. The Lincoln family, which included Abraham's younger sister Sarah, were hardworking farmers who toiled the land, planting corn and other crops. Thomas Lincoln was a simple, uneducated man who was known for his honesty and affable personality. He worked hard to support his family, and all pitched in as best they could. It was from his parents that Abraham Lincoln learned the value of hard work, diligence, and strength of character. They also instilled in him a dislike for the institution of slavery, which they found morally objectionable.

When Lincoln was seven years old, his family moved from Kentucky to Indiana and started another farm. Two years later, Lincoln's beloved mother passed away from brucellosis, which resulted from drinking milk produced by cows that had eaten the poisonous white snakeroot plant. Her passing hit Lincoln hard, and some speculate that his deep sorrow may have been the basis for the depression that would afflict him for most of his adult life, though this is more conjecture than anything else. Less than a year after Nancy's death, Thomas traveled back to Kentucky to find another wife to help him support his farm and children. In Elizabethtown, he became reacquainted with Sarah Bush Johnston, a widow whom he had courted prior to meeting Nancy. They wed quickly, more out of convenience than romantic love; Thomas needed a wife and Sarah needed a husband to help her support her three small children. Thomas paid Sarah's outstanding debts, and they returned to Indiana.

Sarah brought tremendous love to the Lincoln household. She embraced Thomas's children as her own (as he did her children), and Abraham quickly came to accept her as his mother. He never forgot his birth mother, however, and differentiated the two women by referring to Nancy in later years as his "angel mother."

It's common knowledge that Abraham Lincoln received only a few years of formal schooling as a youngster, but he was a very bright student. He wrote well, became proficient at basic mathematics, and excelled at spelling, often stumping his fellow classmates in school spelling bees. Lincoln was also a voracious reader and frequently memorized entire passages from the limited number of books that were available to him in his younger years. Though perhaps ill educated by contemporary standards, Lincoln made the best of what was available to him and used it to further himself personally and professionally for the rest of his life.

Lincoln worked hard to be successful, but most of his early ventures didn't pan out very well. He became a shopkeeper in New Salem, Illinois, when he was 21, but the business didn't flourish as he had anticipated; eventually, his partner died, and Lincoln was left with a heavy debt. He worked a variety of jobs, including surveyor and postmaster, to pay off his creditors, and such endeavors only helped to strengthen his reputation as a man of honesty and integrity. While certainly not averse to hard physical labor, Lincoln soon realized that being a lawyer would be a good way to maintain financial stability, and he started reading law books as a path toward that goal. Two documents that impressed him greatly were the Declaration of Independence and the U.S. Constitution. The men who wrote those words became Lincoln's personal heroes.

EARLY POLITICS

Illinois was a state in the throes of change, and Lincoln was driven to make his mark in state politics. His first political position was a seat on the state legislature, which he won when he was just 23. He would spend four terms in office (from 1832 to 1838), and it was there, during his first years as a political figure, that his reputation as a man of principal and idealism was forged.

Lincoln was especially adept at managing people and calming conflict, and he was selected Whig floor leader at the beginning of his second term. He was a leader in the establishment of the Bank of Illinois and led the campaign to move the state capital from Vandalia to Springfield. Lincoln made his first stand on the issue of slavery in 1837, when he protested a number of resolutions passed by the Illinois legislature condemning abolitionist societies. At that time, Lincoln admitted that he felt Congress could not interfere with slavery in the states in which it already existed, but he personally felt that the institution was founded

Abraham Lincoln

on "both injustice and bad policy" and that steps should be taken to prevent its spread into new territories. This would be Lincoln's personal policy regarding the institution of slavery, right up to the issuance of the Emancipation Proclamation in 1862.

Lincoln passed the state bar in 1836 and set up a law practice in Springfield a year later. He proved to be a talented and well-spoken lawyer and quickly became one of the most prominent attorneys in the area. As a circuit lawyer, Lincoln traveled through 15 counties for 6 months of the year, a situation that allowed him to meet the populace and hear their thoughts on the most important issues of the day. Such folksy socializing enabled Lincoln to really understand what the common man was thinking and feeling and helped him greatly in his capacity as a state legislator.

In 1840, Lincoln did some political stumping for Whig presidential candidate William Henry Harrison and used the platform to promote a central banking system. He solicited the Whig nomination to Congress in 1843 and 1844—losing both times—but was elected to the U.S. House of Representatives in 1846, after campaigning for Henry Clay. In Congress, Lincoln came out against the Mexican War and for the Wilmot Proviso, a piece of legislation that, had it not been defeated by Congress, would have banned slavery in any territory acquired from Mexico. His term ended in 1849, and Lincoln returned to Springfield, Illinois, where he quickly built his law practice into one of the most influential corporate firms in the state.

Lincoln managed to avoid politics for four years, but the Kansas-Nebraska Act pushed him back into the political arena. Lincoln actively campaigned against the act throughout Illinois and was elected to the state legislature as the leader of the Illinois factions opposing the spread of slavery into the territories. However, his stint was short lived. Lincoln quit the state legislature after just a few months to run for the U.S. Senate, a bid that he lost. In 1856, Lincoln joined the Republican Party, which advocated the end of slavery, and he made numerous speeches on behalf of John C. Fremont, the first Republican presidential candidate. Fremont lost the 1856 election to James Buchanan, but he set the stage for Lincoln's presidential run four years later.

THE LINCOLN-DOUGLAS DEBATES

Abraham Lincoln was a gifted public speaker, but he found his talents put to the test in the now famous Lincoln-Douglas debates of 1858. Lincoln had been chosen by the Republican Party to run against Stephen Douglas for the U.S. Senate that year, and in an attempt to get his name out there and generate some much needed publicity, he quietly challenged Douglas—one of the most famous political figures of his time—to a series of seven debates on various issues, primarily the extension of slavery into the territories. Douglas accepted, but knew he was taking a big chance in doing so. The result was a confrontation between two well-spoken, outspoken men that is still remembered today as one of the most thrilling examples of American politics in action.

Slavery immediately became the hottest issue in the debates, and the verbal sparring often got extremely ugly by contemporary standards. Rather than fielding questions from journalists, as is the case today, the candidates themselves decided the tone and content of the debates. From the very beginning, they went at each other like verbal brawlers, often fighting dirty to make the other look silly or stupid. It was grand entertainment, and hundreds of people attended each debate simply to see what would happen.

Douglas immediately went on the offensive. He tried to discredit Lincoln on the issue of slavery by painting him as a rabid abolitionist who wished to put blacks on an equal basis with whites. He also suggested that Lincoln was advocating interracial marriage and hinted that if emancipation were to occur, the Illinois Territory would be overrun with freed blacks who would take jobs away from whites. Lincoln countered by calling Douglas's claims "counterfeit logic." He tried to explain his position as rationally as he could, noting that his call to halt the spread of slavery did not mean he was advocating any type of amalgamation of the races. He also reiterated his long-held belief that slavery was "a moral, social, and political evil" but that the federal government had no right to interfere in the rights of states in which slavery already existed.

Douglas knew that Lincoln was no backwoods bumpkin and that he would have to be in top form in order to win the debates and then the election. Though opponents, each man respected the

LINCOLN ON SLAVERY

It was while accepting the Republican nomination for the United States Senate race against Stephen Douglas in 1858 that Abraham Lincoln made his famous comment regarding the national debate over slavery: "A house divided against itself cannot endure, permanently half slave and half free. I do not expect the Union to be dissolved—I do not expect the house to fall—but I do expect it will cease to be divided. It will become all one thing or all the other."

Stephan Douglas

Stephen Arnold Douglas was short in stature but a giant among the politicians of his time. A gifted orator with a sharp mind, he unwittingly split the nation in half and pushed the two sides toward civil war with the Kansas-Nebraska Act, which, as a senator from Illinois, he introduced to Congress in 1854.

Douglas, who received the nickname "Little Giant," was an expansionist who advocated the acquisition of territory via the Mexican War. He was also quite good at maintaining relations with leaders in the North and the South and was nominated for president in 1852, a race he lost. Douglas remained in the Senate and worked to help the North and South reach compromises on the most important issues of the 1850s.

As chairman of the Senate committee on the territories, he found himself in the center of controversy over the issue of whether new states should be free or slaveholding. Douglas was moderate on the issue, focused more on expanding the nation to the Pacific coast and building a transcontinental railroad. To solve the deadlock over the issue, Douglas proposed the Kansas-Nebraska Act, which repealed the Missouri Compromise and promoted the concept of "popular sovereignty," or allowing the citizens of a territory to decide for themselves. The act was passed, with less than successful results. Proslavery and antislavery advocates in Kansas debated the issue with guns and other weapons, bringing the territory to the brink of civil war and giving it the nickname "Bleeding Kansas." It was hardly the compromise Douglas had envisioned, and he accepted responsibility for the fiasco.

In 1858, Douglas ran for re-election to the Senate. He was opposed by Abraham Lincoln, who at that time was little known outside of Illinois. During the campaign, the two candidates engaged in a series of seven debates over the issue of slavery. Douglas challenged Lincoln's stance on the issue while still promoting "popular sovereignty," which lost him much support among radical Southerners. Douglas won the race but at a heavy cost. His position on slavery continued to alienate him from his fellow Democrats and helped divide the party during the 1860 presidential election, in which Douglas again faced Lincoln. With his party split, Douglas didn't stand a chance, and Lincoln won handily.

other. Douglas described Lincoln as "the strong man of his party—full of wit, facts, dates—and the best stump speaker in the West. If I beat him, my victory will be hardly won." Said Lincoln of Douglas: "Senator Douglas is of world-wide renown. All the anxious politicians of his party . . . have been looking upon him . . . to be President. Nobody has ever expected me to be President."

Lincoln ultimately lost the Senate race to Douglas (who was elected by state legislators, not a popular vote as is the case today), but he ended up a bigger winner in the long run. His excellent showing in the debates and the fact that he provided Douglas with challenging competition made him a national figure and greatly increased his popularity within the Republican Party, which found his moderate stand on the issues a pleasant change from more radical Republicans like William Seward or Salmon Chase. Party officials would demonstrate their approval just two years later by selecting Lincoln as the Republican presidential candidate.

LINCOLN'S FIRST PRESIDENTIAL ELECTION

The presidential election of 1860 was one of the most raucous in American history. The Democratic Party convened in Charleston, South Carolina, in April, to select a suitable candidate, but adjourned without doing so after 50 delegates from the Southern states stormed out when the party refused to include a platform that guaranteed the constitutional protection of slave owners. The Democrats reconvened the following month in Baltimore, but were again unable to reach a suitable compromise on the slavery issue, and, once more, the Southern delegates walked out, taking the majority of the Upper South delegates with them. The remaining Democratic delegates selected Senator Stephen Douglas as their presidential candidate, based on a platform of popular sovereignty, once again pitching Douglas against Abraham Lincoln.

The more than one hundred Southern Democrats who had walked out of the Baltimore convention gathered elsewhere in the city and nominated John Breckinridge of Kentucky as their candidate of choice. Their platform called for the federal government to protect the rights of persons and property in the territories and wherever else its constitutional authority extended. Breckinridge was endorsed by incumbent president James Buchanan and former presidents John Tyler and Franklin Pierce.

Meanwhile, the Republican Party held its convention in Chicago and established a platform that, among other things, opposed the spread of slavery into the territories. Contenders for the nomination included William Seward of New York, who was popularly viewed as a radical abolitionist; Salmon Chase of Ohio; and Edward Cameron of Pennsylvania. Lincoln wasn't the first choice of most of the delegates, but he was the second choice for many of them because of his relatively moderate stand on the important issues. The Pennsylvania delegation switched to Lincoln on the second ballot, and Lincoln took the nomination on the third ballot. Part of his victory may have resulted from a backroom deal that promised Cameron a cabinet post should Lincoln win, and Cameron became Lincoln's first secretary of war.

But that wasn't all. A contentious faction of the Whig party calling themselves the Constitutional Union Party also met in Baltimore; they selected John Bell of Tennessee as their preferred candidate. However, neither the party nor Bell had much to offer voters. Their platform addressed none of the important issues, such as slavery, and merely vowed to uphold the Constitution. As a result, the party came to be jokingly known as the "Do-Nothing" and "Old Man's" Party.

When Election Day rolled around, the race for president had been regionally divided into two specific contests: Lincoln and Douglas in the North (Lincoln wasn't even on the ballot in the Southern states), and Bell and Breckinridge in the South. The candidates campaigned vigorously, and the races contained more than their share of mud slinging and rumor mongering. But in the end, the sharp division within the Democratic Party guaranteed a victory of Abraham Lincoln, who won almost 40 percent of the popular vote and, more importantly, the electoral votes of the largest states in the North and the West.

LINCOLN'S SECOND PRESIDENTIAL ELECTION

Despite doing his best to preserve the Union and bring the Southern states back into the fold, Lincoln almost wasn't reelected in 1864. The public had grown weary of the war, especially the huge number of casualties and the tremendous amount of money required to keep the Union war machine rolling, and they placed blame for the whole mess squarely at Lincoln's feet. The Union had assumed that the war would be over in a matter of months, and the longer it dragged on, the less support Lincoln had among the Northern states. So bleak did things look toward the end that Lincoln himself felt that he would never win the Republican nomination for a second term. The front-runner, at least for a while, appeared to be Salmon P. Chase, who had long held presidential aspirations.

Indeed, Chase did all he could to undermine Lincoln's chances while bolstering his own. As secretary of the treasury, he surrounded himself with a cadre of high-ranking Republicans who believed they were the true power brokers, and he did all he could to curry their favor. However, Chase's bid for the White House was cut short early in the game, when a clandestine attempt to remove Lincoln from the ticket and replace him with Chase became publicly known. The coup made Chase look disloyal to Lincoln, and Chase offered his resignation, which Lincoln accepted a few months later.

Despite growing public dissatisfaction with the war, Lincoln did receive his party's nomination. However, Vice President Hannibal Hamlin was replaced by Andrew Johnson, the Democratic governor of Tennessee. Republican leaders felt that the addition of Johnson increased regional balance and improved Lincoln's chances of winning a second term. The party also temporarily changed its name to the Union Party.

Lincoln's greatest opponent in the 1864 election was George B. McClellan, who won the Democratic nomination during the party's convention in Chicago. The race had all the makings of a true

grudge match, because Lincoln and McClellan, who had commanded the Army of the Potomac, had clashed often during the war. Lincoln eventually dismissed McClellan (who held Lincoln in disdain and never missed an opportunity to say so) over McClellan's frustrating reluctance to pursue the enemy.

McClellan ran on a platform of peace that included a vow to end hostilities with the Confederacy, though personally McClellan believed the war should be continued until the Union won. He felt Lincoln had not proved himself an effective leader during the war, and he also had problems with Lincoln's policy of emancipation. Lincoln countered by portraying the Democratic Party—and its candidate—as disloyal to the Union, and he reiterated the need to preserve the Union at all costs.

One of the biggest thorns in Lincoln's side as the presidential race heated up was the lack of substantial Union victories. Increasingly, Lincoln's leadership and ability to control his fighting forces was called into question, and every Confederate victory was another nail in his political coffin. Newspaper editorials lambasted him at every turn, and his political foes rejoiced at every failure. But the race took a decided turn in Lincoln's favor when William Tecumseh Sherman took Atlanta and David Farragut won the battle of Mobile Bay. Suddenly, the Union was making decisive strikes against the Confederacy, and the end of the war seemed nearer than ever. Lincoln's star shined brighter than ever, and he soundly defeated an arrogant McClellan. Lincoln received 55 percent of the popular vote, and his margin in the electoral college was even more impressive—212 to 21. McClellan had won only his home state of New Jersey and the border states of Kentucky and Delaware.

THE ASSASSINATION OF ABRAHAM LINCOLN

Few events in American history have become so ingrained in the public consciousness as the assassination of Abraham Lincoln. His murder by John Wilkes Booth, coming literally at the end of the Civil War, plunged an already weary nation into deep sorrow.

For many Americans, it was the ultimate tragedy following four years of overwhelming anguish and suffering. Tears at the loss of a great and noble leader flooded the land.

The event began a week after Confederate General Robert E. Lee's surrender to Union General Ulysses S. Grant at Appomattox Court House. An exhausted Lincoln decided to relax by attending a production of a light comedy, *Our American Cousin*, at Ford's Theatre in Washington, D.C. Nearly a dozen people were invited to join the Lincolns at the theater, but only two—Major Henry Rathbone and his fiancée, Clara Harris—did so. Among those who declined were General Grant and his wife. They demurred partly because Mrs. Grant and Mrs. Lincoln did not get along well. Mrs. Lincoln had become extremely jealous of General Grant's popularity and had humiliated Mrs. Grant in public in a fit of pique. Rather than risk another embarrassing incident, the Grants thought it wise to stay home—a decision that probably saved Grant's life.

The Lincolns arrived at the theater with the play already in progress, and the show was stopped briefly so the president and his wife could be welcomed by the audience. The Lincolns, Major Rathbone, and Miss Harris then took their seats and the production continued. Security surrounding the president was light. Though his life had been threatened repeatedly over the course of the war, only a single special guard accompanied him.

At approximately 10 P.M., having finished two snifters of brandy at a nearby bar, John Wilkes Booth, a handsome actor, well known to the theater staff, walked into Ford's and had a friendly chat with the ticket taker, who allowed him in gratis, as a professional courtesy. Around 10:15, during the third act of

John Wilkes Booth

John Wilkes Booth was a rising young stage performer who might have gone on to great success had he not let his despondency over the defeat of the Confederacy and his hatred of Abraham Lincoln overwhelm him.

Booth was born in Maryland in 1838 to a theatrical family. He began his own acting career at age 17 and toured the nation in various productions. He later joined a Virginia militia unit and was present at the execution of radical abolitionist John Brown.

Booth's family was pro-Union once the Civil War began, though Booth was a devout Confederate sympathizer. During the war, Booth gained fame for his dashing good looks and strong voice. Booth and Abraham Lincoln often crossed paths. In November 1863, Lincoln attended a production of *The Marble Heart* at Ford's Theatre, in which Booth was one of the stars. Booth was also an invited guest to Lincoln's second inauguration and can be seen in several photographs of the event.

Booth and a gang of conspirators developed a plan to assassinate the president and several members of his cabinet. Only Booth was successful, killing Lincoln with a single shot to the back of the head during a production of *Our American Cousin*. Booth escaped but was found at a friend's farm in Virginia nearly two weeks later. Refusing orders to give up, Booth was found shot to death, most likely by his own hand.

the play, Booth approached Lincoln's box, which was guarded only by a White House footman named Charles Forbes (the Metropolitan policeman assigned to protect the president had left his post for a few moments), and was admitted in upon showing his calling card. Booth quietly slipped in behind Lincoln, who was leaning forward to more clearly see someone he knew in the audience below, and shot the president in the back of the head with a small single-shot derringer. Major Rathbone quickly stood up to grab Booth, but Booth stabbed him in the arm with a seven-inch dagger, then leaped from the box to the stage below. The jump was an easy one for Booth, who was quite athletic, but his spur caught on the bunting outside the president's box, and he landed awkwardly, breaking his leg. Booth shouted, "Sic semper tyrannis!" ("Thus always to tyrants!") before the stunned audience, then hobbled to the exit, where a horse awaited him. Many members of the audience thought Booth's dramatic entrance was actually part of the production, until people started shouting that Lincoln had been shot. Theater staff immediately identified the assailant as John Wilkes Booth.

The first doctor to attend to Lincoln was a young Army surgeon named Charles A. Leale, who had only recently graduated from medical school. Lincoln was paralyzed, his eyes closed, and Leale initially thought the president was dead. But after Leale probed the bullet wound with his finger, Lincoln showed signs of life and was quickly transported to a home across the street from the theater. He had to be placed diagonally across the bed because he was too tall to fit in it lengthwise.

As word of the attack on Lincoln spread through Washington, a parade of physicians (including Lincoln's personal doctor, Robert Stone) and other medical personnel raced to the house to attend to the president. However, despite their best intentions, it's the consensus of medical experts today that they did more harm than

good. The wound was explored two more times and kept clear of coagulating blood, but there was little else the doctors could do. Lincoln stopped breathing at 6:50 A.M., recovered, then stopped breathing again. He was declared dead at 7:22 A.M. and Vice President Andrew Johnson was sworn in as president within just a few hours.

THE PLOT AGAINST LINCOLN

The assassination of Abraham Lincoln was not the act of a single disgruntled Confederate sympathizer—it was part of a wide-ranging conspiracy to avenge the South. Booth and several associates spent months planning an attack on Lincoln, and his attendance at the theater finally gave them the perfect opportunity. Originally, they had planned to kidnap the president and exchange him for Confederate prisoners of war and possibly a peace treaty between the warring sides. However, as the Confederacy itself started to fall, Booth changed his plans and decided to kill Lincoln instead. Also on the conspirators' hit list were Vice President Johnson, Secretary of State Seward, and General Ulysses S. Grant. A goon named Lewis Powell was sent to assassinate Seward at his home, but he managed only to wound him, thanks in part to the heavy neck brace Seward was wearing at the time of the attack. Powell also wounded two of Seward's sons and his secretary before fleeing.

After shooting Lincoln, Booth escaped by racing over the Navy Yard Bridge. He was met by an accomplice named David Herold, and the men stopped at the home of Dr. Samuel A. Mudd, who set Booth's broken leg. Booth and Herold then fled to the home of a fellow Confederate sympathizer, who hid them from authorities for almost a week. The two men then traveled to Bowling Green, Virginia, where they stopped at the farm of Richard Garrett. A couple of days later, Booth and Herold were surrounded by Union cavalry while sleeping in Garrett's tobacco barn. The soldiers ordered the assassin and his henchman to surrender. Herold immediately gave up, but Booth refused. The barn was set ablaze, and Booth was shot

COULD LINCOLN HAVE SURVIVED?

Could Abraham Lincoln have survived Booth's attack had he received better medical care? Some experts believe so. Dr. Richard A. R. Fraser, in an article in *American Heritage* magazine, speculated that the attending doctors facilitated Lincoln's death by probing the gunshot wound with unsterile fingers and a metal probe, which countered accepted medical practice even for that time. Speculation on the possibility of Lincoln's survival is based on the fact that many Civil War veterans survived gunshot wounds to the head far more severe than Lincoln's.

and killed. A soldier named Boston Corbett took credit for killing Booth, but forensic evidence suggests that Booth actually took his own life.

Not surprisingly, rumors of a large Confederate conspiracy in the death of Lincoln and the attacks on his cabinet swept through Washington. Some rumors suggested that Jefferson Davis and other prominent Confederate officials were in on the plot, but such was not the case; Booth and his cadre of Union haters had worked alone. In trials that reeked more of revenge than justice, all of the conspirators were found guilty, and four of them were executed by hanging. Three others, including Samuel Mudd, the doctor who set Booth's broken leg, were sentenced to life imprisonment, though Mudd served only four years before being pardoned and released. John Surratt, in whose boarding house the bizarre plot was conceived, managed to escape to Canada, then Europe, and finally the Papal States. He was arrested in 1866 and brought home for trial, but a hung jury freed him.

JEFFERSON DAVIS: A SHORT BIOGRAPHY

Jefferson Finis Davis faced a long, arduous, and ultimately losing battle almost from the day he was selected provisional president of the infant Confederate States of America. The position called for a man of tremendous character, well accomplished in both governing politics and military strategy, and Davis was lacking in both areas. However, his military and political background, though less than stellar, and, most importantly, his dedication to the Southern states made him the ideal candidate among the members of the provisional congress, who saw in Davis a more moderate leader than many other aspirants. Davis did his best to establish the Confederacy as a self-sufficient, independent nation, but mercurial public opinion, infighting within his administration and military, his own personality quirks, and a war the South could not possibly win would prevent him from achieving his goals.

CIVIL WAR FACTOID

Lincoln's funeral procession from Washington to Springfield, Illinois, was viewed by millions. His body lay in state in Washington, D.C., New York, Chicago, and other cities and took nearly two weeks to reach its final destination.

Davis was born in Christian County, Kentucky, on June 3, 1808, the youngest of ten children. Though he would become a devout Confederate patriot, he was only a second-generation Southerner; his grandfather had moved from Pennsylvania to Georgia, where Davis's father was born. When Davis was a child, his family moved to Mississippi, where his father owned a small farm. Though a practicing Baptist, Davis attended a Catholic seminary back in Kentucky and entered West Point in 1823. A mediocre student, he graduated in the last third of his class. (Robert E. Lee attended West Point at the same time.)

Upon graduating from West Point, Davis served as an officer in a number of distant posts in Illinois and Wisconsin and saw a little military action during the Black Hawk Indian War (as did Abraham Lincoln), though the conflict did little to enhance Davis's military skills. Davis fell in love with the daughter of one of his post commandants, Colonel Zachary Taylor (who would go on to become the 12th president of the United States), and married her against Taylor's wishes, after resigning from the Army. Sarah Davis died of malaria within three months of their marriage (Davis caught the disease, too, and would suffer from bouts of malarial fever for the rest of his life), and Davis spent the next 10 years working on his plantation in Mississippi. It was during this period that Davis really came to identify with the Southern mentality and lifestyle, including the institution of slavery. He became a proud Southerner and states' rights advocate and, like most of his countrymen, bristled at the thought of any sort of Northern intrusion. During these years, a true Confederate was born.

Davis eventually became involved in politics and won a seat in the House of Representatives in 1845; he was supported and encouraged by his brother Joseph, a man of wealth and national influence. In that same year, Davis fell in love with and married Varina Howell, a pretty and personable daughter of a local gentry.

Davis was in office just a few months before resigning his seat to participate in the Mexican War, where he saw just enough action on the battlefield to convince himself that he was an accomplished military man. Sadly, such was not the case, and Davis's own inflated self-image would spark numerous conflicts with his more battled-seasoned military leaders during the Civil War.

Davis re-entered national politics as a Senator from Mississippi and made a name for himself by strongly supporting Southern causes, including slavery (which he thought should be expanded into the territories) and states' rights. In 1853, President Franklin Pierce appointed Davis his secretary of war and during his three years in that office, Davis assumed an expansionist stance to foreign affairs, a position that reflected his position regarding the expansion of slavery. When his term was completed, Davis returned to the Senate, where he continued his vocal advocacy of slavery.

Despite Davis's unwavering support of Southern causes and his deep love of the South itself, he did not endorse secession and struggled through the Democratic conventions of 1860 to encourage some sort of compromise that would keep the Union whole. But with the election of Abraham Lincoln and the new president's statement that he would not tolerate the spread of slavery into any more territories, Davis knew that the line had been drawn. With a heavy heart, he resigned his Senate seat on January 21, 1861, and joined his fellow Southerners in seceding from the Union.

Davis had hoped to become commander of the Confederate Army and was surprised when he was made provisional president—a position he assumed primarily because the bickering delegates could not agree on any other choice. Davis took the reins of the new republic with an eye toward total independence and international recognition, but he faced so many obstacles that his chances of success were next to nil.

His biggest problem was that he headed the central government of a new nation made up of states that wanted to retain as many rights for themselves as possible. In other words, the states recognized the need for a central government but didn't want to give it any power. Issues such as taxation, conscription of troops, currency, and the suspension of civil laws in the face of a war were a source of constant debate

Jefferson Davis

as the states tried to decide just how much authority their new government should have.

All of this, of course, made preparing for a war with the North all the more difficult for Davis, a man who lacked many of the basic leadership skills that made Abraham Lincoln the best man to lead the Union during this troubling period. By comparison, Davis was easily distracted, too confident of his own limited abilities, unwilling to compromise on important issues, lacking in people skills, and in frail health. Though his heart was in the right place, Davis was a man in over his head from the very beginning.

Worse, the South simply wasn't prepared for a long war. It had no standing army, lacked the manufacturing capability to produce sufficient arms and other necessary goods, and soon suffered from a Northern blockade of its most important ports. Its greatest advantage was its military leadership; many of the U.S. Army's best military minds were from the South and had resigned their posts to join the Confederacy. Left alone, they very well might have been able to resist the North until both sides were ready to talk peace. But Davis wouldn't let them do their jobs. Thinking himself a skilled military strategist, he constantly fought with his commanding officers, who grew increasingly weary of his nonstop meddling. The only officer in which Davis expressed complete confidence was Robert E. Lee. Indeed, Davis was constantly on edge and got into fights and debates with just about everyone around him, military or civilian. As a result, his reputation within the Confederacy suffered greatly over the course of the war, as did the reputations of those who were closest to him.

The South fought valiantly, but the cause seemed all but lost by the winter of 1864–65. The Confederate Army was severely lacking in the most basic necessities, and the North had started several major assaults that threatened to bring the new republic to its knees. But even then, Jefferson Davis was confident that he could broker peace with the Union and save his beloved Confederacy. In February 1865, Davis bragged from the Confederate capital of Richmond, Virginia: "We may well believe that before another summer solstice falls upon us it will be the enemy who will be

CONFEDERATE MONEY

When Jefferson Davis and his cabinet arrived in Danville, Virginia, by train, the Confederate treasury in their possession was given a new value of $327,022— a sum substantially smaller than the estimated value of nearly $550,000 given the treasury when Davis fled Richmond. All attempts to account for the discrepancy proved fruitless, and rumors that Davis had stolen the funds dogged him for years. However, most historians agree that Davis could not and would not have taken the money. Amusingly, the incident ended up as a subplot in Margaret Mitchell's *Gone with the Wind*.

asking us for conferences." But just two months later, Richmond was on the brink of Union capture, forcing Davis and other Confederate leaders to flee.

THE CAPTURE OF JEFFERSON DAVIS

By the end of March 1865, it became evident that despite the best efforts of Robert E. Lee and his dedicated but ragtag army, the Confederate capital of Richmond could not be held. On April 2, Lee warned Davis that he could no longer hold back the Union army and strongly suggested that Davis and his cabinet leave Richmond as soon as possible. Davis and others gathered what they could—including the Confederate treasury's remaining gold worth more than $500,000, Confederate bank notes, negotiable bonds, and a chest full of jewels—and boarded a train for Danville, Virginia. A day later, Union troops entered Richmond and Petersburg.

Davis had hoped to establish a new Confederate capital in Danville and continue the war against the North with Lee at the charge, but it simply wasn't meant to be. Following Lee's surrender to Grant on April 9, Davis and his cabinet scattered to escape arrest. Davis continued south into Georgia, where he was reunited with his wife and family, and planned to travel to either Texas or Mexico, where he and many other members of the Confederacy hoped to find sanctuary. However, the federal army wasn't about to let Davis escape. They pursued him with dogged determination, especially after President Andrew Johnson (wrongly) named him a conspirator in the assassination of Abraham Lincoln.

Davis was finally captured near Irwinville, Georgia, on May 10 by a detachment of the Fourth Michigan Cavalry. He was taken with his wife and children to Macon, Georgia, and along the way was forced to endure the constant taunts of Union soldiers singing, "We'll hang Jeff Davis from a sour apple tree." On May 22, Davis was imprisoned in Fort Monroe, Virginia, and forced into shackles. Still proud and defiant, he resisted being chained and finally had to be subdued by his jailers. Davis sat in Fort Monroe for almost two years without benefit of trial, under constant watch by soldiers who had orders never to speak to him.

Davis suffered tremendously during his incarceration. Already in frail health, captivity only exacerbated his weak physical condition. A light burned constantly in his dank cell, and he was not allowed even a moment of fresh air. It was as if officials in Washington wanted to make doubly sure that the defeated president of the Confederacy was thoroughly punished for his crimes. Davis might have died from this cruel treatment had not Dr. John Craven intervened on his behalf. The physician tended to Davis's health and made sure that his imprisonment was made more bearable by providing Davis with whatever comforts he could arrange.

The national press brought Davis's plight to the world and vocal demands for better treatment helped make Davis's imprisonment a little more tolerable. He was soon allowed to take walks on the prison grounds, and his health gradually improved. Davis was finally released on $100,000 bail. His surety bond was signed by newspaper publisher Horace Greeley and another vocal abolitionist named Gerrit Smith. A free man, Davis found himself with neither a home to return to nor a dollar in his wallet; the proud and defiant president of the Confederacy was now a pauper. All charges against Jefferson Davis were finally dropped by the federal government in 1869.

Davis lived another two decades. He traveled for a while, then settled in Mississippi, where he spent his time writing his memoir, *The Rise and Fall of the Confederate Government.* Davis never retracted a single word, thought, or deed and remained an unrepentant Confederate until his death on December 9, 1889.

CIVIL WAR FACTOID

Jefferson Davis never sought the restoration of his American citizenship following the Civil War. It was finally restored by President Jimmy Carter.

THE VICE PRESIDENTS

HANNIBAL HAMLIN

Hannibal Hamlin, Abraham Lincoln's first vice president, would no doubt be a more prominent figure in American history had he

not been replaced with Andrew Johnson during Lincoln's second term. Upon Lincoln's assassination, Johnson rather than Hamlin became the nation's 17th president.

A devout abolitionist, Hamlin was an influential lawyer and politician in Maine before being selected by the Republican Party as Lincoln's first vice president. In his home state, Hannibal held a number of important political positions, including state legislator, governor, U.S. congressman, and senator. Originally a Democrat, Hamlin severed his ties with the party in 1856 over the issue of slavery and joined the newly founded Republican Party. He was nominated vice president on the second ballot during the Republican convention in Chicago.

Unlike today, when presidential and vice presidential candidates stump together, Lincoln and Hamlin never even met until after the election. During the campaign, opponents angry over Hamlin's stance on slavery attempted to slur his name by suggesting that he was a mulatto trying to pass as white. Hamlin had a dark complexion, which only fueled the wild rumors.

Hamlin and Lincoln got along well, though Hamlin was disappointed that the president didn't push for emancipation and the enlistment of black soldiers earlier in the war. (Two of Hamlin's sons ended up commanding Negro units.) Hamlin also anxiously awaited a more important role within the administration. Lincoln tried to assuage his feelings by seeking Hamlin's opinion on various issues but, for the most part, made the most important decisions himself. One important exception involved the Emancipation Proclamation. Lincoln showed Hamlin an early draft of the document and incorporated some changes in wording that Hamlin had suggested.

Eager for more meaningful work, Hamlin enlisted in the Maine Coast Guard while still holding the office of vice president. He hoped to remain on the ticket with Lincoln in 1864 but was removed by Republican officials as a matter of political expediency; the party sought the support of proadministration Democrats and felt that the addition of Andrew Johnson, a Democrat, would keep them happy.

Hannibal Hamlin returned to the U.S. Senate in 1869, and he served in office for another 12 years before accepting an appointment as U.S. minister to Spain. Hamlin died in 1891.

Lincoln's Gettysburg Address

Few presidential speeches have achieved the acclaim and longevity as the short address Lincoln gave on November 19, 1863, during the dedication of a cemetery at the site of the Battle of Gettysburg in Pennsylvania. Contrary to legend, Lincoln did not hastily write the speech on the back of an envelope during the train trip to Gettysburg; the address was carefully prepared in advance, as were nearly all of Lincoln's most memorable recitations. Following is the complete text of Lincoln's Gettysburg Address:

Fourscore and seven years ago our fathers brought forth on this continent, a new nation, conceived in Liberty and dedicated to the proposition that all men are created equal.

Now we are engaged in a great civil war, testing whether that nation or any nation so conceived and so dedicated can long endure. We are met on a great battlefield of that war. We have come to dedicate a portion of that field, as a final resting place for those who here gave their lives that the nation might live free. It is altogether fitting and proper that we should do this.

But, in a larger sense, we cannot dedicate—we cannot consecrate—we cannot hallow—this ground. The brave men, living and dead, who struggled here, have consecrated it far above our poor power to add or detract. The world will little note nor long remember what we say here, but it can never forget what they did here. It is for us, the living, rather to be dedicated here to the unfinished work which they who fought here have thus far so nobly advanced. It is rather for us to be here dedicated to the great task remaining before us—that from these honored dead we take increased devotion to that cause for which they gave their last full measure of devotion; that we here highly resolve that these dead shall not have died in vain; that this nation, under God, shall have a new birth of freedom; and that the government of the people, by the people, for the people, shall not perish from the earth.

THE EMANCIPATION PROCLAMATION

The Emancipation Proclamation is perhaps the most memorable edict for which Abraham Lincoln is remembered. Many people erroneously believe that the proclamation immediately freed all slaves, but such is not the case; it freed only those slaves in the Southern states involved in active rebellion. The slave states loyal to the United States and those under federal control were exempt. Slavery wouldn't be abolished completely in the United States until the final ratification of the Thirteenth Amendment to the Constitution on December 18, 1865.

Nonetheless, the Emancipation Proclamation was a remarkable move on Lincoln's part and finally made the elimination of slavery a recognized war goal for the Union.

(continued)

ANDREW JOHNSON

Andrew Johnson became the nation's 17th president, after Abraham Lincoln was felled by an assassin's bullet. The Tennessee politician was known for his dislike of the Confederacy, but he showed unexpected sympathy toward the South during Reconstruction. In fact, Johnson was nearly impeached for opposing brutal Reconstruction policies enacted by Congress.

Johnson is an outstanding early American success story. He was born in North Carolina to impoverished parents in 1808 and experienced even greater hardships during his early years than Abraham Lincoln. His family was extremely poor, and Johnson received no schooling as a child. His father passed away when he was three years old. Johnson took a job as a tailor's apprentice when he became old enough to work, and he moved to Tennessee in 1826 to start his own tailor shop. His wife Eliza taught him how to read, and once his business began to flourish, Johnson entered politics. He made a name for himself in local politics and then was elected to the state legislature. Johnson was elected to Congress in 1847, and he later became governor of Tennessee. He was elected to the U.S. Senate in 1857 and made an unsuccessful bid for the presidency in 1860.

Johnson didn't particularly favor emancipation and even owned several house servants, but like many residents of Tennessee, he was vehemently opposed to secession following the election of Abraham Lincoln. In Johnson's mind, the secessionists were nothing more than traitors to the Union, and he stood alone among the senators from the South in refusing to resign his Senate seat— even after Tennessee had left the Union. Johnson supported the Union war effort against the Confederacy, believing it was the only way to preserve the country, but he sponsored a resolution rejecting emancipation as a goal of the war.

Lincoln appointed Johnson military governor of Tennessee in 1862. The state was partially occupied by federal forces, and there was much rancor between rival factions, a situation that made Johnson's job extremely difficult. But Johnson stuck it out for three years, doing his best to keep the peace while attempting to restore a civil government that was loyal to the North. His efforts weren't

for naught; the Republican Party selected Johnson to balance the ticket with Lincoln in the 1864 presidential election. Johnson was recovering from typhoid at the time of his inauguration, and he appeared so unsteady on his feet that many people thought he was drunk, a rumor that angered him greatly. Just six weeks later, Johnson was sworn in as president following Lincoln's death.

Johnson immediately began the arduous task of Reconstruction and initially followed Lincoln's intent of leniency toward the defeated Confederate states. He pardoned thousands of ex-Confederate soldiers and sympathizers and endorsed the rapid readmittance of the seceded states to the Union. However, Johnson's efforts met with great resistance from the Republican-dominated Congress, which resented the new Democratic president despite the fact that he had worked side by side with Abraham Lincoln. Congress wanted to punish the South for its impudence, and it wasn't about to let Andrew Johnson stand in the way. The legislature passed its own Reconstruction acts and policies and merely overrode most of Johnson's vetoes.

As Johnson tried to regain control, Congress attempted to keep him in line with the Tenure of Office Act, which required congressional approval before the president could dismiss any cabinet member. Johnson believed the law to be unconstitutional and fired Secretary of War Edwin Stanton, a Democratic ally of the radical Republicans. Enraged, the House of Representatives used the incident to bring 11 counts of impeachment against Johnson, in February 1868. The trial lasted two months, and Johnson, believing the whole thing to be a sham, refused to attend. He survived only because the Senate came up just one vote short of the two-thirds necessary to remove him from office. Though still president, Johnson found himself almost powerless. One of his last acts—one of defiance more than anything else— was to grant amnesty for all unpardoned former Confederates on Christmas Day 1868.

After leaving the White House, Andrew Johnson attempted two bids to win back his Senate seat and was finally successful with the third in 1874. He served four months there, earnestly battling some of his fiercest enemies, before passing away in July 1875.

THE EMANCIPATION PROCLAMATION

(continued from previous page)

Response to the proclamation was mixed. Many Northern abolitionists wished it was broader in scope but applauded it as a sure sign that slavery as an institution was on its way out. Other Northerners condemned the proclamation, fearing that millions of free blacks would soon invade their states and take away needed jobs. The South, not surprisingly, vehemently denounced the edict, calling it a clear attempt by the Union to promote a slave uprising. And in Europe, the proclamation all but guaranteed that the governments of England and France would never support the Confederacy.

ALEXANDER HAMILTON STEPHENS

Alexander Hamilton Stephens of Georgia was an odd choice for vice president of the Confederate States of America. Though passionately proslavery and favoring states' rights, he was also a Unionist who didn't want to see secession destroy the country. In fact, following Abraham Lincoln's election in 1860, he called for a convention of all Southern states in hopes of preventing secession and attended Georgia's own convention in January 1861 to argue in favor of the Union. Ultimately, however, he signed the Ordinance of Secession.

Stephens was born in Georgia to poor parents and found himself an orphan by age 12. He was raised and educated by an uncle and showed great scholastic aptitude, graduating first in his class at the University of Georgia. Stephens studied law and passed the bar in 1834. Politics soon became a passion, and he was elected to the Georgia legislature in 1836. He served there for all but one year until 1843, working hard on behalf of his constituents. In 1843, Stephens was elected to the U.S. House of Representatives, where he made a name for himself with his unwavering support of slavery and states' rights.

Though he feared that secession would tear the country apart, Stephens had no choice but to follow his countrymen when Georgia split from the Union in January 1861. In February, he traveled to Montgomery, Alabama, and helped to draft the Confederacy's new constitution. His advocacy of issues important to the South, such as slavery, and generally moderate stand on most others made him appealing to the delegates of the provisional congress, and he was selected to be vice president under Jefferson Davis.

Stephens and Davis could not have been more different, and they did not get along personally or politically. Stephens found Davis's personality difficult to deal with, at one time referring to him as being "weak and vacillating, timid, petulant, peevish, obstinate." In addition, as a long-time advocate of states' rights, Stephens could not abide Davis's attempt to create a controlling centralized government or his nationalistic approach to the war.

He also disapproved of Davis's attempts to institute a draft, impose taxes, and suspend the writ of habeas corpus. As a result of these differences, Stephens spent very little time in the Confederate capital of Richmond, preferring instead his home state of Georgia.

During his tenure, Stephens tried to provide a strong national voice and advocated a number of sound political policies, such as the quick sale of cotton to Europe before the Union blockade of Southern ports went into effect. He also pushed for peace between the warring regions and led the Southern delegation at the failed Hampton Roads Conference in February 1865. During that meeting with Abraham Lincoln and Secretary of State Seward, Stephens urged the North and the South to end their differences and unite to fight the French in Mexico. His pleas were ignored.

At the war's end, Stephens was arrested and imprisoned at Fort Warren in Boston until October 1865. After being freed, he returned to Georgia and was again elected to the U.S. Senate in 1866. However, he was refused his seat by radical Republicans in Congress seeking to punish the seceded states. In 1871, Stephens bought a newspaper in Atlanta and used it to attack what he saw as unfair Reconstructionist policies. Two years later, he was elected to the House of Representatives, where he served until 1882. Stephens was then elected governor of Georgia, but he died in 1883, just a few months into his term. In addition to his political successes, Alexander Hamilton Stephens wrote a very successful book on the Civil War entitled, *A Constitutional View of the Late War Between the States*.

THE PRESIDENTIAL WIVES

Mary Todd Lincoln and Varina Howell Davis shared, as did their husbands, a great many similarities as well as a great many differences. Both women loved their husbands and doted over them, both women lost a child during the war, both women were accused of being sympathetic to the enemy, and both women would face public ridicule while their husbands were in office.

Being the First Lady during wartime, whether it was for the Union or the Confederacy, was an extraordinarily difficult task, but both women coped as best they could, considering they had little to prepare them for what lay ahead.

MARY TODD LINCOLN

Mary Todd Lincoln was born in 1818 into a life of privilege. Her father was a wealthy banker in Lexington, Kentucky, and Mary grew up well educated and socially ambitious. At the age of 21, she moved to Springfield, Illinois, to live with her married sister. Her sister's father-in-law, Ninian Edwards, was the governor of Illinois, and Mary quickly became one of the most popular girls in their social and political set, which included a number of influential politicians.

It was in Springfield that Mary met Abraham Lincoln, by then a prominent lawyer with strong political ambitions and the drive to make them a reality. Mary realized Lincoln had great potential as a husband and politician, but their courtship was rocky, due primarily to their emotional differences; Mary tended to be nervous, tense, and temperamental, and Lincoln was often moody, depressed, and absentminded. However, they managed to overcome these differences and were soon engaged to be married. Their first attempt to wed was called off at the last minute, when Lincoln got cold feet. They tried again—successfully—on November 4, 1842. Lincoln was 33, Mary just 23.

Mary gave birth to Robert, the first of their four sons, just nine months after she and Lincoln were wed. Sadly, Robert would be the only child to survive into adulthood. Their second son, Edward Baker, was born in 1846, but he died four years later. The Lincolns would lose another child, 11-year-old William, in 1861 to fever and a third, Tad, in 1871 to tuberculosis. The death of William was a devastating blow to the Lincolns, and Mary, already delicate and over-wrought, suffered a nervous breakdown that kept her bedbound for nearly 3 months. She eventually recovered but refused to enter William's room again. She began consulting spiritualists and seers in an attempt to contact William in the spirit world and later told her half sister Emili that the ghosts of both Edward and William visited her in the White House.

The relationship between Mary and Abraham Lincoln has been greatly dissected over the years. Some historians have stated that their relationship was troubled throughout their marriage because of their mutual emotional problems and the supposition that Mary considered herself superior to her husband's relatively humble lifestyle. However, while the Lincolns certainly had their ups and downs (perhaps more than most married couples), there is little doubt that Lincoln loved Mary despite her often stubborn and jealous nature.

When Lincoln was elected president, Mary did her best to fit in, but her snooty manner and taste for extravagance only alienated her from the general public. Mary was also prone to outbursts of temper and jealousy that greatly embarrassed her husband and his staff. One of the victims of her temper was the wife of General Ulysses S. Grant; Grant's wife couldn't stand to be in the same room with Mary.

The war placed Mary in great conflict. As the wife of the president of the United States, she was an avowed and dedicated Unionist. But four of her brothers and three of her brothers-in-law served in the Confederate Army, resulting in a great deal of criticism that Mary found difficult to take. Still she persevered, attempting to maintain some degree of social life during the war's grimmest months—another issue that resulted in public criticism. No matter what Mary did, it seemed that there were always those ready to take her to task for it.

Her husband's assassination was one of the greatest emotional blows suffered by Mary Todd Lincoln. She was devastated by the incident, so overcome by grief that she was unable to accompany his body to Springfield, Illinois, for burial. Mary was left a wealthy woman after Lincoln's death, but she spent a great deal on frivolous things and found herself almost penniless after a few years. Congress took pity on her and granted her a liberal pension, which allowed her to live well, if not exactly in the wealthy manner to which she had become accustomed.

Mary Todd Lincoln

Following Tad's death, Mary plunged into such a state of depression that her eldest son, Robert, had her institutionalized for several months. Mary traveled some after that, then spent her remaining years with her sister in Springfield, in the same house in which she had met her husband some four decades before. Mary Todd Lincoln died on July 16, 1882.

VARINA HOWELL DAVIS

Varina Howell Davis was a source of tremendous support for her husband, Confederate President Jefferson Davis, and for the Southern cause during the Civil War. It was a very difficult task, but she performed it with wit, humor, and grace.

Varina Howell was born in Mississippi in 1826. Her father was a wealthy plantation owner with Northern roots—her grandfather was an eight-term governor of New Jersey—and Varina grew up in a life of privilege and education. A bright and vivacious girl, she spent two years at a girls' finishing school in Philadelphia. At age 17, she was introduced to Jefferson Davis, a widower twice her age. They married in 1845, and Varina enjoyed the social whirl that came with being the spouse of a rising star within the Democratic Party. When the couple moved to Washington D.C., Varina fit in quite well and received some renown as a charming and witty hostess with a penchant for throwing spectacular parties. With her husband preoccupied with politics, she also oversaw the affairs of their plantation in Mississippi.

After her husband was elected president of the Confederate States of America, Varina packed up and moved with their family to join Davis in Richmond, Virginia. Her role as First Lady of the new republic was considerably more difficult than anything she had previously experienced, but she proved adept at juggling her many responsibilities, most notably sustaining her husband during the course of the Civil War, a cause both knew was desperate from the start.

Like Mary Todd Lincoln, Varina Davis faced an onslaught of criticism from the press and the public. Because her background was from the North, there were those who felt that Varina didn't fully

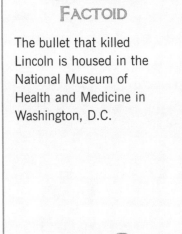

CIVIL WAR FACTOID

The bullet that killed Lincoln is housed in the National Museum of Health and Medicine in Washington, D.C.

support the Confederacy—a false allegation. She was alternately accused of entertaining too lavishly during wartime and not doing enough to lift the spirits of her countrymen. In addition, because she was intelligent and strong willed, she was often accused of meddling too much in her husband's affairs of state. The Civil War era was a time when women were expected to be quiet and do as they were told, and Varina Davis chafed at such restrictions. Still, she was a wonderful wife to Jefferson Davis, a man who was often cantankerous and moody. She bore him six children, cared for him during his frequent periods of illness, and offered support and love during periods of overwhelming stress. Varina also faced challenges in her personal life. In 1864, her five-year-old son, Joe, fell to his death from the rear balcony of the presidential mansion in Richmond.

Varina was with her husband when he was captured by federal troops near Irwinville, Georgia, in May 1865. She spent the next two years fighting for his release from prison and even met with President Andrew Johnson, who was sympathetic to her plight. When Davis was finally released, he and Varina settled at an estate near Biloxi, Mississippi; the estate, named "Beauvoir," was given to them by a benefactor. Upon Davis's death in 1889, Varina turned the estate into a home for Confederate veterans and went to live with her daughter in New York City.

Varina Howell Davis published her memoirs in 1890 and continued to write for various magazines and newspapers. She died in 1906 and was buried in Richmond, next to her husband, who was well remembered by the people of the South.

4

Military Leaders
of the
North and South

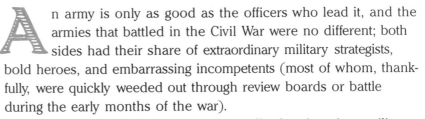

An army is only as good as the officers who lead it, and the armies that battled in the Civil War were no different; both sides had their share of extraordinary military strategists, bold heroes, and embarrassing incompetents (most of whom, thankfully, were quickly weeded out through review boards or battle during the early months of the war).

What sets the Civil War apart from all other American military conflicts is that many of the opposing officers knew each other, had studied together at West Point, fought side by side in the Mexican War, and, prior to secession, had even been friends. At the First Battle of Bull Run, for example, Pierre G. T. Beauregard, who was second in the class of 1838 at West Point, battled Irvin McDowell, who had graduated twenty-third in the same class. Likewise, George B. McClellan, West Point class of 1846, would find himself facing classmate Thomas J. "Stonewall" Jackson.

Without question, the Mexican War (1846–1848) proved to be an effective battlefield primer for many officers who would end up on opposite sides of the Civil War. During the Mexican War, in which American forces were commanded by General Winfield Scott, Captain Robert E. Lee, and regimental Quartermaster Ulysses S. Grant both saw battle.

But when the South seceded in 1861 and the war call came, fraternity was forced to give way to national allegiance. Lines were formed, the enemy declared, and the fight was on. Officers on both sides deeply regretted having to do battle with former comrades, but friendship meant little in the throes of combat. All were fighting for their lives and the preservation of their beloved nations.

POLITICS AND GENERALS

In today's U.S. Army, rank is determined by experience and expertise. But things were a little different during the Civil War. It was an era in which political favors were often repaid with military appointments, and, as the war began to heat up, President Abraham Lincoln found himself under constant pressure to appoint men with little or no military experience. Many of the Union's early military officers were loyal Republicans, influential War Democrats, or everyday people demanding payback for some favor granted earlier. As might be expected, the majority of officers so appointed had no right leading men into battle, and during their relatively brief command, they only served to embarrass themselves and their respective war departments. The First Battle of Bull Run resulted in a humiliating Union rout when inexperienced officers panicked and ran in the face of the enemy, abandoning their men.

General Benjamin Franklin Butler is a prime example of wartime incompetence. A prominent Boston attorney and influential Democrat, Butler used his influence to grab a military appointment. He managed some early successes but embarrassed himself mightily when, as military governor of New Orleans, he ordered the confiscation of Confederate property and was accused of stealing silverware from area homes and churches. Butler also succeeded in angering the entire population of New Orleans with his controversial "Woman Order," which stated that any woman who insulted or berated a Union soldier would be treated like a common prostitute. Butler was recalled by his superiors in Washington in December 1862 after corruption and bribery by Northern speculators became commonplace in the city under his administration. Butler was later given a field command in Virginia, and his embarrassments continued to mount throughout the rest of the war.

Not surprisingly, the incompetence demonstrated by many appointed officers did little to instill pride or confidence in the men who served under them, and morale in such units was often very low. In many cases, the battle experience of common soldiers far exceeded that of their commanders. Personal behavior was also an issue. Many officers drank heavily, frequented prostitutes, and generally behaved quite badly, setting a horrible example for their men.

The diary kept by a soldier in the 75th New York, which was camped near Baltimore as it traveled to Washington, offers a glaring example: "Tonight not two hundred men are in camp. Capt. Catlin, Capt. Hurlburt, Lt. Cooper and one or two other officers are under arrest. A hundred men are drunk, a hundred more at houses of ill fame. Col. Alford is very drunk all the time now."

But not every military appointee proved to be an embarrassing incompetent. More than a few realized the responsibility of the

MILITARY ORGANIZATION

Since a great many of the leaders in the Confederate army had served in the Union army prior to the war, they instituted a similar system of organization. Four infantry regiments typically formed a brigade, commanded by a brigadier general. Three brigades comprised a division, commanded by a brigadier or major general. Two or more divisions formed an army corps, commanded by a major general in the Union army and by a major or lieutenant general in the Confederate army. A small army might consist of a single corps, though the principal armies contained two or more.

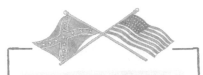

WHAT MAKES AN INFANTRY

Ideally, the full strength of an infantry regiment was 1,000 men, 4,000 men for a brigade, 12,000 men for a division, and 24,000 or more men for a corps. Confederate divisions and corps were typically larger than those in the Union army because a Southern division often contained four brigades and a Southern corps contained four divisions.

positions they were given and worked long and hard to prove themselves. They read military textbooks, studied military strategy, trained their men well, and did all they could to advance the war effort. One example is Francis Preston Blair (brother of the Union's Postmaster General), who received glowing recommendations from both William T. Sherman and Ulysses Grant for his performance during the war.

The day after the Union defeat at the First Battle of Bull Run, Congress authorized the formation of military review boards to evaluate officers and remove those found to be unfit for command. Several hundred officers were let go or resigned in the following months, making room for leaders with more experience. The practice of appointing officers, or electing them from the ranks (a common practice in volunteer units), continued, but at least the review boards helped establish minimum standards of competence.

The bad apples aside, many officers in both the Union and the Confederate armies proved to be outstanding leaders and military strategists. They led their men from the front rather than the rear, defined bravery in the face of overwhelming odds, and did all they could to advance their side to victory. This chapter offers a brief look at some of the most prominent officers on both sides of the conflict.

UNION OFFICERS

WINFIELD SCOTT

General Winfield Scott was a lifelong soldier with an illustrious career when the Civil War broke out in 1861. By that time he had served as general-in-chief for nearly 20 years and, at age 75, was nearing the end of his ability to lead effectively. Stricken by gout and vertigo and weighing nearly 300 pounds, Scott could no longer ride his horse, and there are some indications that he was experiencing the early signs of dementia. Nonetheless, Scott commanded tremendous respect among most Union leaders.

Scott was born in Virginia in 1786 and joined the military early in life. He served in the War of 1812 and was captured by

enemy forces, but the incident made him a hero, and his renown was second only to that of Andrew Jackson. Scott also fought in the Indian wars and the Mexican War, in which he led the army into Vera Cruz (Robert E. Lee, then a captain, was praised by Scott for his performance during the campaign). Scott emerged from the Mexican War a triumphant hero and became the first lieutenant general in the U.S. Army since George Washington. Like many men before and after him, Scott hoped to parlay his heroic reputation into a career in politics. He was the Whig candidate for president in 1852, but he lost the race to Franklin Pierce, a Democratic senator from New Hampshire.

His political aspirations shot down, Scott rejoined the military. He was nicknamed "Old Fuss and Feathers" for his unwavering conformity to military pomp and regulations. When war with the South seemed inevitable, it became apparent that Scott would need a field commander. He recommended fellow Virginian Robert E. Lee for the position, but Lee turned down Scott's personal request, resigned his commission, and joined the Confederate army instead. George McClellan was then appointed to the field commander position, but the appointment didn't work out well for Scott. McClellan, who was known for his arrogance, resented Scott and took to contradicting him at staff meetings and avoiding him in public.

The early days of the war took the shine off of Scott's armor. He was blamed and severely chastised by the press and public for the Union's early losses, and his proposal for defeating the Confederacy—a naval blockade intended to squeeze the Confederacy while the Union bolstered its forces for an extended struggle—was roundly ridiculed when it became public (see the Anaconda Plan).

With the Union army seemingly unable to win a decisive victory during the early months of the war, Scott presented Lincoln with a standing offer to step down; following the Confederate victory at Ball's Bluff, the president accepted. George McClellan was appointed commander of the Union army the same day, and Scott, a proud warhorse his whole life, found himself put out to pasture.

Winfield Scott spent his retirement writing a lengthy two-volume autobiography and traveling through Europe. He died in 1866, having

> ### CIVIL WAR FACTOID
>
> Union General Lew Wallace became a writer after the war. One of his best-known novels was *Ben-Hur: A Tale of the Christ*, first published in 1880. It was made into two motion pictures.

CAVALRY

Cavalry regiments usually had 12 rather then 10 companies, known as "troops." Cavalry regiments, brigades, or divisions were placed with divisions, corps, or armies, as battle situations dictated. Field artillery batteries consisting of four or six guns were also attached to brigades, divisions, or corps as required. Approximately 80 percent of the Union fighting forces were infantry, 14 percent cavalry, and 6 percent artillery. The Confederate army had a similar proportion of artillery but a slightly higher proportion of cavalry.

watched his much-ridiculed Anaconda Plan play an integral role in the Union's final victory against the Confederacy.

GEORGE B. MCCLELLAN

Had George Brinton McClellan been as good a soldier as he thought he was, the Civil War might have come to a much faster conclusion. Unfortunately, the cocky and arrogant general was prone to chronic hesitancy, allowing the enemy to retreat and rebuild time after time. President Lincoln became so frustrated by McClellan's failure to follow through on the battlefield that he eventually removed him from command of the Union army.

McClellan was born in Philadelphia in 1826, the scion of a wealthy family. He entered West Point at age 16 and graduated second in his class. His classmates saw great things in McClellan, and he was voted "most likely to succeed." Upon graduation, McClellan was appointed brevet second lieutenant in the engineer corps and shipped off to hone his military skills in the Mexican War. He fought well and received commendations for his performance in several important battles, including the battle of Cerro Gordon. He later was promoted to the rank of captain.

After the Mexican War, McClellan taught practical engineering at West Point for four years, then was transferred to the West for a two-year stint. In 1855, he was sent to Europe to report on the Crimean War. Upon his return, he resigned from the military to pursue a career as a civil engineer in the railroad industry.

In 1861, as the Civil War heated up, McClellan was made major general of the Ohio Volunteers, commanding the Department of the Ohio. One of his first victories was to rout the Confederate army from western Virginia, laying the groundwork for the creation of the new state of West Virginia. As a result of his success, McClellan was promoted to major general of the regular army.

After the Union army was sent fleeing at the First Battle of Bull Run, Lincoln appointed McClellan commander of the Army of the Potomac. His earlier military successes suggested that McClellan was the man to whip the Union army into shape and bring the war to a quick conclusion, but such was not to be. The reasons for McClellan's failures are many. His arrogance and sense of self-importance alienated him from many, and he was openly disdainful of Abraham Lincoln, whom he ridiculed in public. The soldiers under his command, however, respected the authority and obedience that he brought with him, and after several months of much-needed training, they were ready to prove themselves.

But McClellan balked. While the president and the nation pushed him to attack the Confederates at Manassas Junction (the site of the First Battle of Bull Run) and then push on to Richmond, McClellan was convinced that he was dramatically outnumbered and refused to move until his army was bolstered to 270,000. In truth, McClellan's army was nearly twice that of opposing forces, and he could have won a solid victory if he had advanced as advised. Lincoln was disappointed and angry, but remained convinced that McClellan was a brilliant military leader, and he promoted McClellan to general-in-chief of all of the federal armies upon the resignation of General Winfield Scott.

In January 1862, Lincoln gave McClellan a direct order to move out and face the enemy, but McClellan continued to stall for another two months, claiming his soldiers weren't ready and that he needed still more troops and supplies. McClellan finally began his Peninsular Campaign against Robert E. Lee and won a number of victories, though his aggravating reluctance to pursue retreating enemy forces only prolonged the conflict. McClellan, the frequent victim of misinformation, continued to believe that he was outnumbered and finally retreated back to the Potomac in July 1862. At his wit's end, Lincoln replaced McClellan with General Henry Halleck, placed John Pope in charge of all Union troops north and west of Virginia, and left McClellan in charge only of the Army of the Potomac.

However, Pope suffered a demoralizing defeat at the Second Battle of Bull Run on September 1, and McClellan was once again

George B. McClellan

placed in charge of all federal troops. He worked hard to rebuild his army, then moved out to meet Lee, who was threatening to invade the North. A rapid assault by McClellan probably would have destroyed Lee's army, but once again McClellan hesitated, allowing troops under Stonewall Jackson to take the Union garrison at Harpers Ferry just in time to meet up with Lee at Antietam. (Many historians believe that the only reason Lee was unable to capture Harrisburg, Pennsylvania, as planned was because his orders accidentally fell into McClellan's hands. Had McClellan not been so fortunate, it's likely that Lee would have succeeded.)

McClellan met Lee at Antietam on September 17, 1862, and the two engaged in one of the fiercest, bloodiest one-day battles of the entire war, with a combined total of more than 27,000 casualties. Had McClellan forced one final push against Lee at the end of the day, it's very likely that he could have crushed the Confederate forces and brought an early end to Lee's assault against the North. But again, his hesitancy cost him greatly.

Lincoln met with McClellan in Sharpsburg on October 1 to encourage him to push forward; later, Lincoln would make his request a direct order. But McClellan refused to proceed, still convinced that he was greatly outnumbered and that he needed more troops and supplies. When a month passed with McClellan still in position, Lincoln removed him from command and forced McClellan into civilian life.

McClellan quickly entered politics, where his arrogance and sense of self-importance were an asset. He wooed the Democratic Party and was nominated its presidential candidate in 1864. McClellan campaigned hard, but a number of important Union victories helped Lincoln win the election with little difficulty.

A three-year tour of Europe followed McClellan's presidential defeat. He re-entered politics upon his return and was elected governor of New Jersey in 1878, serving a single term. McClellan then left public office to once again work as an engineer, during which time he penned his own version of events during the war in a book entitled *McClellan's Own Story*. George McClellan died on October 29, 1885.

ULYSSES S. GRANT

Ulysses Simpson Grant came out of the Civil War the savior of the Union and a true hero. So popular was he at the war's end that he was elected president in 1868, an astonishing achievement for a man who, prior to the war, failed at almost everything he attempted.

Grant was born Hiram Ulysses Grant in Georgetown, Ohio, in 1822. His father was a hardworking tanner and his mother a devoutly religious woman who had great hopes for her son, though Grant was a bit of a disappointment as a child. Preferring horses to studying, he proved a skilled rider but did poorly in school. However, despite his poor grades, Grant managed to make it into West Point thanks to a recommendation from his local congressman, who mistakenly referred to him as Ulysses Simpson Grant in his letter to the academy. Grant liked the name and kept it.

Grant continued his tradition of mediocre grades while at West Point, graduating 21st in a class of 39, and was commissioned brevet second lieutenant. He was assigned to the infantry and sent to Jefferson Barracks, near St. Louis, Missouri, where he learned how to be a soldier. It was there that he met Julia Dent, who would soon become his wife. A year later, he was sent to the Southwest frontier, where he served until the beginning of the Mexican War. During that conflict, he served under Zachary Taylor and Winfield Scott. Both men taught Grant much about military strategy and combat, lessons that would serve him well later in life.

Following the Mexican War, Grant was assigned to a variety of distant posts, a situation that did little to instill in him a passion for the military as a career. He started drinking heavily while stationed at a post on the Pacific coast and resigned from the army after being reprimanded by his commanding officer.

Grant moved with his family back to St. Louis, where he tried a number of occupations with little success. Finally, his two brothers hired him as a clerk at their leather store, and there he stayed until the beginning of the Civil War. When the first shots were fired on Fort Sumter, Grant eagerly volunteered for the Union army but had great difficulty getting someone to assign him to a true command. Finally, in June 1861, he was made colonel of a regiment of

GRANT NOT A TEETOTALER

Ulysses S. Grant was both famous and infamous for his drinking, though history proved that liquor did not adversely affect his ability to win battles, a fact well recognized by Abraham Lincoln. According to legend, in response to a temperance committee that found Grant's drinking immoral, Lincoln said, "Would you tell me what brand of whiskey Grant drinks? I would like to send a barrel of it to my other generals."

volunteers from Illinois. Three months later, Grant was promoted to brigadier general and assigned to a command in Illinois.

The first military action Grant saw in the war was an attack on a Confederate camp at Belmont, Kentucky. However, the attack almost turned into a disaster when the enemy started to regroup as Grant's men broke rank to ransack the camp. Luckily, Grant was able to pull them together in time. In February 1862, Grant led a very successful campaign against Fort Henry and Fort Donelson in Tennessee. During the latter attack, he uttered his now famous proclamation, "No terms except an unconditional and immediate surrender can be accepted." From then on, the "U.S." in his name came to stand for Unconditional Surrender.

Thanks to his successful campaign against Forts Henry and Donelson, Grant was promoted to major general by President Lincoln. He fought in the Shiloh campaign, but his success there was almost accidental; it was superior Union numbers more than anything else that defeated more skilled Confederate troops. Union casualties were heavy during the battle, and Grant received more than his share of criticism. But Lincoln stood by him, noting, "I can't spare this man—he fights."

The Shiloh campaign tarnished Grant's reputation, but he was able to redeem himself and prove his skill as a military strategist with his amazing capture of Vicksburg in July 1863. This much-needed victory opened the Mississippi River to the Union and split the Confederacy in half. Four months later, Grant won additional victories at Missionary Ridge and Lookout Mountain in Tennessee. Congress was so grateful for Grant's successes that he received a gold medal and was promoted to lieutenant general. More importantly, Lincoln made Grant general-in-chief of the armies of the United States.

Finally in charge, Grant developed a plan to attack the Confederate army on three fronts: Meade and the Army of the Potomac would face Lee, Butler would lead the Army of the James against Lee's support, and Sherman would lead the Army of the Tennessee against Joe Johnston and finally into Atlanta. Rather than stay in Washington, where he felt out of place, Grant chose to lead by example and went into combat with the Army of the Potomac.

Ulysses S. Grant

The Confederacy did not roll over under Grant's three-pronged assault. Both sides fought valiantly, and many battles resulted in extremely heavy Union casualties. But the officers under Grant's command did their jobs well, and the strategy eventually proved effective. Sherman managed to cut a wide swath through the South, severing Confederate supply lines and destroying anything that could be used to sustain the Confederate war machine. By April, the Confederate army was in desperate straits, with many of its soldiers literally starving. On April 9, 1865, Grant accepted Robert E. Lee's surrender at Appomattox Court House, effectively ending the war.

With the war's end, Grant was a national hero. He assisted in the Reconstruction effort, leaning toward a more moderate stance and chafing at many of the overly punitive policies instituted by Congress. In 1868, he ran for president as a Republican and won the election with little difficulty. However, Grant was always more of a military man than a politician, and his two terms in office were marred by scandal and accusations of corruption within his administration, though Grant himself came out relatively unscathed.

Sadly, Grant's final years were less than successful. He failed at a number of ventures and found himself so poor that he was forced to sell his treasured war mementos and write his memoir to put food on the table. His autobiography, *Personal Memoirs*, was a huge success, but Grant died from throat cancer in 1885 before he could enjoy any financial reward.

> ### CIVIL WAR FACTOID
>
> Is Ulysses S. Grant really buried in Grant's Tomb in New York City? Yes, and so is his wife, Julia, who was interred there in 1902.

WINFIELD SCOTT HANCOCK

Winfield Scott Hancock was one of the most respected and admired generals in the Union army. He participated in many of the Civil War's most important battles, including Gettysburg, and proved himself a confident, fearless, and adept officer who had an uncanny knack for being where he was needed most.

Hancock was born in Pennsylvania in 1844. He graduated from West Point at age 20 and, as a second lieutenant, served on the frontier at Fort Towson before being assigned to Mexico shortly before war there was declared. Under the command of Winfield

Scott, Hancock participated in four major battles over the course of the Mexican War and was awarded a brevet, or honorary command, to first lieutenant. Following the Mexican War, Hancock continued to hone his military skills during a number of regional conflicts, including the Seminole Indian wars in Florida in 1855 and the Kansas uprising in 1857–58.

Hancock was chief quartermaster of the Southern District in California when the Civil War began. Eager to participate in the brewing conflict, Hancock requested a transfer to active duty in the East and was made brigadier general of volunteers. He also helped organize the Army of the Potomac. Under General George McClellan, Hancock served well in numerous battles of the Peninsula Campaign, including the battles of Williamsburg and Frazier's Farm. He also commanded the first division of the 2nd Army Corps during the Battle of Antietam and participated in the Battle of Fredericksburg.

Hancock's star rose as the war continued. Following the Battle of Chancellorsville, President Lincoln appointed Hancock commander of the entire 2nd Army Corps as Union forces tried to stop Robert E. Lee's push into the North through Pennsylvania. Sensing the need for change within the Union war machine, Lincoln also replaced General Joseph Hooker with General George Meade. Immediately after the appointments, the two men would face tenacious Confederate forces during the three-day Battle of Gettysburg.

Hancock's participation in the Battle of Gettysburg would be instrumental in helping the Union win. He assisted Meade in choosing a splendid defensive position during the first day of combat, and his own army successfully repulsed Lee's attack on the Union's left flank during the second day. Always in front rallying his troops, Hancock was wounded during the fighting at Gettysburg and would suffer from his wounds for the rest of his life.

However, Hancock was nothing if not a trouper, and after a six-month convalescence, he returned to his corps and saw repeated combat during the Virginia campaigns in 1864. In the Battle of the Wilderness, Hancock managed to rally his troops to victory after they were nearly overrun by infantry led by James Longstreet. Instead of retreating as others probably would have done, Hancock ordered his troops to form another line of battle along a road on which the Confederate forces were advancing. When the Confederates arrived, Hancock's men stopped them in their tracks and pushed them back.

Hancock participated in a number of other major battles, and his courage was rewarded with an appointment to brigadier general in the regular army on August 12, 1864. Later that month, however, Hancock's troops were nearly crushed in a Confederate attack during the Petersburg campaign. An exhausted Hancock was brought back to Washington to recruit a corps of veterans. He remained in Washington for the rest of the war, except for a short stint as commander of the Middle Military Division of Virginia.

A soldier to the end, Hancock was promoted to major general in the regular army in July 1866 and went on to fight in the Missouri Indian wars. He later was assigned to a post in the South to help with the Reconstruction effort in Texas and Louisiana. However, Hancock was less than pleased with much of the military participation during Reconstruction and angered his superiors by refusing to act on orders he found offensive or unnecessary. He was eventually transferred back north and placed in command of the Department of the East.

Like most great war heroes of the time, Hancock was approached for political office; he was nominated for president by the Democrats in 1880 but lost to Republican James Garfield, also a veteran. In 1885, Hancock conducted the funeral of Ulysses S. Grant, under whom he had been corps commander. It was Hancock's last official public duty of note. He died on Governor's Island, New York, in February 1886.

Montgomery Meigs

A great deal of the Union army's success in the Civil War must be credited to Montgomery Meigs, who was appointed quartermaster general of the army in June 1861. A graduate of West Point, Meigs had a remarkable flair for efficiency and was responsible for supplying the army with almost everything it needed, except food and weapons.

The logistics of wartime supply were daunting; the Union Army was at a disadvantage because it was in foreign territory, but Meigs proved quite adept at keeping supply lines open and maintained. As a result, the average Union soldier was better fed and better equipped than his Confederate counterpart.

Many of the programs and policies Meigs instituted during his tenure as quartermaster general made their way into civilian life. For example, he furnished clothing manufacturers with a series of graduated uniform measurements, which later were used to "size" civilian clothing. And the army's insatiable demand for shoes resulted in the widespread use of the new Blake-McKay sewing machine for attaching uppers to soles.

WILLIAM TECUMSEH SHERMAN

William Tecumseh Sherman stands out as one of the Union's most valuable military officers. With drive and unflagging determination, he succeeded in cutting the Confederacy in half, first taking Atlanta by siege, then continuing on to the sea and through the Carolinas. In the North, Sherman was considered a hero; in the South, which suffered greatly during his famous march, he was nothing less than a monster. But opinion aside, he was more than instrumental in helping to bring the Civil War to an end.

Sherman was born in Ohio in 1820. He was named Tecumseh, after the great Shawnee chief, by his parents but was given the new first name of William by Senator Thomas Ewing, who raised Sherman upon his father's death. Sherman graduated from West Point and went on to serve in the Mexican War. He resigned from the army in 1853 to pursue a career in law and banking. However, he found the work boring and, in 1859, he became superintendent of a military school in Louisiana.

Sherman's affection for the South didn't stop him from rejecting a commission in the Confederate army when the Civil War broke. A Unionist, he joined the federal army and was appointed a colonel in the infantry. Sherman saw combat in the First Bull Run campaign in July 1861, during which Union forces suffered a humiliating defeat. A month later, he was promoted to brigadier general and assigned to Kentucky. In October 1861, Sherman was made commander of the Department of the Cumberland, but he found himself in constant fights with his commanding officers and the press. After being accused of being unstable, Sherman found his command severely restricted and even contemplated suicide. However, he was able to overcome his depression and was given a new chance as commander of the 5th Division, Army of the Tennessee, in March 1862.

Sherman participated in the Battle of Shiloh, during which he was wounded and had three horses shot out from under him. The battle went poorly for the Union, and some newspapers tried to place the defeat on Sherman's command, but General Grant and

William Tecumseh Sherman

THE ARMIES OF THE NORTH AND SOUTH: A PORTRAIT IN NUMBERS

According to carefully kept government records from 1861 to 1865, the Union army consisted of approximately 2,200,000 men. They ranged in age from 18 to 46, with the average age being in the mid-20s. The majority of these men had been farmers before the war broke out, and very few of them had any previous military experience. The average height of a Union soldier was 5 feet 8 inches, and the average weight was 145 pounds. A little more than 75 percent of Union soldiers had been born in the United States, and nearly all of them were volunteers; the various drafts held throughout the war added only about 6 percent to the total numbers in the field.

Statistics are not so readily available regarding the makeup of the Confederate army, because many records were destroyed during the final days of the war. It is known, however, that many of the Confederate soldiers who enlisted were younger or older than their Union counterparts, especially as the war dragged on and the need for fighting men became increasingly desperate.

The few remaining records that do exist suggest that Confederate officers were usually elected from among middle-class or upper-class men with previous military experience, either in the U.S. Army before the war or via Southern military academies. The average Southern soldier tended to be a farmer and considerably more rural than the average Northern soldier; few came from large cities. It can also be assumed that the typical Confederate soldier had less education than his Union counterpart, but what he lacked in schooling, he more than made up in riding and shooting ability, since most farmers also tended to be skilled huntsmen.

Their reasons for joining the Confederate army were fairly clear-cut: preservation of home and family and the right of their states to engage in self-government. Many Southern soldiers also distrusted and disliked Northerners, perceiving them as evil and insidious. (This opinion changed as the war progressed and the opposing sides came to know each other better. Soon both sides realized they had more similarities than differences, and it wasn't uncommon for foes to meet, barter, and visit between battles.) The preservation of slavery was secondary to most, since the majority of Confederate soldiers were not slave owners.

CIVIL WAR FACTOID

The word *sideburns* was derived from Union General Ambrose Burnside, who was renowned more for his impressive muttonchops than his skill as a field commander.

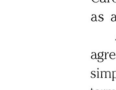

General Halleck had only praise for Sherman's bravery and quick thinking. In July 1862, Sherman was placed in charge of the District of Memphis and, along with Grant, participated in a number of important battles leading to the capture of Vicksburg, the last Confederate hold on the Mississippi River.

In March 1864, after Grant was placed in charge of the entire Union army, Sherman was given command of the Military Division of the Mississippi. His orders were to capture Atlanta, one of the South's leading centers of industry and manufacturing. After spending several weeks gathering supplies and amassing his forces, Sherman began his campaign against Confederate forces protecting the city, wearing them down bit by bit in a series of small maneuvers. Eventually, the city fell, and Sherman marched in. He had all civilians evacuated and then ordered anything that might be used to aid the enemy burned to the ground. With Atlanta no longer a threat, Sherman took his army on his now famous march to the sea, destroying virtually everything that might be used against the North along the way. The devastation was massive, but Sherman was intent on completely breaking the South and severing all supply lines. He ordered his men not to harm private property or harass civilians, but there were numerous violations as angry Union soldiers took revenge against the states that started the war. After taking Savannah on December 21, 1864, Sherman marched his troops through South Carolina and North Carolina, continuing his strategy of total warfare as a way of bringing the conflict to a faster end.

After Lee surrendered to Grant, Sherman negotiated a surrender agreement with Confederate General Joseph Johnston. But even this simple act generated criticism as Sherman added a number of political terms to what should have been just a military surrender. Sherman was angry at the scolding he received from his superiors and the Republican administration and refused to shake hands with Secretary of War Stanton during a review of the federal army in Washington.

Sherman took a number of different military assignments following the conclusion of the Civil War, including succeeding Grant as commander in chief of the U.S. Army in 1869. He retired from active duty in 1883 and died on February 14, 1891.

DAVID FARRAGUT

David G. Farragut is one of the few genuine naval heroes to come out of the Civil War, and is probably best remembered today for a statement he made during the Battle of Mobile Bay: "Damn the torpedoes! Full speed ahead!"

Farragut was born in Tennessee in 1801 and was taken in as a foster child by Commodore David Porter, a respected naval hero. Farragut loved the sea and served under his adopted father at a very young age. When he was just 12, Farragut participated in the War of 1812; he was captured by the British but eventually released. Farragut also served in the Mediterranean and just missed fighting in the Mexican War.

Farragut had been in the Navy nearly 50 years by the time the Civil War started. He was stationed at the Norfolk Navy Yard when Virginia seceded in April 1861 and quickly moved to New York. His first orders, to serve on a naval review board that selected officers for retirement—were less than spectacular. But things changed in January 1862, when Farragut was appointed commander of the squadron ordered to break down the naval defenses guarding New Orleans and take the city. It was a formidable task; the river approach to New Orleans was guarded by two forts and numerous Confederate gunships. But Farragut was confident the city could be captured and began his attack in April. After an attempt to destroy the cannons guarding the mouth of the Mississippi failed, Farragut defied orders and tried a direct assault. He ordered his armada through the Confederate defenses and succeeded with the loss of only a couple of ships and 37 casualties. On April 25, Farragut's ships sailed into New Orleans and captured the now defenseless city with a minimum of difficulty.

The capture of New Orleans made Farragut a naval hero and national celebrity. He was promoted to rear

Ely Parker

Ely Parker was the highest ranking Native American officer in the Union army, and had the unique distinction of transcribing the terms of Robert E. Lee's surrender at Appomattox Court House on April 9, 1865.

A full-blooded Seneca, Parker was born on a tribal reservation in New York. When the Civil War began, Parker tried to enlist in the Union army, but he was denied a commission. However, the army—desperate for qualified personnel—changed its mind.

Grant made Parker his military secretary, with a rank of lieutenant colonel, during the 1864 Petersburg campaign. However, despite his rank, Parker was often the subject of racial bigotry and was frequently referred to by his fellow officers as "the Indian."

While meeting with Grant to discuss surrender terms, Lee appeared startled by Parker's presence, witnesses recalled, and at first mistook Parker for black, because of his dark complexion. Upon learning that Parker was a full-blooded Seneca Indian, Lee said, "I am glad to see one real American here." Parker replied, "We are all Americans."

LEE'S FAVORITE HORSE

One of Confederate General Robert E. Lee's most trusted companions during the war was his horse, Traveller. Lee first saw the Confederate-gray stallion during his West Virginia campaign in 1861 and bought the animal from its owner for $200 a year later.

Originally named Jeff Davis, Lee renamed the 16-hand-high horse Traveller and spent much of the rest of the war perched upon its back. Lee rode Traveller in almost every important battle and

(continued)

admiral and participated in a number of other water battles, including Vicksburg and Port Hudson. Then came the orders he had been waiting for: Destroy the defenses around Mobile Bay. Farragut began his assault on August 5, 1864, commanding 4 iron-clad and 14 wooden ships. It was a fierce battle, and Farragut lost one of his ships, the *Tecumseh*, to a water mine, known then as torpedoes. The loss of the ship temporarily confused Farragut's men, who hesitated in their assault. Farragut, tied high up in the rigging of his flagship so that he could see better, was warned of other torpedoes, to which he gave his now famous response, "Damn the torpedoes! Full speed ahead!" Farragut's armada managed to push past the defending cannons of Fort Morgan and inflict heavy damage on the waiting Confederate vessels. Before long, Mobile Bay lay in Union hands, though the city itself remained under Confederate control until the following April.

The victory was cause for celebration in the North, and Farragut was promoted to the new rank of vice admiral, which was created just for him. He was also given a purse of $50,000 from several wealthy families in New York as a reward for his heroic success. His health failing, Farragut participated only marginally during the rest of the war.

When the war was over, Farragut toured Europe, where he was warmly received. In 1870, he suffered a heart attack and died while touring the Portsmouth Navy Yard in New Hampshire. His funeral in New York was attended by thousands of people, including President Grant.

CONFEDERATE OFFICERS

ROBERT E. LEE

Robert Edward Lee stands out as one of the most conflicted commanding officers of the Civil War. A dedicated Southerner who turned down command of the Union army to remain faithful to his home state of Virginia, he emerged from the war a hero to the South despite numerous losses and near escapes on the battlefield. Though a fine leader and military tactician, a great deal of Lee's success during the war must be attributed to luck. Nonetheless, Lee managed to rally his army in the face of overwhelming odds and continued to fight valiantly long after the cause was lost. His remarkable dedication to the war effort typifies everything that made the South such a formidable foe during the four-year conflict.

Born in Virginia in 1807, Lee descended from a family that had more than its share of influential statesmen and soldiers. His father, "Lighthorse Harry" Lee, was a former governor of Virginia and a cavalry officer during the Revolutionary War. However, Harry Lee's death, when Robert was only 11, left the family somewhat impoverished, and Robert was raised by his mother, Anne, to whom he was extremely close.

A good student, Lee entered West Point in 1825, his admittance all but guaranteed by a testimonial letter signed by five senators and three representatives. Lee studied hard and graduated second in his class (and without a single demerit) in 1829. Because of his high grades, he was assigned to the corps of engineers (less talented students were usually assigned to the infantry) and traveled to a number of different posts over the next 17 years. During this time, he married Mary Ann Randolph Custis and started a family.

During the Mexican War, Lee was commended for his commitment to the various combat assignments to which he was appointed, and in 1848, he was placed in charge of the construction of Fort Carroll in Baltimore Harbor. Four years later, he was made superintendent of West Point. It was a highly coveted assignment, but Lee found the work unexciting and was transferred to the 2nd Cavalry Division in 1855, spending much of his time in Texas.

As the Civil War began to heat up, Lee realized that although he wasn't an advocate of either slavery or states' rights, he had to follow his heart and remain faithful to his home state of Virginia. His superiors in Washington tried desperately to keep him as the Southern states began to secede and even offered Lee the command of the Union army, but he refused and resigned his commission. By June 1861, Lee was appointed a general in the Confederate army and advisor to Confederate President Jefferson Davis.

As the war began in full force, Lee worked hard to bolster and place the Confederate army. He stopped a Union advance from

LEE'S FAVORITE HORSE
(continued from previous page)

over thousands of miles as the war raged on.

Lee liked to relieve the stress of the day by taking his horse for an evening ride. He once noted in a letter to his wife, "Traveller is my only companion; I may say my only pleasure." Traveller outlived Lee by several years and, according to lore, finally succumbed to lockjaw. Traveller's skeleton is preserved at the Washington and Lee Museum.

Robert E. Lee

western Virginia and organized defenses along the coasts of Georgia and South Carolina. On May 31, 1861, Lee took command of the Confederate army after General Joseph Johnston was wounded in the Battle of Seven Pines. He renamed it the Army of Northern Virginia and set about preventing Union forces from taking Richmond. It appeared to be a no-win situation, since Union General George McClellan had more than one hundred thousand men at his command, Major General Nathaniel Banks was moving on several important Confederate supply forces in the Shenandoah Valley, and Major General Irvin McDowell was camped just a stone's throw away in northern Virginia. In all cases, the Union forces far outnumbered the Confederate forces.

Lee's strategy was simple: He would combine his entire army against one of the opposing threats, defeat it, and thus disrupt the remaining Union forces. With more than a little luck on his side, Lee managed to push back McClellan's army. He then turned north to attack the Union army in the Second Battle of Bull Run. Both times, Lee was ably assisted by Thomas "Stonewall" Jackson, who so admired Lee that he once noted, "I would follow him onto the battlefield blindfolded."

The morale of his soldiers was remarkably high as a result of these victories, so Lee decided to continue his offensive with a northern invasion. Jackson captured Harpers Ferry, Virginia, but Lee's plans accidentally fell into McClellan's hands, forcing him to take a defensive position at Antietam Creek, Maryland. The ensuing battle was the bloodiest single-day fight in the war, and both sides took heavy losses. Lee was forced to retreat back to Virginia, where he was harshly criticized by the press.

However, things went better for Lee three months later, when he defeated Union forces at the Battle of Fredericksburg in Virginia. Troops led by Ambrose Burnside took longer than anticipated to attack, allowing Lee to secure important defensive positions in the nearby hills. The result was a devastating blow to the Union. Lee again saw victory against overwhelming forces in the Battle of Chancellorsville in May 1863, but success came with a heavy price: the death of corps commander Stonewall Jackson.

Lee was on a roll, and in June he attempted another invasion into the North. He succeeded in capturing the entire Cumberland Valley and other parts of Pennsylvania. But Lee's luck ran out in the Battle of Gettysburg, where he suffered a huge number of casualties in three days of heavy fighting and was forced to retreat.

In the spring of 1864, Lee faced Grant for the first time, in what became known as the Wilderness campaign. Lee was overpowered 120,000 men to just 60,000, and his troops were crushed by Grant's better-equipped soldiers in several battles. Despite his best efforts, Lee was forced to retreat to Petersburg, where he tried desperately to protect the Confederate capital of Richmond from Grant's ceaseless onslaught. His forces dwindled on an almost daily basis, but still Lee fought on.

In February 1865, Lee was placed in charge of all of the Confederate armies. It was a no-win situation, and everyone knew it. In hindsight, Jefferson Davis probably should have surrendered and tried to broker a peace treaty, but he felt confident that Lee could rally the troops and push on. For three hard months Lee did his best to protect Richmond, but Grant's overwhelming numbers and Lee's inability to get needed supplies finally took their toll. His men starving, Lee surrendered to Grant on April 9, 1865.

After the war, Lee was paroled home and indicted for treason. However, he was never brought to trial and was finally pardoned. He spent his remaining years as president of Washington College (later named Washington and Lee College) in Lexington, Virginia. There, among other accomplishments, he established the nation's first journalism and business schools. Robert E. Lee died on October 12, 1870, and was buried in the chapel he built on the university campus.

JEB STUART

James Ewell Brown "Jeb" Stuart became renowned for his leadership and daring as one of the Confederate army's most skilled cavalry commanders. Vain and prone to showing off, he was a

JOHN BROWN'S EXECUTIONERS

Robert E. Lee just happened to be in Washington, D.C., when radical abolitionist John Brown and his followers captured the federal arsenal at Harpers Ferry, Virginia, on October 16, 1859. He was assigned to lead the troops that finally brought Brown into custody; helping him was Jeb Stuart. Interestingly, Thomas "Stonewall" Jackson was in command of cadets from the Virginia Military Institute sent to witness Brown's execution. Little did Lee, Stuart, and Jackson know that less than two years later they would all be fighting against the Union.

gifted horseman and brave soldier who understood the importance of military strategy and instilled astounding loyalty in the men who served under him.

Stuart was born in Virginia in 1833. His father was a wealthy lawyer, and Stuart received a good education. He entered West Point in 1850 and graduated 13th in his class. He was made a second lieutenant in the Mounted Rifles and was assigned to the Texas frontier, where he stayed until he was promoted to first lieutenant.

In 1856, Stuart and his men were sent to Kansas to help control the border conflict in that state. The next year, he was seriously wounded while fighting the Cheyenne Indians. During his recuperation, Stuart, a talented inventor, created a new saber attachment that was adopted by the War Department. During his stay in Washington, Stuart volunteered to serve with Robert E. Lee when Lee was sent to bring radical abolitionist John Brown into custody at Harpers Ferry, Virginia. That job accomplished, Stuart returned to Kansas, where he stayed until Virginia seceded from the Union in 1861. At that time, Stuart resigned his commission and volunteered for the Confederate army; he was made a lieutenant colonel in the 1st Virginia Cavalry. Like many soldiers in the war, Stuart had family members on the other side—his father-in-law was a general in the Union army.

Stuart and his regiment helped turn back the Union army at the First Bull Run campaign, and Stuart was promoted to brigadier general in September 1861. During the Peninsular campaign, Stuart and his cavalry troops (1,200 in all) provided Robert E. Lee with invaluable information regarding General George McClellan's troops by making a complete circuit of the Union forces over a three-day period, capturing numerous prisoners, arms, and equipment along the way. The information he obtained helped the Confederates win the Battle of Gaines's Mill.

Stuart's reputation continued to strengthen, and he was promoted to major general in July 1862. He was also placed in command of all cavalry forces in the Confederate army of Northern Virginia, which he led through a number of important battles, including Second Bull Run, Antietam, and Fredericksburg. When Stonewall Jackson was

Josiah Gorgas

Josiah Gorgas was one of the unsung heroes of the Confederacy during the Civil War. As the Confederate army's head of ordnance, it was his job to arm the fighting forces, and he did an incredible job, considering the limited resources with which he had to work.

Gorgas was born in Pennsylvania in 1818, attended West Point, and served in a variety of federal arsenals early in his career. With the secession of the Southern states in 1861, Gorgas resigned his commission with the U.S. Army and agreed to become the Confederate army's chief of ordnance. His job was to keep the Confederate army supplied with weapons and ammunition, as well as with the raw materials needed to manufacture them—a daunting task, considering the South's lack of factories and manufacturing facilities.

When Gorgas took the job, the South had only one foundry large enough to make heavy artillery and just a handful of factories capable of manufacturing rifles. But because of his ingenuity, new arsenals, rolling mills, and factories were built throughout the South. He also used a corps of agents who purchased guns and other equipment from manufacturing plants in the North and in Europe, and employed his own fleet of blockade runners to smuggle the weapons past Union gunships guarding Southern ports.

Gorgas realized that a wealth of weapons could be taken from the enemy, and encouraged Confederate soldiers to seize during battle all the usable small arms and artillery they could. This plan proved so successful that more than one hundred thousand Union rifles were procured in just one year. In addition, Gorgas turned to the citizens of the Confederate states for raw materials, such as iron, with which to make weapons. He even encouraged farmers and others to save animal manure and human waste for leeching into niter.

The Confederate army experienced shortages of food, clothing, and other goods over the course of the war, but thanks to Gorgas's tireless efforts, Confederate soldiers never lacked weapons and ammunition.

killed during the Battle of Chancellorsville in May 1863, Stuart briefly took command of 2nd Corps of the Army of Northern Virginia.

After the Confederate victory in Chancellorsville, Lee proposed another invasion of the North and turned to Stuart to provide reconnaissance. On June 9, 1863, Stuart and his troops came across a Union cavalry patrol, which led to the Battle of Brandy Station, Virginia; it was the largest cavalry engagement in American history. When the dust cleared, Stuart stood the clear victor.

The Battle of Gettysburg, however, would severely tarnish Stuart's reputation. Prior to the battle, Lee sent Stuart and his troops to scout the enemy. Stuart decided on his own to do another ride around McClellan's army but found himself pushed farther east than he had anticipated. As a result, Stuart was unable to contact Lee for nearly 10 days. He returned on the second day of fighting at Gettysburg but was unable to offer much help. Had Stuart and his men been in position when the fighting started, the battle might have taken a different turn. But they weren't, and Lee's army took a pounding. Stuart stayed close by Lee for the next several months, monitoring Grant's movements during the Wilderness campaign.

Jeb Stuart was mortally wounded on May 11, 1864, during the Battle of Yellow Tavern, in which Stuart and his troops—outnumbered nearly three to one—took on the Union cavalry commanded by Philip H. Sheridan as it rode toward Richmond. Stuart was immediately taken to the Confederate capital, where he died the following day. Robert E. Lee was devastated by the loss of his close friend and trusted cavalry commander.

THOMAS "STONEWALL" JACKSON

Thomas Jonathan "Stonewall" Jackson was one of the finest officers in the Confederate army, a consummate professional who, though a strict disciplinarian who never drank or smoked, earned the respect and loyalty of all who served with him. So famous are his exploits on the battlefield that his name is practically synonymous with the Civil War, even though he died in battle midway through the conflict.

Jackson was born in Virginia (in a region that is now West Virginia) in 1824; he was orphaned as a youngster and raised by an uncle. Though he received little education as a child, Jackson managed to secure a spot at West Point and studied with such vigor and determination that he graduated 17th in a class of 59.

Jackson's first taste of combat was in the Mexican War; under John B. Magruder, he fought in numerous battles, including Vera Cruz, Contreras, and Chapultepec. Jackson showed exemplary skills as a soldier and was promoted to major within 18 months. After the Mexican War, Jackson was transferred to a number of different posts, including Florida, where he helped quell the Seminole uprising. In 1852, Jackson resigned his commission to become a professor of military tactics and natural philosophy at the Virginia Military Institute.

A religious man with strong convictions and few bad habits, Jackson enjoyed a number of quiet personal pursuits, including travel, until the Civil War started in 1861. When his home state of Virginia seceded, Jackson went with it and joined the Confederate army. One of his first tasks was to train infantry at Harpers Ferry, and by June 1861 he was promoted to brigadier general.

Jackson received his now famous nickname at the First Battle at Bull Run in July. According to reports, Jackson and his men fought off a Union advance with such courage that General Barnard Bee supposedly called out to his troops, "Oh men, there are Jackson and his Virginians, standing behind you like a stone wall! Let us determine to die here, and we shall conquer. Follow me." Jackson immediately became known as "Stonewall," a name that followed him for the rest of his life. (There are conflicting opinions as to whether Bee actually made the "stonewall" comment and, if so, whether it was really meant as a compliment. Some historians speculate that Bee was complaining that Jackson was not coming to his aid. However, Bee never got a chance to explain himself; he was mortally wounded moments later and died the next day. The newspapers in Richmond picked up on the story, and the legend of Stonewall Jackson was born).

Thomas "Stonewall" Jackson

In October 1861, Jackson was promoted to major general and placed in command of the Army of the Shenandoah Valley. Beginning in March 1862, he began a march through the valley, facing a number of armies that greatly outnumbered his own. But what he may have lacked in manpower Jackson more than made up for in brilliant strategy. Deploying his men quickly and for optimum effect, Jackson managed an impressive diversion that effectively kept Union forces in northern and western Virginia from attacking Richmond.

Jackson and his men were then transferred to the Richmond area, where they participated in the Seven Days' campaign. Jackson didn't perform as well as he had earlier and made several crucial missteps during the campaign that hurt the Confederate effort. At Mechanicsville and White Oak Swamp, for example, he failed to position his troops as ordered by Robert E. Lee, placing the Army of Northern Virginia in serious jeopardy.

However, Jackson redeemed himself at Second Bull Run. He and his men made a grueling 51-mile march through Virginia to Manassas Junction in just two days. After arriving at the scene, Jackson performed a disappearing act that thoroughly confused Union General John Pope, who was never able to accurately pinpoint Jackson's location. This gave Jackson and the other Confederate troops the upper hand, and though facing superior numbers, they managed an impressive victory.

Jackson proved invaluable again during the Battle of Antietam; he arrived just in time to save Robert E. Lee's army from complete annihilation. A month later, in October 1862, Jackson was promoted to lieutenant general and placed in charge of the 2nd Corps of the Army of Northern Virginia. In December, Jackson led his men to victory at the Battle of Fredericksburg, then took some time off to visit his wife, who had just given birth. However, his time home was cut short when Jackson received news that more than one hundred thousand Union troops were flooding across the Rappahannock on both sides of Fredericksburg. Jackson divided his forces and sent one division to halt Major General John Sedgwick's left flank while he rode to join Lee. With their forces combined, Lee and Jackson were able to push the federals all the way back to Chancellorsville on May 1, 1863. The next day, through a brilliant military maneuver in which they divided their forces and attacked on two sides, Lee and Jackson were able to send the Union forces running, thus securing a needed victory.

The Battle of Chancellorsville was Jackson's last. Returning to camp as dusk fell, he was mistaken for the enemy by one of his own men and shot in the arm. The wounded limb was amputated in a desperate attempt to save his life, but Jackson died of pneumonia on May 10. Once again, Lee had to face the death of a close friend and one of his most important officers.

DABNEY MAURY

Dabney Herndon Maury originally wanted to be a lawyer, until he discovered that he didn't like law. So he transferred from the University of Virginia to West Point, where he found the life of a soldier more to his tastes. During the Civil War, after a number of important victories, he gained fame as a hero in the Western theater.

Maury was born in Fredericksburg, Virginia, in 1822 to a family of influence. His ancestors were Huguenots who moved to America in the early 1700s, and his paternal uncle was Matthew Fontaine Maury, a famed Navy officer, oceanographer, and hydrographic researcher who also lent his talents to the Confederate cause.

After developing a distaste for his original pursuit, Maury managed to get into West Point, graduating in 1846. One of his classmates was George Pickett, who would gain fame years later for his ill-fated charge during the height of the Battle of Gettysburg. Upon graduating from West Point, Maury served in the Mexican War as a lieutenant in the Mounted Rifles and was given the honorary rank of first lieutenant for bravery in the siege of Cerro Gordo; the rank would become permanent not long after.

Maury served as an instructor of military tactics and a professor of geography, history, and ethics at West Point between 1847 and 1852. A stint in Texas followed, then Maury returned East to marry and become superintendent of the cavalry school in Carlisle Barracks, Pennsylvania. In 1860, he was appointed assistant adjutant

STONEWALL'S SICKNESS

Stonewall Jackson was one of the South's greatest military leaders. He was also a hypochondriac prone to eccentric behavior. Among his many idiosyncrasies, Jackson refused to eat pepper because he thought it made his left leg ache. He always sat upright and rigid to keep his internal organs in "alignment," he often held his right arm in the air for several minutes at a time, he habitually sucked lemons, he napped before battle, he believed Northerners were devils, he preferred strolling through camp handing out Sunday school leaflets to engaging in other forms of recreation, and he refused to write a letter that would be in the mail on a Sunday.

general of the Department of New Mexico, but he resigned his commission the following year when Virginia seceded from the Union. He joined the Confederate army as a cavalry captain, and by early 1862 had been promoted to colonel and an aide to General Earl Van Dorn, commander of the Trans-Mississippi Department.

Maury fought in the Battle of Pea Ridge, Arkansas, on March 7–8, 1862, and was rewarded for his bravery with a promotion to brigadier general. Maury also fought gallantly in the Battle of Iuka, the Battle of Corinth, and the Battle of Hatchie Bridge; he was promoted to major general in November 1862. At the Battle of Corinth, Maury and his troops fought with such ferocity that they drove the Union forces out of town and then continued to harass the fleeing soldiers in their retreat. In July 1863, Maury was placed in charge of the District of the Gulf, taking command in Mobile. He did his best to defend the Gulf, but toward the end of the war, he was forced to surrender to overwhelming odds.

After the war, Maury had little going for him. His personal fortune was long gone, and because he was branded a traitor for joining the Confederacy, the U.S. Army was closed to him. He worked as a teacher at various schools for a while, then went into business in New Orleans. When the city was hit with a cholera epidemic, he closed his shop and volunteered as a nurse in the city's hospitals. In the 1880s, Maury was appointed minister to Colombia and also served on the National Guard Association's executive committee for several years.

Dabney Maury wrote numerous magazine articles and books over the years, including a history of Virginia for children and his memoir, *Recollections of a Virginian*, which was published in 1894. He died in 1900 in the home of his son and was buried in the Confederate Cemetery in Fredericksburg, Virginia.

PIERRE G. T. BEAUREGARD

Pierre Gustave Toutant Beauregard was one of the Confederate army's best officers and one of its first heroes, but a rancorous relationship with Confederate President Jefferson Davis kept him from achieving the fame—and commands—that went to many of his associates.

Beauregard was born in Louisiana in 1818 to a wealthy and prosperous Creole family. A gifted student, he attended West Point and graduated second in his class. Like most of his contemporaries, he honed his military skills during the Mexican War and spent many years with the corps of engineers. As the army's chief engineer in New Orleans, he supervised the dredging of the mouth of the Mississippi.

In January 1861, Beauregard was appointed superintendent of West Point, but the job didn't last long. Beauregard was dismissed after just five days because of his vocal prosecessionist views. When Louisiana seceded, Beauregard—an ardent Confederate—joined the Confederate army as a brigadier general.

Beauregard commanded the Confederate troops that captured Fort Sumter and, as a result, became the South's first war hero. He was also a commander at the First Battle of Bull Run, and helped achieve the Confederate army's first battlefield victory, though Jefferson Davis berated Beauregard for not pursuing the panic-stricken Union soldiers all the way into Washington.

That was the first of many problems Beauregard would have with the cantankerous Davis. In another instance, Beauregard assumed command when General Albert Johnston was killed during the Battle of Shiloh, and he ultimately lost the battle at Corinth. Davis accused Beauregard of being too elaborate in his military strategy and relieved him of command.

Beauregard was reassigned to Charleston, South Carolina, where Jefferson felt he could do no harm. However, Charleston became a frequent target of attack by Union forces, and Beauregard fought valiantly to protect it. In April 1864, Beauregard was sent back to Virginia, where he played a crucial role in stopping two potentially devastating Union attacks: an advance on Richmond in May and an attack on Petersburg in June. In the latter, Beauregard and his small army of just 2,500 men managed to hold off Northern forces until Robert E. Lee arrived with reinforcements.

However, Jefferson Davis failed to recognize the important role Beauregard played in the Battle of Petersburg, and rather than being

CIVIL WAR FACTOID

Confederate General Pierre G. T. Beauregard, in addition to being a skilled military tactician and soldier, designed the Confederate army's "Southern Cross" battle flag.

rewarded, he was shipped off to a relatively unimportant administrative position in the West. In 1865, Beauregard was brought East, yet again, to act as Joe Johnston's second in command in the hopeless task of halting William T. Sherman's unstoppable assault through the Carolinas.

After the war, Beauregard was offered military commissions from Romania and Egypt but declined them both, preferring instead to return to New Orleans, where he became active in the railroad industry and other public works. He also wrote extensively and published a number of books on military theory and his recollections of the Civil War years. Beauregard died in Louisiana in 1893.

JUBAL A. EARLY

Jubal Anderson Early may not have met the image of a top military strategist and fighter—he suffered from arthritis and was even more unkempt than the average Confederate soldier—but he proved himself well on the battlefield and became one of the South's favorite officers.

Early was born in 1816 to an aristocratic Virginia family. He attended West Point and graduated 18th in his class of 1833. He fought in the Mexican War and the Seminole uprising in Florida but didn't want to make the military a career and retired to become a lawyer and state legislator. In 1861, he attended the Virginia secession convention and voted to remain in the Union.

However, once the war began, Early willingly leapt into the fray. He joined the Confederate army and after proving his mettle at the First Battle of Bull Run was promoted to brigadier general. Early commanded a brigade during the Peninsula campaign in Virginia in the spring of 1862 and was wounded in the shoulder. After a fast recovery, Early led a division in a number of important battles, including Antietam, Fredericksburg, Gettysburg, and the Wilderness.

Early was a feisty commander who often behaved unpredictably and impulsively on the battlefield. But he proved himself an able leader who was well liked by his troops, and he was quickly promoted to lieutenant general. In June and July 1864, Early led an astoundingly daring attack on Washington, D.C., that proved disastrous for the Union. Riding up from the Shenandoah Valley, his corps of 14,000 men seized or destroyed property throughout Maryland. (He also collected more than $200,000 in ransom money by threatening to burn the villages of Hagerstown and Frederick).

Early met little resistance in his march toward Washington, crushing a tiny federal force near the Monocacy River in early July. Within two days, he stood less than five miles from the nation's capital. Luckily, federal reinforcements arrived in time to prevent Early and his troops from capturing the city. Realizing he couldn't win, Early quickly withdrew back into the Shenandoah Valley.

But Early wasn't done. He continued to harass the North, raiding various towns in Pennsylvania, including Chambersburg, which he burned to the ground when the townspeople refused to pay a ransom of $500,000. Grant finally sent forces led by Philip Sheridan into the Shenandoah Valley to stop Early's campaign of terror.

Early suffered greatly in subsequent battles. In the Battle of Winchester on September 19, 1864, he lost nearly a quarter of his troops, and Sheridan routed Early's remaining forces three days later at Fisher's Hill. Early tried one last attempt to hold the Shenandoah Valley, with a surprise attack on Union forces at Cedar Creek on October 19. It appeared early in the battle that Early would be the victor, but Sheridan's forces pitched a fierce counterattack that decimated Early's troops and brought the valley under Union control. In March 1865, Early was defeated yet again by Sheridan at the Battle of Waynesboro, forcing Robert E. Lee to relieve him of command. Early then was sent to join the fighting in Texas, but the war ended before he arrived.

With the cessation of hostilities, Early traveled to Mexico, Cuba, and Canada, where he wrote his memoirs. He returned to Virginia in 1869 and resumed his law practice. An unrepentant Confederate, Early always remained faithful to the Southern cause and was the first president of the Southern Historical Society. He died in 1894.

CIVIL WAR FACTOID

Nathan Bedford Forrest had 30 horses shot out from under him and was himself wounded four times in battle.

CIVIL WAR
FACTOID

Confederate General Joseph
E. Johnston moved his unit
by railroad to Manassas
Junction for the First Battle
of Bull Run in July 1861. It
was the first time in history
that soldiers were trans-
ported to a battle via train.

JOSEPH E. JOHNSTON

Joseph Eggleston Johnston was another talented Confederate officer who had recurrent problems with Jefferson Davis. However, he was a very effective, well-liked leader who held important commands in the eastern and western theaters throughout the war and did his very best against all odds.

Johnston was born in Virginia in 1807. He attended West Point and saw quite a bit of combat following graduation, including service in the Seminole War and the Mexican War. He was wounded during both of those actions, but he always came back for more. In the 1850s, he saw duty in the Kansas Territory during the bloody conflict there and was made quartermaster general of the U.S. Army in June 1860. However, he resigned his commission in April 1861, when Virginia seceded from the Union.

Johnston was made a brigadier general in the Confederate army in May 1861 and was the commander of the Confederate troops that won the First Battle of Bull Run in July (though Johnston deferred the planning of strategy to Pierre G. T. Beauregard, who had a greater knowledge of the battlefield). It was the first military victory for the Confederate army and a stunning and unexpected blow against the overly confident Union.

The following month Johnston was named a full general and appointed to command the Department of the Potomac. He was wounded in the Battle of Seven Pines in May 1862 and temporarily relieved of duty while he recuperated. In November, Johnston was appointed commander of the Department of the West, but Jefferson Davis refused to support his battle strategy, and Johnston suffered humiliating defeats at Stones River, Vicksburg, Chickamauga, and Chattanooga. As a result of these losses, Johnston's reputation among Confederate leaders in Richmond suffered greatly.

Johnston was brought back East to command the Army of Tennessee and ordered to stop William T. Sherman's march toward Atlanta. Johnston did his best against the Union general, but Confederate officials felt he wasn't aggressive enough, and Johnston was replaced in July 1864 by General John B. Hood. Johnston was reassigned to command the Army of Tennessee in February 1865 and led his troops against Sherman's march through the Carolinas. By that time, the South was all but lost, and Johnston was little more than an annoyance to Sherman, whose troops considerably outnumbered Johnston's. On April 26, Johnston surrendered to Sherman, despite orders from Davis to move south and continue fighting.

After the war, Joseph Johnston held a number of jobs. He worked in insurance and for a railroad company, served a term in the U.S. Congress, and became a federal railroad commissioner. And like most of his contemporaries, he wrote his memoirs. Johnston was a pallbearer during William T. Sherman's funeral, which was held on a bitterly cold day. He refused to wear a hat out of respect and contracted pneumonia, from which he died in 1891.

OTHER IMPORTANT MILITARY FIGURES

The armies of the Union and the Confederacy were commanded by a large number of men, only a handful of which are discussed above. Following is a short list of other military figures of note.

THE UNION

- ✪ George G. Meade (1815–77) saw action at Mechanicsville, Gaines's Mills, and White Oak Swamp, where he was badly wounded. He returned to lead his brigade in the Second Battle of Bull Run and the Battle of Antietam. Meade replaced Joseph Hooker as commander of the Army of the Potomac on June 28, 1863—just in time to lead it during the Battle of Gettysburg.

- ✪ George Henry Halleck (1815–72) was appointed major general in charge of the newly formed Military Department of Missouri and later was placed in command of the Departments of Kansas and Ohio. He took command of Union forces after the Battle of Shiloh, with instructions to crush Beauregard's army but acted with such hesitancy that Beauregard was able to retreat. Lincoln appointed Halleck general-in-chief of all the armies of the North, where he proved more skilled as an administrator than commander.

○ Joseph Hooker (1814–79) was known by the nickname "Fighting Joe Hooker," which he greatly disliked. He led the Union attack at Antietam and was wounded; he recovered to command a corps in the Battle of Fredericksburg just three months later. He was appointed to command the Army of the Potomac in January 1863. Hooker lost to Lee in the Battle of Chancellorsville in May 1863. He was removed from the Army of the Potomac in June 1863, just before the Battle of Gettysburg. Hooker saw combat in the Battle of Chattanooga and the Siege of Atlanta.

○ Philip Sheridan (1831–88) was one of the youngest commanders to serve in the Civil War. He was known for his skill and bravery as a cavalry commander. Sheridan fought in numerous battles in both the East and the West but was most famous for his "scorched earth" policy during his Shenandoah Valley campaign between 1864-65.

○ Ambrose Everett Burnside (1824–81) raised a brigade that fought well at the First Battle of Bull Run and was instrumental in the capture of several vital Southern coastal positions some months later. Promoted to major general, Burnside twice refused offers to take over the Army of the Potomac from McClellan, with whom he was friends, but he finally accepted when Lincoln offered him the position in 1862. However, Burnside proved unskilled for the job and led the Union army to a devastating defeat at the Battle of Fredericksburg.

○ George Custer (1839–76) is remembered more for his last stand at Little Bighorn in 1876 than his participation in the Civil War. Custer proved to be an adept and skilled soldier. At 23, he became the youngest general in the Union army. He distinguished himself on the second day of the Battle of

---

CIVIL WAR FACTOID

Contrary to legend, the word *hooker* as slang for prostitute was not derived from General Joseph Hooker, who was known for his many vices. In truth, the word *hooker* was in common usage long before the Civil War began.

Gettysburg, with a series of daring frontal attacks that held back Jeb Stuart's advance on Culp's Hill. Custer and Stuart met again at the Battle of Yellow Tavern, in which Stuart was killed.

THE CONFEDERACY

- Nathan Bedford Forrest (1821–77) rose from private to lieutenant general in the Confederate army and became one of the war's most feared cavalry commanders because of his "lightning raids" on enemy camps. His cavalry successfully covered the Confederate withdrawal following the Battle of Shiloh, even though Forrest was seriously wounded. He saw combat at the Battle of Murfreesboro and the Battle of Chickamauga, among many others. Forrest led the extremely controversial capture of Fort Pillow, in which his men were accused of slaughtering more than two hundred unarmed troops, primarily black soldiers who had already surrendered.

- Albert Sidney Johnston (1803–62) was a very skilled commander who was killed during the Battle of Shiloh in April 1862. Johnston was appointed commander of the Confederate Department of the Mississippi when the war broke out, and though undermanned, he managed to establish a bulkhead in Kentucky to protect Tennessee from a Union offensive. He held the position until January 1862, when he was overrun by Grant's superior numbers.

- John Bell Hood (1831–79) was a courageous fighter. Hood nonetheless lacked the strategic skills necessary to command an army. Under his leadership, the Confederate Army of the Tennessee was pretty much annihilated trying to stop Sherman late in the war. Before that, however, Hood fought well in a number of battles, including the Seven Days' campaign, Second Bull Run, and Antietam. He was wounded at Gettysburg and lost his right leg in the Battle of Chickamauga.

CIVIL WAR FACTOID

George Custer was present during Lee's surrender to Grant at the home of Wilmer McLean in Appomattox Court House, Virginia. Custer stole a small table as a souvenir of the climactic event,

- Braxton Bragg (1817–76) was greatly disliked by his superiors as well as those who served under him. Bragg showed flair as a military tactician but also demonstrated potentially fatal indecision on the battlefield. He commanded the coast between Pensacola and Mobile during the first summer of the war and was promoted to major general of the regular army in September 1861. Bragg served under Albert Johnston as chief of staff and participated in the Battle of Shiloh. He was promoted to commander of the Confederate army of the Mississippi in June 1862, replacing Pierre Beauregard. Bragg had initial successes in Kentucky but lost the opportunity for more gains by wasting time trying to set up a secessionist government in Frankfort. He also participated in the Battle of Murfreesboro, the Battle of Chickamauga, and the Battle of Missionary Ridge.

- John B. Magruder (1810–71) was known for his need to always be in the spotlight. Magruder's star rose early in the war, only to plummet when he was blamed for a crucial Confederate defeat on the last day's battle at Malvern Hill during the Seven Days' campaign of June–July 1862 (he accidentally led his division down a road away from the battle). He was transferred to command the District of Texas in October 1862, where he saw action in minor battles. At the end of the war, Magruder moved to Mexico, where he served as a general under Emperor Maximilian.

5

The Major Battles
of the
Civil War

Today's soldiers are professionals, highly trained and skilled in everything they do. But things were a lot different during the Civil War. At the beginning of hostilities, the U.S. Army was fairly small (totaling about 15,000 men) and widely spread out, hardly ready to invade and conquer the rebellious South. And the Confederacy was even worse off. As a fledgling nation, it didn't even have a standing army, much less a war machine, nor did it have the weapons to fight even if it wanted to.

On both sides, the Civil War was essentially a war of amateurs. For the most part, the commanding officers were trained military men, a great many of them graduates of West Point and veterans of the Mexican War and other military conflicts. But the men serving under them were almost all volunteers, farmers and businessmen who put down their tools, picked up their guns, and marched off to do battle for a cause they believed in: the preservation of their beloved republics.

General Winfield Scott, Lincoln's general-in-chief at the beginning of the Civil War, greatly disliked volunteer soldiers. He had fought with them during the Mexican War and found them to be generally more trouble than they were worth. They were untrained, unskilled, and ill behaved. In short, they were not the type of soldiers he wanted.

However, the Union desperately needed their services; though it had plenty of weapons, it lacked the manpower to engage in a full-scale war. So on April 15, 1861, Lincoln put out a national call for 75,000 militia to sign up for a three-month enlistment, the length of time he felt would be needed to restore order and bring the South back into the Union. The call was met with enthusiasm, and the Union army soon had far more than 75,000 volunteers, eager if not ready, to fight. In the South, Jefferson Davis enlisted 100,000 men for one year.

General Scott begged for more time to train the volunteer forces (as well as organize the supply services required to keep them armed, fed, and clothed in the battlefield). He knew from experience that, though enthusiastic, few of the new recruits had the skill and training necessary to fight an armed enemy. They would require extensive training in the use of firearms, strategy, and combat, and these were things that couldn't be taught in a day. But while Lincoln may have concurred with Scott in his evaluation of the Union's volunteer militias, he was also facing heavy pressure from Congress, the press, and the public to get matters underway and bring the war to a quick end. As a result, most volunteer soldiers received a minimum of training, if any, before shipping out for battle.

The Confederate army was slightly better off when it came to volunteer soldiers. They, too, received a minimum of drilling and instruction, but because most Confederate soldiers were farmers and outdoorsmen, they tended to be much more skilled with a rifle. They were also fighting on home turf and knew the terrain much better than the invading Union soldiers. This gave the Confederate army a decided home-field advantage.

When the fighting started in earnest, however, the volunteer forces on both sides quickly came to know the bitter taste of fear. It's one thing to be able to pick a squirrel off a tree branch at 50 yards, but it's quite another to fire and advance while other men are shooting at you. Most of their commanding officers had become battle hardened in the Mexican War and other conflicts, but the typical foot soldiers had not. For them, it was literally a trial by fire, and many found warfare more frightening than they ever imagined. In many cases, campfire braggadocio gave way to blind panic in the face of enemy bullets. But those who survived the first battles of the war became better soldiers, and they helped teach and inspire the constant flood of new recruits. In some cases, the volunteers proved to be even better fighters than the soldiers in the regular army, and some officers came to prefer them on the battlefield. Noted General Thomas J. Wood, who commanded a division at the Battle of Chickamauga: "[The volunteers] will 'stick' you; you can fight them as long as you please . . . The regulars are too sharp. They know when they are whipped but the volunteers don't; they will fight as long as they can pull a trigger."

NORTHERN RECRUITS

One of the strangest aspects of Northern recruitment was the concept of substitutes, in which wealthy men of fighting age could either pay a flat "commutation" fee of $300 or hire someone to fight in their place. In theory, this practice allowed professionals and those with various skills to work for the war effort while still providing able-bodied soldiers. But as might be expected, the program was rife with corruption, and it wasn't uncommon for men to accept money to act as a substitute, then move to another city and get paid again. In addition, many healthy men bribed their doctors to get them out of military service for medical reasons.

REBEL YELL

One of the most effective weapons on the Confederate side was the "rebel yell," a shrill cry that helped rally the troops as well as frighten and disorient the enemy.

Historians believe the rebel yell was first heard during the First Battle of Bull Run in July 1861. After nearly 14 hours of fighting, a corps of soldiers under Pierre G. T. Beauregard began a counterattack against Union forces and launched the now-famous wail. When the Union forces saw—and heard—what was coming at them, they panicked and fled in retreat. The rebel yell was heard during nearly every major battle after that.

THE CHANGING FACE OF WARFARE

As noted earlier, the Civil War was the first "modern" war in that it incorporated technological advances that would change the face of combat forever. The use of gunpowder and firearms was introduced into warfare in the fourteenth century, and up until the Civil War, soldiers typically stood like pickets on a fence, shooting at each other across fields with single-shot muskets and other imprecise weapons. It was awkward and time consuming and not particularly effective.

But the Civil War changed all that. The traditional musket, which could take up to a minute to reload even by a skilled soldier, was replaced with a variety of more modern weapons, including breechloading rifles and carbines that offered greater accuracy, distance, and firepower. Within a year of the war's onset, it became considerably easier to kill or be killed. Unfortunately, many military leaders failed to take these advances into account and used old tactics of attack that put their soldiers in considerable jeopardy from a much more distant enemy. The result was an unexpectedly high number of casualties.

The Civil War also saw a large number of other unique innovations. The use of trains to ferry soldiers and equipment from one place to another was a historical first, as was the use of the telegraph by commanders in the field to transmit information and stay in touch with their fellow officers. Not surprisingly, a lot of time and energy went into destroying enemy train tracks and telegraph wires.

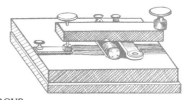

In naval combat, the most important innovation of the Civil War was the creation and use of ironclad ships. In the past, warships were all made of wood, which was very susceptible to enemy artillery. In comparison, the ironclads, while somewhat unwieldy, were practically indestructible. The two-hour battle between the Union ironclad *Monitor* and the Confederate ironclad *Virginia* (formerly the *Merrimac*) outside of Norfolk Harbor in March 1862 is a prime example of how sturdy the ships could be. Hundreds of shots were fired from both ships, but when

How the Civil War Was Funded

Both sides poured millions of dollars into their war machines, with the citizens of the Union and the Confederacy ultimately taking the brunt through ever-increasing taxes.

Most people believe a federal income tax is a relatively new phenomenon, but in truth, it was first enacted by Secretary of the Treasury Salmon B. Chase as a way of funding the war effort. In the beginning, money was provided through loans from private financiers, then war bonds marketed by Philadelphia banker Jay Cooke, which brought the government more than a billion dollars. When the sources of private capital disappeared, Chase was allowed to print a national currency under the Legal Tender Act. The money, known as greenbacks, was backed by treasury gold. (Previously, each state had printed its own money.)

Congress passed the first Internal Revenue Act at the same time it passed the Legal Tender Act. This was necessary because the government's international credit rating had plummeted as a result of early Northern defeats (no one wants to fund a loser), and money for the war effort, which was costing an estimated $2.5 million a day by 1862, was growing tight. The first income tax rates were just 3 percent, but the government also enacted other taxes as well, including a sin tax on tobacco and liquor, a luxury tax on jewels and other items, and a license tax. In short, the government dug deep into the pockets of its citizenry in a desperate attempt to keep its war machine going.

Funding for the war was even more difficult for the Confederacy. Christopher Memminger, a South Carolinian of German descent, was appointed the first secretary of the treasury and ordered to find a way to keep the war funds coming. At first, lacking the internal organization to establish taxes or tariffs, Memminger turned to the sale of war bonds, which could be redeemed when the war was over. The bonds sold briskly following the capture of Fort Sumter, but sales dried up as it became increasingly evident that the effort was doomed, and soon, they were worthless.

Ultimately, its inability to get funding from overseas forced the Confederate government to tap its citizens, who found themselves paying a series of taxes that made those imposed by the federal government look positively friendly. In addition to a federal income tax, the Confederacy also required a 10 percent "tax in kind," which required farmers to turn over to the government a portion of all the crops they grew.

the smoke cleared, neither ship had been penetrated or seriously damaged. Both sides claimed victory, but in truth, the duel had been a draw—and clear evidence that naval warfare would never be the same.

This chapter takes a chronological look at the major battles of the Civil War. Of course, this is far from a complete analysis. There were hundreds of small skirmishes and minor battles between the major battlefield events, far too many for us to discuss here. What follows are the battles of greatest importance, the battles that, for whatever reason, helped push the war to its inevitable conclusion.

THE FALL OF FORT SUMTER
APRIL 12–13, 1861

COMMANDERS ROBERT ANDERSON (UNION) AND PIERRE G. T. BEAUREGARD (CONFEDERACY)

It could be said that the Civil War officially started with the Confederate attack on Fort Sumter in Charleston Harbor, South Carolina. It was a relatively one-sided "battle" because the Union fort was low on men and supplies, but it signaled to the world that the South meant business in its conflict with the North.

When Abraham Lincoln was inaugurated, he vowed that the federal government would not start a war with the South, nor would it try to take back federal facilities held at that point by Confederate forces. He did promise, however, to "hold, occupy, and possess" forts and other installations still under federal control within the Confederacy, and that included Fort Sumter.

Lincoln was thrown into the first serious crisis of his presidency the day after his inauguration, when he received a frantic wire from Major Robert Anderson, the commander of Fort Sumter, stating that the facility had less than a six-week supply of food. The fort would be impossible to hold if new supplies were not sent immediately.

General-in-Chief Winfield Scott told Lincoln that resupplying the fort would be impossible, and Secretary of State William

CIVIL WAR FACTOID

Robert Anderson, the commander of Fort Sumter in 1861, retired from the regular army in 1863 as a result of ill health. After the Union capture of Charleston in 1865, he took part in a ceremony in which he raised the same American flag he had lowered four years earlier.

Seward advised that it simply be evacuated in an attempt to cool growing hostilities in South Carolina, which had been the first state to secede from the Union. Lincoln chose an option he hoped would appease both sides: He would resupply the fort but not reinforce its defenses. He then sent a message to Francis Pickens, the governor of South Carolina, telling him of his decision.

Jefferson Davis, however, was not in a conciliatory mood. He wanted nothing less than the surrender of the fort, the presence of which he saw as an insult to the Confederacy, and ordered Beauregard to take it by force if necessary. Beauregard sent Anderson a message informing him of his intent to bombard the fort if it were not evacuated, to which a pragmatic Anderson replied, "Gentlemen, I will await the first shot and if you do not batter the fort to pieces about us, we shall be starved out in a few days." Anderson then informed Beauregard's emissary that he would evacuate the fort by noon on April 15 if he did not receive additional orders or supplies by that time. Anderson was told the terms were not acceptable.

On April 12, at 4:30 A.M., a single mortar was fired to signal the 43 Confederate guns around Fort Sumter to begin their assault. More than four thousand shells were fired at the fort, but amazingly, no one within was injured. On the second day of the bombardment, hot shells set portions of the fort on fire. Realizing there was no way he could mount any type of reasonable defense, Anderson ordered the American flag lowered and replaced it with a white flag of surrender.

During the fort's evacuation the next day, Anderson ordered a cannon salute to the flag. During the ceremony, one of the big guns exploded, killing Private Daniel Hough. Another soldier, Private Edward Galloway, was gravely injured in the explosion and died a few days later. They were the war's first military casualties, victims of an accident.

On April 15, Abraham Lincoln proclaimed a state of insurrection rather than a state of war and issued a call for 75,000 volunteers to quell the rebellion. The Civil War had officially begun.

CIVIL WAR FACTOID

Abner Doubleday, Anderson's second in command, is often credited with inventing the sport of baseball in 1839. In truth, baseball in various incarnations had been around long before.

THE FIRST BATTLE OF BULL RUN
⊶ JULY 21, 1861 ⊷

COMMANDERS IRVIN MCDOWELL (UNION) AND
PIERRE G. T. BEAUREGARD (CONFEDERACY)

The First Battle of Bull Run was the first real battle of the war. Union officials felt it would be an easy victory and would lead to a quick conclusion to the war, but history proved otherwise. At the end, the Confederacy was the winner, routing inexperienced Union forces and sending them fleeing all the way back to Washington.

The battle was set more for political than military reasons. Confederate leaders were eager to prove their mettle against the more industrial North and announced their intentions to move the capital of the Confederacy to Richmond, Virginia, a situation that greatly angered Northern politicians. Meanwhile, the press and the public were loudly pushing for the Union to move "on to Richmond" and end the war as quickly as possible. More importantly, by the time the battle was set, many of the 75,000 volunteer recruits were nearing the end of their 90-day enlistment and were getting ready to go home.

Union General Irvin McDowell's strategy for the battle was simple: His plan was to invade Virginia, crush the Confederate forces, and push on to Richmond. Opposing him in this endeavor was Confederate General Pierre G. T. Beauregard, already a Confederate war hero as a result of his role in the fall of Fort Sumter. If the Confederacy could win the first battle of the war, Beauregard reasoned, it might impress upon the Union the strength and fortitude of the Confederate army and result in a truce that in turn might lead to an early peace.

Each side was divided into three armies. McDowell had 30,600 troops along the Potomac facing 20,000 Confederate soldiers under Beauregard, who had amassed his forces behind a creek called Bull Run near Manassas Junction. Union General Robert Patterson had 18,000 men facing 12,000 Confederates under Joseph E. Johnston near Harpers Ferry. And Union General Benjamin Butler commanded 10,000 men

in Fort Monroe at the tip of the Virginia peninsula, guarded by a small unit of Confederates under John B. Magruder (neither Butler nor Magruder would play a role in Bull Run).

McDowell's first objective was to attack Beauregard and drive him from Manassas Junction by feigning an attack on the Confederate center, then clobbering the Confederate left. He ordered Patterson to keep Johnston busy at Harpers Ferry so that Johnston couldn't join Beauregard, thus giving McDowell a decided advantage in numbers. However, Johnston gave Patterson the slip and was able to come to Beauregard's aid, as did others.

McDowell left Washington for Manassas Junction on July 16, 1861. But his army was large and slow, due primarily to a huge number of supply wagons and the carefree attitude of the neophyte soldiers, who often broke rank to gather berries or rest in the shade, and he didn't arrive until July 18. On that day, Union reconnaissance troops sent to feel out the enemy were met and driven back by Confederate forces at Blackburn's Ford; it was a small Confederate victory that demoralized the green Union troops.

The battle itself began on July 21. Beauregard's grand plan to attack McDowell, based on Napoleon's strategy at Austerlitz, was a dismal and immediate failure because of the inexperience of his troops. McDowell's army gained an early advantage thanks to its greater numbers, and it appeared the Union would win; several Confederate units were defeated as Union infantry advanced on a small plateau called Henry House Hill (it was here that Stonewall Jackson was given his famous nickname).

But just when a Union victory seemed assured, Johnston's army arrived from Harpers Ferry to reinforce Beauregard's army. Fighting aggressively, the Confederate forces caused the Union line to crumble. Retreat was called, and the Union soldiers, most of whom had never been in battle before, began to race to the rear as the Confederates shot at them. The retreat turned into a rout as officers abandoned their troops, terrified soldiers fled in panic, and the entire Union supply train became a horrible, tangled mess of carts, trucks, and ambulances. Chaos reigned, and the situation was made worse by the presence of hundreds of sightseers, many with picnic baskets in hand, who had arrived from Washington in carriages and

SUBSTITUTES

As a symbolic gesture to encourage the practice of hiring substitutes during the war, President Lincoln paid $500 to a 20-year-old Pennsylvanian named John Summerfield Staples, who had been discharged from the Union army because he had contracted typhoid. Future Presidents Chester A. Arthur and Grover Cleveland, both of draft age, also avoided military duty by paying others to do it for them.

buggies, to watch from a grassy slope a few miles away what was assumed to be a forgone Union victory. It would have been comical if it hadn't been so tragic. Federal losses totaled 2,896 men dead, wounded, or missing. Confederate losses totaled 1,982.

The First Battle of Bull Run would foreshadow a great many other battles in which outmanned and outgunned Confederate forces would defeat the Union army through skill, bravery, and sheer battlefield tenacity. It also proved to Lincoln and others that the short, clean war they had hoped for was not going to happen.

THE BATTLE OF SHILOH
⚔ APRIL 6–7, 1862 ⚔

COMMANDERS ULYSSES S. GRANT (UNION) AND ALBERT SIDNEY JOHNSTON (CONFEDERACY)

This battle, the bloodiest of the war up until that date, is considered an important Union victory, though Ulysses S. Grant was greatly criticized for his efforts. The Union originally called this engagement the Battle of Pittsburg Landing, after the Tennessee River embankment the Union forces were defending, but both sides eventually named it Shiloh, after the Methodist log meeting house near the site of some of the bloodiest fighting.

Grant was stationed with 42,000 troops on the west side of the Tennessee River near the Mississippi border. He remained there for nearly a month, waiting for the arrival of Don Carlos Buell's army. Their combined forces were to head south to attack an important Confederate railroad center called Corinth, which was being protected by Confederate General Albert Sidney Johnston. However, Johnston decided to attack first, hoping to catch Grant's troops before Buell arrived. Johnston's second in command, Pierre G. T. Beauregard, liked the idea at first but then changed his mind; he felt that 20,000 soldiers on a 20-mile march would be too easily detected and that Grant would be reinforced before they arrived.

But when Johnston's army arrived at Pittsburg Landing on April 6, they found no signs of Buell's arrival. The Confederate forces caught the Union troops off guard (Grant was away from the front receiving treatment for an injured leg), and after three hours of brutal, bloody fighting, they managed to overrun the divisions commanded by William T. Sherman and Benjamin Prentiss near Shiloh Church. The battle could have turned into a rout, but Johnston's army lost its momentum when his soldiers started rummaging through the now abandoned Union camps looking for food and supplies.

The battle became increasingly disorganized, and soldiers on both sides scrambled to find their correct units. One major battle turned into numerous smaller skirmishes, with both sides taking heavy casualties. In many cases, confused Confederate troops dressed in both blue and gray fired on their own men, and hundreds of panic-stricken soldiers on both sides ran from the battlefield in terror.

When Grant arrived on the scene, he ordered his remaining men to hold their positions in a dense thicket at all costs. With Grant barking orders and doing his best to rally them, the Union soldiers managed to repel more than a dozen hard Confederate charges. Johnston, who was directing the assaults, took a bullet in the foot and bled to death at 2:30 P.M. Three hours later, the 2,200 defenders of the thicket, which came to be known as "the Hornet's Nest" because of the constant gunfire, were ordered to surrender as they came under fire from Confederate artillery. But it was growing dark, and it had started to rain, so Beauregard, who assumed command upon Johnston's death, decided to delay a final assault until the next morning. The decision would cost him greatly.

During the night, Grant was greatly reinforced by Don Carlos Buell's army, and Beauregard awakened the following morning to face an army nearly twice as strong as before. Fighting resumed around 7:30 A.M. and the Union forces were able to recapture almost all of the ground they had lost the day before. The Confederates made one counterattack but were pushed back. Late in the afternoon, Beauregard ordered a withdrawal back to Corinth, covered by Nathan Forrest's cavalry.

Grant's army won the battle, but Grant was strongly rebuked for being caught by surprise. His superior officer, Henry Halleck, accused Grant of being drunk at the time (an accusation that was not true, but was typical of Halleck) and also blamed him for the large number of Union casualties. More than 13,000 Union soldiers were killed, wounded, or missing in the battle, compared to 10,694 on the Confederate side; this loss was more than twice the number of dead in all previous engagements combined.

THE CAMPAIGN AND SECOND BATTLE OF BULL RUN
AUGUST 26–SEPTEMBER 1, 1862

COMMANDERS JOHN POPE (UNION) AND ROBERT E. LEE (CONFEDERACY)

The Second Battle of Bull Run was fought in the same region and ended pretty much as the first one did—that is, with a Confederate victory over superior Union numbers. The key to Confederate success was exceptional leadership and better planning.

The Confederate army had managed to protect Richmond during George McClellan's Peninsular campaign and the Seven Days' Battle but had not been able to advance very far. Robert E. Lee, with support from his best generals, intended to change that with a daring offensive that he hoped would move the war from the James River to north of the Rappahannock.

Meanwhile, the North was undergoing a much needed military reorganization. McClellan's recurrent hesitancy was wearing thin on Lincoln, who turned to other leaders to move the Union army forward and, he hoped, to win some important battles. He appointed Major General Henry Halleck general-in-chief of all federal forces and placed General John Pope in charge of the newly created Army of Virginia, which was formed to launch another attack on Richmond as quickly as possible. McClellan's army remained positioned at Harrison's Landing, Virginia, where McClellan refused to budge until his numbers were reinforced.

Lee had a formidable job ahead of him: He had to prevent Pope and McClellan's forces from hooking up and overpowering his smaller army of just 55,000 men. His plan was simple but fraught with danger. He would split his troops and send Stonewall Jackson with 24,000 to capture the Union supply depot at Manassas Junction. Lee and Major General James Longstreet would follow the next day with 30,000 soldiers to meet Jackson at Manassas.

Pope, who had lost track of Lee and Longstreet's division, met Jackson in Manassas and engaged in a heated two-day battle between August 28 and 30. The Confederate forces managed to successfully repel attack after attack by the right half of the Union army, and Jackson pulled back some of his exhausted troops at the end of the day. Pope mistook Jackson's move as a retreat and wired Washington that he was about to pursue. Unknown to Pope, however, Lee and Longstreet had joined Jackson on August 29, bringing nearly 30,000 fresh troops. When Pope tried to cut off the Confederate "retreat," he was met with a tremendous assault that crushed his army and forced him to retreat. Troops from the Army of the Potomac, commanded by McClellan, arrived on August 31, but there was little that they could do. Pope was forced to retreat all the way back to Washington, giving the Confederacy a much needed victory. However, it came with a heavy price: A combined total of more than 14,500 men were killed or wounded between August 16 and September 2.

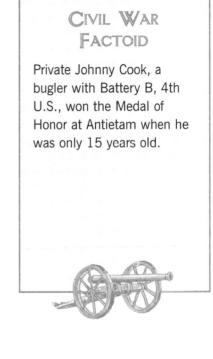

CIVIL WAR FACTOID

Private Johnny Cook, a bugler with Battery B, 4th U.S., won the Medal of Honor at Antietam when he was only 15 years old.

THE BATTLE OF ANTIETAM
⊸⊜ SEPTEMBER 17, 1862 ⊜⊷

COMMANDERS GEORGE MCCLELLAN (UNION) AND ROBERT E. LEE (CONFEDERACY)

The Battle of Antietam was the single bloodiest day of fighting in the Civil War, with a combined total of more than 27,000 casualties. It was also a decisive victory for the Union and gave Abraham Lincoln the confidence he needed to issue his Emancipation Proclamation, which effectively changed the Union's war aims to include the abolition of slavery and increased manpower by allowing black soldiers to participate.

Prior to Antietam, Robert E. Lee, riding high on the Confederate victory at the Second Battle of Bull Run, planned an invasion of the North through western Maryland. His goals were many: to take some of the pressure off of Virginia, which was being smashed by Union forces; to attract recruits in Maryland, a border state with strong Confederate sympathies; and to win a major victory on Union soil with the intent of forcing Lincoln to bargain for peace.

Lee's primary goal, however, was the capture of the Union railroad center in Harrisburg, Pennsylvania. He hoped to take the town by dividing his army. While he moved into Pennsylvania, Stonewall Jackson would capture the Union garrison at Harpers Ferry, then hook up with Major General James Longstreet's three divisions and join Lee near Harrisburg.

The plan might have worked, considering Union commander George McClellan's hesitancy to strike in the face of what he thought were superior numbers. But, through an incredible quirk of fate, McClellan came into possession of a copy of Lee's plans, which had been found wrapped around some cigars near an abandoned Confederate camp. However, McClellan considered that the orders might be a trap and failed to act on them for nearly 16 hours.

Lee, meanwhile, was informed that his plans were now in the hands of the enemy and worked hard to protect his three vulnerable flanks. But fighting broke out in a number of locations along the planned route, and the Confederates experienced heavy casualties. On September 15, Lee was planning a retreat back into Virginia when he learned that Jackson had taken Harpers Ferry and collected some much needed supplies. Lee quickly changed his mind and ordered all of his divisions to meet in Sharpesburg. McClellan, again overly cautious, allowed Lee's forces to converge. On September 17, he finally attacked; 75,000 Union troops faced just 40,000 Confederates.

Lee's left flank, led by Stonewall Jackson, was almost annihilated during the Union onslaught, led by Joseph Hooker, Joseph

Mansfield, and Edwin Sumner. The rebel soldiers took a horrible pounding until they were reinforced by two fresh Confederate divisions, who fought back with amazing vigor. Within just 20 minutes, an astounding 2,200 Union soldiers were killed or wounded in an area known as the West Woods, and Sumner was forced to retreat.

Later in the day, the Union army focused on decimating the Confederate center, led by Major General Daniel Hill. Sumner's remaining divisions attacked Hill's line for three brutal hours, resulting in such carnage that the narrow street on which it occurred became known as Bloody Lane. The assault broke the Confederate center, and Union forces under the command of General Ambrose Burnside crossed Antietam Creek to attack Lee's right flank. Lee's army probably would have been destroyed during the ensuing battle if it hadn't been reinforced by a division led by A. P. Hill, which arrived after a grueling 30-mile march from Harpers Ferry. Upon arrival, Hill's men launched a blistering counterattack that helped keep the Union forces at bay.

Had McClellan continued his assault, it's very likely that he could have completely devastated Lee's army. But instead of making one final push, he let his troops rest, as did Lee. Lee retreated back to Virginia on the evening of September 18, having lost nearly a quarter of his army at Antietam.

THE BATTLE OF CHANCELLORSVILLE
MAY 1–4, 1863

COMMANDERS JOSEPH HOOKER (UNION) AND ROBERT E. LEE (CONFEDERACY)

Many historians consider the Battle of Chancellorsville to be one of Lee's greatest victories. Greatly outnumbered, he outplanned and outmaneuvered his opponent so skillfully that Hooker never knew what hit him. This victory helped the South make some strategic gains in the eastern theater and put the Union on the defensive.

Joseph Hooker replaced Ambrose E. Burnside as commander of the Army of the Potomac on Lincoln's orders, following the Union's winter defeat in Fredericksburg and the embarrassing "Mud March" that resulted. Lincoln was looking for a skilled commander who would aggressively pursue Lee's army, and Hooker, who was arrogant and vain but well liked by his men, had fought well in the Peninsula campaign and at the Battle of Antietam and showed tremendous promise. Hooker, shortly before a planned offensive against the Confederate general near Fredericksburg, wrote a letter to the present in which he stated, "May God have mercy on General Lee, for I will have none."

Hooker decided to attack Lee on two fronts. He left a third of his 115,000 troops near Fredericksburg to keep Lee's army busy and took the remainder of his men up and across the Rappahannock and Rapidan to engage Lee's relatively unprotected left flank and rear.

Hooker arrived in Chancellorsville, at a house in the middle of a clearing about 10 miles west of Fredericksburg, on April 27 and set up camp. He was confident that he could destroy Lee's army with overwhelming numbers but failed to take into consideration Lee's considerable skills as a strategist. With just 60,000 troops at his disposal, Lee used the same tactic that brought victory at the Second Battle of Bull Run: He divided his troops, leaving 10,000 men at Fredericksburg and taking the rest to defend his vulnerable flank.

The armies first clashed on May 1. Hooker's men were climbing through dense woods toward the Confederate line when they were met with a surprise attack by Stonewall Jackson. Startled, Hooker lost his nerve and, against the advice of his corps commanders, immediately ordered a withdrawal into the woods, which had been nicknamed the Wilderness. Major General Jeb Stuart notified Lee that Hooker's right flank was vulnerable, so Lee took a huge risk and divided his forces yet again, ordering Jackson to attack with 26,000 men.

Hooker had been advised of Jackson's movements by scouts, but he didn't think Jackson posed much of a threat and failed to act. As the sun was about to set on the evening of May 2, Jackson and his men attacked troops under General Oliver O. Howard. The soldiers were caught completely unaware and forced into a two-mile withdrawal before Union artillery stopped Jackson just short of the Chancellorsville house.

It was a grand victory for Lee's outnumbered army, but there was little celebrating because Stonewall Jackson had been shot in both arms by some of his own men as he returned to camp in the approaching darkness. Jackson's left arm was amputated in a desperate move to save him, but he died of pneumonia in Richmond a few days later. Jeb Stuart assumed command of the infantry and launched another attack against Hooker's army on the morning of May 3, pushing them all the way back to the Rappahannock and Rapidan.

As Stuart attacked Hooker, Lee found that his rear was being threatened by Union troops led by Major General John Sedgwick. On May 4, a portion of Lee's army in Fredericksburg attacked Sedgwick's forces at Salem Church, engaging in a brutal day-long battle that ultimately pushed Sedgwick across the Rappahannock. Hooker joined Sedgwick in his retreat the following day, giving the Confederate army an amazing win against overwhelming odds—and the Union a humiliating defeat that never should have occurred, considering it held the advantage in sheer manpower. The Union army suffered more than 17,000 casualties in the relatively brief engagement; the Confederacy lost about 13,000. Joseph Hooker was removed from command of the Army of the Potomac a month later.

CIVIL WAR FACTOID

Astoundingly, only one civilian (a young woman who was struck by a stray bullet) was killed during the three-day battle at Gettysburg.

THE BATTLE OF GETTYSBURG
JULY 1–3, 1863

COMMANDERS GEORGE MEAD (UNION) AND ROBERT E. LEE (CONFEDERACY)

The three-day Battle of Gettysburg is perhaps the best remembered clash of the entire Civil War. It was a literal bloodbath, with both sides taking heavy casualties (a combined total of more than 50,000 men dead, wounded, missing, or captured), and it put a quick end to the second (and final) Confederate invasion of the North.

Lee's decision to take the war into the North was based on a number of factors. First, he wanted to bring some relief to Virginia, which had seen more than its share of battle and was running low

on supplies. Second, it was hoped that a solid victory in Union territory would bring the Confederacy some much needed international recognition by proving it was a force to be reckoned with.

Lee got things going by advancing his 70,000 troops northeastward from Fredericksburg on June 3. Four days later, Confederate and Union cavalry engaged in a heated battle at Brandy Station, near Culpepper, Virginia. The Confederates won, but they were greatly surprised by the skill and daring of the Union horsemen.

The Northern army spent the next two weeks regrouping as commanders waited for Lincoln to name a replacement for the disgraced Joseph Hooker. During this time, the Army of the Potomac, 100,000 strong, monitored the movements of Confederate troops and placed a heavy guard around Washington, D.C., which was at risk of Southern attack.

Lee realized that once again he faced superior numbers, so he had to plan his strategy carefully. He turned to cavalry commander Major General Jeb Stuart to determine the location, size, and extent of the Union army, but this time Stuart didn't come through. Instead of making a quick reconnaissance trip, he led his men on a ride around McClellan's army and found himself pushed so far east that he was unable to rejoin Lee for nearly 10 days.

As a result of Stuart's inaccessibility, Lee had no way of determining the size of the army he was going to fight. More importantly, he did not know until June 28 that Union forces led by Major General George Meade, who had replaced Hooker, had crossed the Potomac heading northwest. The appointment of Meade had re-energized the flagging Union troops, which now marched toward Harrisburg, Pennsylvania, with renewed vigor.

Lee no longer held the element of surprise, so he ordered his troops to stop their advance and converge west of Gettysburg until Stuart returned with more information. On July 1, Confederate soldiers entered Gettysburg looking for shoes and were spotted by Union cavalry commander Brigadier General John Buford, whose troops were camped on a hill southwest of town. Buford sent his men to engage the Confederates, led by Major General Henry Heth, while he called for reinforcements. The Confederate soldiers raced back to camp with news of the Union troop movements, and a Confederate attack on the Union cavalry line was ordered. So started the Battle of Gettysburg.

The Union army had been reinforced with fresh troops from the 1st Corps, led by Major General John Reynolds, when Heth's division attacked at McPherson's Ridge. Reynolds was killed in the ensuing battle, which laid waste to the Iron Brigade of the West, one of Reynolds's best fighting units. The Confederates took the ridge and pushed the Union troops back to Seminary Ridge. As all of this was going on, troops from both sides were being drawn to the battle, with Union troops converging from the south and east and Confederate troops from the north and west.

The Confederate army greatly outnumbered the Union forces during the first day of fighting and used their advantage to drive Union troops led by Major General Winfield Scott Hancock through the town of Gettysburg to Cemetery Ridge, which lay to the south. The Confederates might have enjoyed a tremendous victory had they engaged in one last assault on the hills, but General Richard Ewell decided not to attempt another attack because nightfall was approaching.

Darkness allowed the armies on both sides to regroup. When morning broke, the Union army had formed its men into a giant fishhook, with the shank located at Cemetery Ridge, the bent part curving around the ridge and the barb on Cemetery Hill and Culp's Hill. The Confederate commanders were unsure how to attack the Union position. Lieutenant General James Longstreet wanted to engage in a flanking movement that he hoped would force the Union army to attack, but Lee argued for a more offensive approach. His goal was to capture some of the high hills so that heavy artillery could be mounted on them.

The battles on that second day were determined more by accident than by strategy. Union Major General Daniel Sickles decided on his own to move his corps a mile forward from the main line to occupy a peach orchard and wheat field, weakening the Union left just as the Confederates were planning to attack. Luckily, Longstreet delayed his assault until around 4 P.M., allowing Meade time to reinforce Sickles's position.

In the late afternoon and evening hours, bloody battles were waged in the peach orchard, in the wheatfield, and in a clump of boulders that came to be known as Devil's Den. Meade maneuvered to protect the hills and secure the Union position. Confederate troops made several assaults on Cemetery Hill and Culp's Hill, but they were overwhelmed by blistering Union fire. The sun finally set with neither army making much headway. Again, both sides rested and regrouped.

The third day of fighting began early in the morning on the north end of the line, with Union General Henry Slocum's troops retaking their position near Culp's Hill. Both armies prepared for another major assault. Longstreet again suggested a flanking maneuver that would force the Union to take the offensive, but Lee nixed the idea. In his mind, the Confederate forces had only two options: They must retreat or try one last big attack.

Lee finally ordered an attack on the center of the Union line at Culp's Hill, to be led by 15,000 fresh soldiers under the command of Major General George Pickett and others. It was then that Jeb Stuart finally returned, and Lee ordered him to attack the Union rear with his cavalry.

The last battle of the vicious, bloody engagement started at 1 P.M. with a deafening artillery duel. The cannons roared until both sides were nearly out of ammunition, and at 3:30 P.M., Pickett and his men started a charge against Union forces at Cemetery Ridge. The charge was pure suicide; Pickett's men marched across an open field, only to be slaughtered by Union artillery that had been held in reserve. A handful of men made the crossing successfully and managed to capture a short stretch of the Union line, but they were unable to hold it.

Jeb Stuart's assault on the Union rear flank, which lasted nearly three hours, was equally unsuccessful. Despite his best efforts, Stuart was unable to make much headway, and he, too, suffered heavy casualties. By the end of the day, Lee knew he had been defeated and decided to pull his army back into Virginia. Unable to carry his wounded, Lee left nearly 7,000 injured soldiers in Union care. Had Union forces pursued him in his retreat the following day, they might have been able to completely disable the Confederate war machine and bring the conflict to a quick close. However, Meade and his men were exhausted, and he opted to let Lee go. As a result, the war would endure for another two years. A month after his defeat at Gettysburg, Lee offered his resignation to Jefferson Davis. Davis refused to accept it.

THE BATTLE OF CHICKAMAUGA
⟹ SEPTEMBER 19–20, 1863 ⟸

COMMANDERS WILLIAM ROSECRANS (UNION) AND BRAXTON BRAGG (CONFEDERACY)

The Battle of Chickamauga, named after a creek in northwest Georgia, proved to be the region's bloodiest engagement. It was an important Confederate victory that nearly destroyed the Union's war effort in the western theater.

Over the previous month, the Army of the Cumberland, under the command of Major General William Rosecrans, had engaged in a successful campaign that concluded with the occupation of Chattanooga, Tennessee, an important gateway to the southeastern region of the Confederacy. Rosecrans was eager to press his foe, Confederate General Braxton Bragg, who commanded the Army of Tennessee, but he fell victim to misinformation that the Confederate troops were retreating and quickly sent his army in pursuit. In truth, Bragg was gathering reinforcements in northern Georgia with the goal of retaking Chattanooga. When James Longstreet arrived, Bragg's forces outnumbered Rosecrans's by nearly 10,000 men.

Worse for Rosecrans, he had to divide his army into three columns during its advance through the treacherous terrain around

the city. They would have made easy pickings for Bragg's army, but delays and poor planning kept Bragg's subordinates from launching an effective attack, and several small skirmishes alerted Rosecrans to Bragg's trap.

> **CIVIL WAR FACTOID**
>
> Among those killed during the Battle of Chickamauga were a teenaged girl who had disguised herself as a soldier so that she could fight with the Union forces, and Confederate Brigadier General Ben Hardin Helm, Mary Lincoln's brother-in-law and a good friend of President Lincoln.

On September 13, Rosecrans began regrouping his troops on the west bank of Chickamauga Creek, just across the Georgia border. Patrols from both sides engaged in a number of small skirmishes near the creek on September 18, and the Battle of Chickamauga began with a vengeance the next day.

Bragg's strategy was to attack Rosecrans's left flank and smash the Union army by forcing it into a valley from which it could not retreat back to Chattanooga. However, assaults by Confederate troops were met with a withering response from soldiers commanded by George Henry Thomas. The day's fighting in the area's thick woods degenerated into vicious hand-to-hand combat that brought the Confederates only very small gains and heavy casualties on both sides.

Confederate Lieutenant General Leonidas Polk was instructed to perform a sideways attack against Thomas early on September 20, but Polk delayed the assault. Bragg then ordered Longstreet to conduct an all-out frontal attack, which proved very successful. Rosecrans, unable to see a large section of his troops, erroneously believed there was a break in his lines and sent an entire division to fill it, leaving a gap on the Union right. Longstreet's forces barreled through the weakened Union line, overrunning Rosecrans's headquarters and forcing more than half of his army into a retreat back to Chattanooga.

Rosecrans himself was swept up in the retreat, leaving George Henry Thomas to command what was left of the Union force. Thomas bravely refused to retreat and rallied his troops to form a defensible line on the ridge of Snodgrass Hill. For the remainder of the day, Longstreet and Polk sent wave after wave against the Union forces, but they were unable to dislodge them. As a result of his stalwart defense, Thomas received the nickname "The Rock of Chickamauga."

Thomas finally realized the futility of his position and ordered his men to withdraw back to Chattanooga as night fell. The Confederates were handed a victory, but Thomas's bravery in the face of overwhelming odds helped keep the Union army from being completely destroyed as it retreated. Nonetheless, the casualties on both sides were enormous. More than 16,000 Union sol-

---

CIVIL WAR FACTOID

The artillery duel between Union and Confederate forces on the third day of fighting at Gettysburg was so loud it could be heard as far away as Pittsburgh.

diers were killed, wounded, missing, or captured, and more than 18,500 Confederate soldiers—nearly 30 percent of the troops involved in the battle—met similar fates. The Confederate dead or wounded included ten of Bragg's generals, a situation that so depressed him that he failed to attack the Union forces in retreat toward Chattanooga. Bragg's inaction, which allowed the Union forces to regroup and fortify in Chattanooga, greatly angered his subordinates; Longstreet and Polk demanded that he be dismissed, and Nathan Bedford Forrest refused to serve under him any longer.

But despite Bragg's failure to strike a decisive blow against the Union army, the Confederate victory at Chickamauga did wonders to revive the flagging spirits of the South, which had suffered greatly as a result of defeats at Gettysburg and Vicksburg.

The Campaign and Battle of Chattanooga
⇒ October–November 1863 ⇐

Commanders Ulysses S. Grant (Union) and Braxton Bragg (Confederacy)

The Union forces were able to hold off Confederate assaults on their fortification in Chattanooga, so Confederate General Braxton Bragg ordered a siege. Supply lines to the city were severed in early October, and within weeks, the entrenched Union soldiers found themselves perilously low on food and other supplies.

To the rescue was Major General Ulysses S. Grant, recently appointed commander of the Military Division of the Mississippi. Grant replaced William Rosecrans with Major General George Thomas as commander of the Army of the Cumberland, then, with his chief engineer, William F. Smith, he developed a daring plan to break the Confederate siege. The first part of his

strategy was to open a supply line by attacking Confederate forces on the east bank of the Tennessee River, then establishing a bridgehead at Brown's Ferry. Supplies could then be shipped by boat to

Brown's Ferry and transported across Moccasin Point to the waiting troops in Chattanooga.

Grant was able to force the Confederates off Raccoon Mountain and put his so-called "cracker line operation" into effect on October 26. Confederate forces assaulted the new line at Wauhatchie on October 28 and 29, but the first supply ship still arrived safely on November 1. As he waited for reinforcements to arrive from Memphis and Vicksburg, Grant planned the next step of his offensive: He must force the Confederates off their dangerous position on Missionary Ridge, along the northeastern and southeastern sides of Chattanooga, and from Lookout Mountain on the southwestern side.

At the same time that Grant was forming his strategy, the Confederate army underwent some dramatic changes. Lieutenant General Leonidas Polk, Daniel H. Hill, and Thomas C. Hindman, disgusted with Bragg's slowness at Chattanooga, complained to the War Department and were granted transfers. Bragg also picked this time to send several divisions and 35 cannon under the command of Lieutenant General James Longstreet eastward to help troops in West Virginia in their campaign against Union General Ambrose Burnside. This move severely weakened his lines on Missionary Ridge just as the Union army was getting ready for a major assault.

Grant's plan went into action on November 23 with the arrival of fresh troops under the command of William T. Sherman. Grant's first goal was Orchard Knob, which was the forward position in the center of the Confederate line on Missionary Ridge. The battle began with an ingenious ruse on Grant's part: He dressed his divisions as if for a military parade and had them march below the hill. When curious Confederate soldiers on the knob moved down for a closer look, the Union soldiers attacked and, following a heated battle, took control of the hill.

Grant made Orchard Hill his headquarters for the coming fight and ordered Sherman's divisions to cross the Tennessee River and attack the Confederate right on the north end of Missionary Ridge. He also ordered Hooker to take Lookout Mountain on the Confederate left. Early on the morning of November 24, Hooker engaged the enemy in a battle made difficult by rain and fog; hours later, he emerged the victor. Sherman, delayed by the rain, made slower progress and didn't arrive on Bragg's right until that afternoon.

As Sherman approached, Bragg ordered half of his troops to the bottom of the hill with instructions to fire a volley when the Union army was within 200 yards and then withdraw up the slopes. But Bragg wasn't known for his outstanding communication skills, and he failed to inform all of his men of the plan.

The Battle of Missionary Ridge began on the morning of November 25. Sherman's forces and artillery struck repeatedly at the Confederate line along the north end, but they were repelled. To draw the Confederates away from Sherman's front, Grant ordered Thomas to attack the Confederate forces at the base of the ridge. The wiser Confederate soldiers realized what was happening and withdrew immediately, but many stayed and fought, only to be overrun by Union troops. Having taken the Confederate line, the Union soldiers, acting without orders, decided to pay back the Confederates for the Union defeat at Chickamauga by racing up the mountain slope in an unexpected attack that successfully drove the rebels into a full retreat. Chattanooga was saved.

The defeat at Chattanooga was an important nail in the coffin of the Confederate cause. It cost the South important communication and supply lines and opened the door for Sherman's Atlanta campaign.

> **CIVIL WAR FACTOID**
>
> During the Battle of the Wilderness, fighting was halted on several occasions as both sides tried to rescue wounded comrades from the uncontrolled brushfires that threatened to burn them alive.

THE BATTLE OF THE WILDERNESS
MAY 5–7, 1864

COMMANDERS ULYSSES S. GRANT (UNION) AND ROBERT E. LEE (CONFEDERACY)

The Battle of the Wilderness in Virginia's Rapidan basin was the first battle between Ulysses S. Grant and Robert E. Lee and was the beginning of a 40-day campaign that would include some of the bloodiest fighting of the entire war. Grant, who had been appointed general-in-chief of the Union army, had one thing on his mind: a final battle between Meade's Army of the Potomac and Lee's Army

of Northern Virginia that, he hoped, would be instrumental in bringing the Confederacy to its knees.

Union troops started crossing the Rapidan River and heading south to confront Confederate forces near the site of the Battle of Chancellorsville. In order to reach their destination, the Union army had to pass through the dense forest known as the Wilderness, where Lee had won a decided victory almost exactly a year earlier. As Grant's troops trudged through the forest and brush, they came across countless reminders of that previous battle, including bleached bones, firearms, and other debris. It was Grant's hope that his men could clear the Wilderness before engaging Lee.

However, Lee had other plans. He realized the value of the Wilderness and planned to use it to his advantage, since his army was outmanned 115,000 to 60,000. The battle started on May 5 when Union and Confederate troops accidentally found each other while the Union soldiers were still crossing the forest. Both sides quickly called for reinforcements, and around 1 P.M., the Union army prepared a major assault. However, the forest was so thick that soldiers on both sides became entangled and separated from regiments, and entire units found themselves completely lost. Visibility was also severely hampered by the thick underbrush and smoke from brushfires ignited by bursting shells. Chaos reigned as frightened soldiers soon started shooting at anything that moved in the thickets, often hitting their own men.

As Lee had hoped, the familiar terrain gave the Confederate soldiers a strong advantage over their Union counterparts. However, the Union forces had far more men and were able to absorb greater casualties while continuing to fight. Grant ordered assault after assault against the Confederate lines, all of which were repelled with heavy casualties on both sides. But by the end of the first day of fighting, Grant had succeeded in weakening Lee's right flank, which he hoped to destroy with one more major attack.

At dawn the following day, Union forces began hammering the Confederate center, pushing their way forward until they were almost on top of Lee's field headquarters. But by this time, Lee had received much needed reinforcements from James Longstreet and others, and a counterattack was mounted, to be led by John Gregg,

who had assumed command of Hood's Texas Brigade. Lee himself wanted to lead the charge, but the Texas troops refused to budge until Lee was safely behind the lines.

Longstreet's troops, fresh and rested, managed to push back the Union forces through much of the morning, and a massive attack on the Union's left flank was put in motion. However, the momentum of the moment was broken when Longstreet was accidentally wounded by one of his own men. By the time Lee was able to coordinate a new assault later that afternoon, the Union forces had regrouped and were able to successfully defend themselves.

At the same time, a late attack on the Union's right, led by Confederate commander John Gordon, was able to drive the Union army back one mile, though the federal soldiers quickly reclaimed all the land they had lost and were almost back in position by nightfall. However, the temporary setback demoralized Grant's headquarters.

Neither Grant nor Lee were particularly happy with the way the battle had gone. The Union experienced more than twice the casualties as the Confederacy (17,500 to 7,750), but Lee hadn't gained much ground.

The two armies went at it again the following morning with a number of small skirmishes. Lee had expected Grant to retreat, considering the fact that he had assumed such heavy losses and gained little in the bargain, but Grant was resolute. Rather than pull back, he ordered an advance, his plan now being for George Meade's army to move south past Lee's right and position itself between Lee's army and the Confederate capital of Richmond. The Battle of the Wilderness ended in a tactical draw, only to resume a day later in the small crossroads town of Spotsylvania Court House.

CIVIL WAR FACTOID

The first federal paper money, printed under the Legal Tender Act of 1862, carried the image of Secretary of the Treasury Salmon P. Chase, who aspired to be president and saw the greenbacks as a multitude of tiny campaign posters. Sadly for Chase, his dream of living in the White House never materialized.

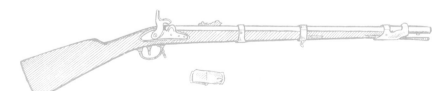

THE BATTLE OF SPOTSYLVANIA
⟶ MAY 8–19, 1864 ⟵

COMMANDERS ULYSSES S. GRANT (UNION) AND
ROBERT E. LEE (CONFEDERACY)

The Battle of Spotsylvania, a small crossroads town in Virginia, came almost immediately after the Battle of the Wilderness and once again pitched Grant and Lee in a vicious, bloody brawl that would result in heavy casualties on both sides. Many of Grant's sub-ordinates believed that Grant was intentionally throwing his soldiers in the line of fire, risking heavy losses simply to wear down the outnumbered Confederate forces, but such

was not the case. Grant loathed the heavy casualties these battles incurred, but he was a soldier with a plan: He had to lure Lee's army out of the forests and into the open, where they could be wiped out by the Union's superior numbers and firepower.

Following the Battle of the Wilderness, which concluded with a heavy loss of life and not much else for either side, Grant ordered his men to advance further south in the hope of blocking Lee's path back to Richmond. Lee anticipated this move and raced south too, arriving at Spotsylvania ahead of Grant and with sufficient time to build protective fieldworks. This forced Grant to take the offensive, and he promised to "fight it out on this line if it takes all summer."

Grant first tried an unsuccessful assault on Lee's left flank, then ordered an attack on an area known as the "Mule Shoe," located near the center of the Confederate line. Supported by a heavy artillery barrage, a Union division commanded by Colonel Emory Upton made a running charge late in the day on May 10, breaking through the enemy defense and capturing an astounding number of Confederate prisoners before being driven back.

Grant was pleased with the results of this attack and ordered a larger assault on the center of the Confederate line two days later. Hoping to catch the Confederate forces by surprise, 15,000 men led by Winfield Scott Hancock stormed the enemy line at 4:30 A.M. on May 12, capturing almost an entire infantry division and splitting

Lee's army down the middle. The Confederates were no match for Hancock's corps and were pushed back almost half a mile as the Union forces rested and regrouped in trenches formerly occupied by gray-clad rebels.

Lee assembled a countercharge and planned to lead it himself, but cooler minds prevailed upon him to remain safely behind the line. (Had Lee led the charge as he wanted to, history suggests he probably would have been killed in battle.) The two armies met in a battle that lasted more than 20 hours and involved some of the bloodiest hand-to-hand combat seen in modern warfare. Ground, soaked by rain and blood, was won and lost by the foot, with enormous casualties on both sides. As the hours passed, the soggy battlefield literally became covered with the bodies of the dead and wounded. The gunfire was so intense during portions of the battle that trees two feet thick were shorn in half by flying bullets.

Both sides fought with all they had, refusing to give an inch until after midnight, when Lee finally ordered his bone-weary troops to fall back to a new line of freshly dug protective earthworks. Grant tried to flank Lee's army over the next few days, but he met with little success. On May 18, he attempted another frontal assault that did little but kill still more Union soldiers. The following day, May 19, Lee took the offensive and mounted a daring assault on Grant's right. Grant's troops managed to hold their ground, and Grant finally accepted the fact that he would not be able to bring Lee into the open at that time. The next day, he ordered the Army of the Potomac to move south to Hanover Junction, Virginia, forcing Lee's Army of Northern Virginia to again race ahead in the hope of establishing a line of defense at the next point of engagement. Neither army had much time to rest before the fighting began anew.

The Battle of Spotsylvania took a huge toll on both sides. More than 17,500 Union soldiers were killed, wounded, missing, or captured, and nearly 10,000 Confederate soldiers were also taken out of action. But while the Confederate numbers may have been smaller, they had a more dramatic impact because the South's forces were diminishing rapidly, the victims of battle attrition.

CIVIL WAR FACTOID

According to a 1993 congressional commission report, 43 percent of the Civil War's major battlegrounds are privately owned, and only 4 percent are largely protected by local, state, or federal government.

THE CAMPAIGN AND SIEGE OF ATLANTA
⤳ MAY 1—SEPTEMBER 2, 1864 ⤲

COMMANDERS WILLIAM T. SHERMAN (UNION) AND
JOHN B. HOOD (CONFEDERACY)

The fall of Atlanta after a four-month campaign and siege was a devastating blow to the South and signaled the end of the war in the western theater. Once Atlanta was under Union control, Sherman set out on his infamous march to the sea and then into the Carolinas, destroying anything he felt could be used to sustain the Confederate war effort. This strategy, combined with Grant's campaign against Lee's Army of Northern Virginia, would ultimately lead to a Confederate surrender. But getting to that point wasn't easy.

Atlanta was vital to Confederate manufacturing and communications, and Sherman knew that taking the city would be a huge step toward ending the conflict. His policy was all-out war, which meant anything that could be used against the North would have to be eliminated. Facing Sherman's 100,000 man army was Confederate General Joseph Johnston, who commanded a considerably smaller army of 62,000 men. Johnston knew he wouldn't stand a chance if he faced Sherman directly, so he tried a different strategy: He planned to keep Sherman away from Atlanta as long as possible, at least until the November elections. If Lincoln were defeated, he reasoned, a new president, tired of the war, might decide to bring hostilities to an end and broker a lasting peace. In the beginning of May, Johnston's army was firmly entrenched along Rocky Face Ridge, a rock wall surrounding a canyon leading into Chattanooga. The lower six miles of the ridge formed the east wall of the Snake Creek Gap, the site of an earlier battle between forces led by Union Major General James B. McPherson and Johnston's army. McPherson couldn't establish a strong offense and was finally forced to fall back, allowing the Confederates to retreat farther south. Sherman pursued Johnston's army, and another heavy battle occurred at Resaca on May 14–15. Several weeks of additional fighting at a variety of locations forced Johnston to pull back to Kennesaw Mountain, where he was finally able to establish strong defensive positions along the mountain's steep slopes and repel a frontal assault by Sherman on June 27. More than 2,000 Union

Sherman's March to the Sea

The fall of Atlanta was just the beginning of Sherman's grand scheme to bring about a Union victory by splitting the Confederacy down the middle. Once the city was under his control, he ordered all civilians evacuated and anything that could be used by the enemy destroyed. His goal was to crush not only the Confederate army but also the spirit of its supporters; in short, victory at any cost.

Sherman had two options: He could confront John Bell Hood's army to the west or continue eastward to Savannah and the Atlantic coast. He chose the latter, using his infamous march to continue the destruction of anything that could be used against Union forces, including crops that might feed Confederate soldiers, who were already on the verge of starvation.

Sherman's March to the Sea began on November 15. Atlanta was torched as he moved his men out, and smoke filled the skies as the city was reduced to rubble. Sherman's 62,000-man army marched in two columns that presented a front 25 to 60 miles wide. Like army ants, they swarmed over the countryside, destroying railroads, bridges, telegraph lines, manufacturing plants, plantations, and anything else that Sherman deemed of value to the Southern war effort.

The trek cut Sherman's army off from Union supply lines, and his troops foraged off the land, simply taking whatever food and livestock they found. While Lee's army starved for lack of provisions, Sherman's army had more food than it could possibly consume and extra supplies were either abandoned or given to the growing contingency of runaway slaves who eagerly followed the army that had liberated them.

Sherman gave orders not to steal from private citizens, but these orders was not strictly enforced, and many violations occurred as Union soldiers took it upon themselves to punish Southern citizenry. Families and entire towns fled the approaching army, rightfully fearful of retribution; they often returned to find everything they owned gone and their homes and farms destroyed.

Sherman's army was so large that it faced little opposition from Confederate forces, aside from a small number of state troopers, militiamen, and cavalry. There were occasional skirmishes, but Sherman's army quickly overran any opposing forces in its path. Sherman reached the Atlantic coast, after a march of 300 miles, on December 10, having inflicted an estimated $100 million worth of damage along the way.

The taking of Savannah was Sherman's next objective, but as he prepared a major assault, Confederate General William S. Hardee withdrew his greatly outnumbered 10,000-man army rather than face certain annihilation. Sherman marched into Savannah on December 22 and wired Lincoln two days later to offer the city as a Christmas present. Lincoln was elated by Sherman's tremendous success.

From Savannah, Sherman turned his attention to the Carolinas, continuing his slash-and-burn policy. South Carolina took the brunt of the damage from Sherman's forces, who greatly wanted to punish the first state to secede. In the minds of many, the entire war was South Carolina's fault.

soldiers were killed by withering Confederate cannon and rifle fire during that engagement. Confederate losses numbered just 500.

Sherman refused to give up and continued to push Johnston's smaller army, forcing it back bit by bit until Johnston was just seven miles from Atlanta. He later withdrew south of the Chattahoochie River, the last natural barrier between Sherman's army and Atlanta. Confederate President Jefferson Davis was disappointed with Johnston's tactics and, looking for someone more aggressive and willing to fight, replaced Johnston with Major General John B. Hood.

Hood leapt into the fray with everything he had, launching a major offensive on July 20 against Sherman's army, which had been split at Peachtree Creek. Hood's men fought bravely, but they were simply outnumbered. More than 4,800 Confederate soldiers were killed or wounded in the ill-fated assault, and Hood was forced to retreat to Atlanta.

Sherman mistakenly believed that Hood had abandoned Atlanta, and he sent McPherson to the south and east of the city to attack Hood in retreat. On July 22, William Hardee's infantry division, hoping to catch Sherman by surprise, attacked Sherman's forces in what became the Battle of Atlanta. But once again the Confederate forces were outmanned and outgunned, losing more than 8,500 men. Union losses during the battle were lighter, but Sherman lost a valued corps commander with the death of James McPherson.

Sherman replaced McPherson with Major General Oliver Howard and sent him around the western side of Atlanta with orders to sever Hood's communication lines. Hood fought back on July 28 with a heated battle at Ezra Church. He successfully protected the railroad there, which was an essential supply line, but he lost another 2,500 men in the process. At this point, the Confederate army numbered fewer than 45,000 men. Facing overwhelming numbers, they fell back behind Atlanta's defensive lines and waited for Sherman to attack.

However, rather than risking a frontal assault, which would have resulted in huge casualties, Sherman laid siege on Atlanta, bombarding the city with heavy artillery for more than a month and doing all he could to destroy its supply lines. But the South refused to give in that easily; Confederate cavalry commander Joseph

Wheeler skillfully kept many supply lines in operation until the end of August.

The standoff came to a head on August 28, when Sherman attacked the Montgomery & Atlanta Railroad south of Atlanta. Hood, realizing the importance of keeping the line open, attacked the Union flank at nearby Jonesborough but ultimately lost after a valiant battle. With no remaining line of defense, Confederate forces evacuated Atlanta on September 2, and Sherman's troops marched in the following day.

The once proud city of Atlanta had been all but destroyed during the siege and final evacuation. Buildings once used for manufacturing had been demolished by Union artillery or burned to the ground by fleeing Confederate troops, who also ransacked stores for all the supplies they could carry. If Atlanta had to fall, the Confederates were not going to let the invaders enjoy any of the fruits of their labor. For all intents and purposes, Atlanta became a ghost town that was no good to anyone.

THE BATTLE OF NASHVILLE
➤ DECEMBER 15–16, 1864 ➤

COMMANDERS GEORGE H. THOMAS (UNION) AND JOHN BELL HOOD (CONFEDERACY)

The Battle of Nashville proved to be the undoing of Confederate General John B. Hood and his Army of Tennessee. It brought to a close the major fighting in the war's western theater.

Hood had experienced a devastating defeat at Franklin, about 75 miles south of Nashville, on November 30, but he refused to retreat from Tennessee. He clung to the desperate but doomed hope that he could retake the state and collect enough reinforcements to confront Union forces in Virginia and the Ohio Valley.

Despite his loss at Franklin, Hood marched his ragtag troops (a quarter of whom didn't even have a pair of shoes to call their own) on to Nashville, where Union forces, under the command of George Thomas, awaited. The ensuing battle was devastating to the Confederates. Thomas's army,

CIVIL WAR
FACTOID

During the siege of Petersburg, the Confederate army was so desperate for able bodies to man its defenses that it ultimately resorted to using old men, young boys, and two unwilling members of Jefferson Davis's cabinet.

combined with that of John Schofield, fresh from Franklin, was nearly twice the size of Hood's. Worse, federal forces had occupied Nashville since early 1862 and had fortified the city to the point where it was nearly impenetrable.

Hood and his army arrived in the hills south of Nashville on December 2 and found themselves in a serious quandary. They lacked the manpower and weapons to attack or lay siege, and they couldn't go around the city without exposing their rear flank. So Hood did the only thing he could do: He formed a defensive line and waited for Thomas to attack, hoping and praying that reinforcements would arrive before the inevitable battle started.

But Thomas wasn't in a rush. He knew Hood's position was desperate, realized he didn't pose much of a threat, and decided to take his time in planning his assault. This delay greatly angered Grant, who was still in Virginia. He ordered Thomas to attack, fearing Hood's Army of Tennessee might try to prolong the waning war by invading territory in the North. But Thomas, who was waiting out a sleet storm, ignored the command. Livid, Grant finally decided to go to Tennessee himself to relieve Thomas and get the matter over with once and for all.

However, Thomas attacked Hood's position before Grant arrived. On the morning of December 15, three Union corps smashed the Confederate left while supplemental infantry and cavalry drew the attention of Confederate troops at the other end of the defensive line. Hood's army fought as best it could against overwhelming numbers but finally was forced to fall back to a new position between two hills about two miles away.

In the darkness, Thomas couldn't tell if Hood's army had merely pulled back or had actually retreated, so he waited until the following afternoon to renew his attack. Hood's men managed to successfully push back a charge on Overton Hill, but by 4 P.M. Hood's entire left flank was surrounded by Union infantry and artillery. As a hard rain began to fall, the Union troops managed to smash through the Confederate line with frightening force, routing the panic-stricken rebels. Nearly an entire division, including its artillery, was captured in the fray, along with a large amount of other supplies. The remaining soldiers of the Army of Tennessee found themselves pursued by Union horsemen after the rout. They ran for nearly two weeks, covered in the rear by Nathan Bedford Forrest's cavalry, until they reached Mississippi.

The Battle of Nashville was a resounding success for the Union and was won with relatively light casualties—about 400 Union soldiers killed and approximately 1,500 Confederates killed or wounded. Hood resigned his command in January, and his remaining troops were reassigned to the eastern theater, where they were give the hopeless task of stopping Sherman's march through the Carolinas.

THE SIEGE OF PETERSBURG
JUNE 15, 1864–APRIL 3, 1865

COMMANDERS ULYSSES S. GRANT (UNION) AND ROBERT E. LEE (CONFEDERACY)

Grant and Lee spent the final months of the war in a deadly game of cat and mouse. Grant outmanned and outgunned his Confederate counterpart, but he never seemed able to get Lee's army into a position in which it could be destroyed once and for all. The fighting culminated in the Siege of Petersburg, a 10-month standoff that ended only after the Confederate army, worn down by almost nonstop fighting, could no longer defend itself against a frontal assault.

Lee had handed Grant a humiliating defeat at the Battle of Cold Harbor, Virginia, on June 3, 1864, and nine days later, much to Lee's bewilderment, Grant quietly began moving his Army of the Potomac. His destination was Petersburg, a town about 20 miles south of Richmond that was vital to the Confederate capital's railway supply lines and communications. Grant knew that if he could take Petersburg, Richmond would not be far behind.

A 2,100-foot pontoon bridge was quickly built by army engineers so that Union troops could cross the James River, and on June 15, an advance guard of more than 10,000 men commanded by William F. Smith stood ready to descend on Petersburg. The city was defended by a tiny Confederate army of just 2,500 men, led by Pierre G. T. Beauregard, but Smith didn't know that. Assuming the opposing army to be much larger, he proceeded with extraordinary

caution, coming close to taking the city. However, Beauregard's soldiers managed to hold off the Union assault just long enough for Lee and the Army of Northern Virginia to come to their rescue.

Grant's hopes for a quick victory in Petersburg (and a quick end to the war itself) were destroyed. Having no other recourse, he laid siege on the city, bombarding it daily with heavy artillery in the hope that he could drive Lee to surrender. Lee, meanwhile, grew increasingly frustrated. He knew that his army was greatly outnumbered and that his stand at Petersburg in defense of Richmond was a losing cause. He could hold out for a while, but not forever.

Grant tried to hasten the situation by extending his offensive line, a complicated maze of trenches, more than 40 miles around to the southwest of Petersburg. Lee was forced to follow suit, stretching his defenses to the very limit. Life in the trenches was no picnic for either side. It was tremendously boring duty, made hazardous by the constant threat of enemy snipers and heavy artillery. The trenches were broiling hot during the summer months and bitter cold during the winter. They were also filthy, and many a soldier succumbed to disease. All in all, though, the Union soldiers had it a bit easier than their Confederate counterparts. They received good rations and decent clothing, whereas the Confederate soldiers were lucky if they had a sweet potato and a blanket to share between them. As a result, desertion was rampant on the Confederate side, continually diminishing Lee's manpower. Yet despite these hardships, Lee's fortifications were incredibly solid and successfully repelled repeated Union assaults.

As the siege continued, Union forces slowly and methodically increased their stranglehold on the enemy by severing vital supply lines. In August, they successfully captured the Weldon Railroad, and in October, the Union army beat down a Confederate attempt to retake two important roads, though they were unable to capture the Southside Railroad. Grant also increased his numbers, and by the winter of 1865, his army had grown to 125,000; Lee's army had shrunk to just 50,000 men.

Lee realized that he had little chance of successfully holding off Grant's growing army and formed a plan that involved leaving the trenches around Petersburg and joining forces with Joseph E.

THE BATTLE OF THE CRATER

Petersburg was under siege, and Grant and his officers were eager for any way to open up the Confederate line to a Union assault. Members of a regiment of Pennsylvania coal miners suggested digging a tunnel beneath a Confederate stronghold 150 yards away, packing the mine with explosives, and blowing it up. The resulting confusion would allow a few federal divisions to move through the rebel center and into Petersburg.

Colonel Henry Pleasants liked the idea and proposed it to his corps commander, Ambrose Burnside. Burnside saw the plan as a way to mend his tattered reputation and gave the okay, even though his superiors, George Meade and Ulysses Grant, were skeptical.

The tunnel was started on June 25 and completed nearly a month later. Amazingly, the construction went completely unnoticed by Confederate troops, even though they were just a short distance away. The completed shaft was 511 feet long and extended directly under the Confederate line.

Burnside, seeing an easy victory, assigned his only fresh division, which consisted of black soldiers who had received special training and were anxious to prove themselves in combat, to lead the attack. However, for reasons only his own, Meade overruled Burnside and ordered a white division to lead the assault with the black

soldiers to follow. Around 5 A.M. on July 30, four tons of gunpowder that had been packed into the shaft exploded with a tremendous roar, creating a crater 170 feet long and 30 feet deep. The impact on the troops above was devastating. Several Confederate units were flung into the air, an entire regiment and an artillery battery were buried, and soldiers ran screaming from the area.

Unfortunately, the Union attack that was to immediately follow the blast was held up for nearly an hour. When the federals finally did advance, many of the soldiers inadvertently jumped into the crater rather than going around it, finding themselves hopelessly trapped. By this time, the Confederate forces had regrouped and soldiers had spread out around the crater's rim, picking off the helpless Union troops as if they were fish in a barrel. The black unit avoided the crater but were met with a strong rebel counterattack.

The losses during the ill-fated Battle of the Crater were staggering: 3,798 Union soldiers and approximately 1,500 Confederates dead. Grant called the incident "the saddest affair I have ever witnessed in the war." He dismissed James H. Ledlie, commander of the division that led the attack, for being drunk while his troops advanced and placed Burnside on extended leave.

Johnston's army in North Carolina. On March 25, John Gordon attacked the Union line east of the city in a desperate attempt to carve out a path by which Lee's army could escape. The rebel forces managed to capture Fort Stedman and nearly a half mile of Union trenches, but they were finally forced back by a Union counterattack.

Grant extended his offensive line several miles to the west in an attempt to break Lee's already weakened defenses. On April 1, infantry and cavalry from both sides met at Five Forks Junction, and after a heated battle, George Pickett's Confederate division was broken and routed. That opened the door for Grant's final attack. At 4:30 A.M. on April 2, Union forces started a massive assault along the entire Confederate defensive line. The horribly outnumbered Confederate troops couldn't hold off the onslaught, and Union troops broke through at several places. Petersburg had fallen.

Lee had no recourse but to retreat. He sent word to Jefferson Davis that Petersburg would soon be in Union hands and that Richmond should be evacuated immediately, then headed west along the Appomattox River in search of food and some way to join Johnston's army. Grant, unwilling to let Lee's troops escape and regroup yet again, followed close behind. The two commanders skirmished for several more days, but Lee quickly realized there was no way he could win against Grant's much larger army. On April 9, the two men met in the home of Wilmer McLean in Appomattox Court House to discuss terms of surrender.

APPOMATTOX COURT HOUSE

NAVAL WARFARE

Though most of the major battles in the Civil War occurred on land, naval warfare also played an integral role in the conflict's final outcome, especially in the western theater. The navies on both sides developed startling new innovations, such as the ironclad ship and the submarine, and changed forever the way sea battles would be fought.

The first naval involvement was a blockade of Southern ports ordered by President Lincoln just a few days after the attack on Fort Sumter. Lincoln believed a blockade would strangle the new republic's ability to do business with foreign powers and thus force it toward a quick peace. But while Lincoln's intentions may have been good, the U.S. Navy's ability to carry out the plan was not.

At the onset of the war, the U.S. Navy's fleet was in shambles. It had only 90 ships, and most of them were obsolete. In fact, when Lincoln first called for a blockade, only three ships were available for immediate duty—three ships to cover more than 3,500 miles of Southern coastline. In addition, the majority of Union navy personnel were spread across the world and unavailable for immediate service (and of those that were, nearly 10 percent resigned their commission to join the Confederacy). As a result, Confederate blockade runners, which were typically painted gray to avoid detection, came and went with impunity for the first couple of years of the war.

The Union blockade became more effective as the war progressed. In 1861, at the beginning of the war, only one in ten blockade runners was captured. By 1864, that number had risen to one in three. A number of different types of blockades were used. Some Southern ports were close-blockaded and attacked by a combination of army and navy forces. Out at sea, a cruising blockade was often established in international waters, along well-traveled sea lanes and in neutral ports. Not surprisingly, the Confederate government balked at cruising blockades, calling them a violation of international law. But the Union found them effective.

The U.S. Navy also patrolled inland waterways such as rivers and bays, often assisting army forces in penetrating Confederate

CIVIL WAR FACTOID

The first federal income tax law was enacted during the Civil War but died after the war was over. It wasn't until 1913 and the ratification of the Sixteenth Amendment that the income tax became part of the U.S. Constitution.

defenses, especially along the Mississippi River. More than once, naval forces played an important role in deciding the outcome of a battle.

The Union navy may have been less than adequate at the onset of the war, but even with its many faults, it was still superior to the Confederate navy. Stephen Mallory, Confederate secretary of the navy, described the Confederate navy in 1861 as consisting only of an unfurnished room, in which naval policy was formed, in Montgomery, Alabama. However, under Mallory, the Confederate navy quickly made up for its deficiencies and soon proved a viable threat to the Union war effort. It's estimated that one-sixth of Confederate naval officers came from the North at the beginning of the war, among them navigator Matthew Fontaine Maury and Franklin Buchanan, former commandant of the Washington Navy Yard.

The Confederate naval forces consisted primarily of two types: commerce destroyers (modeled after the pirate-like privateers that preyed on British merchant ships during the Revolutionary War and the War of 1812) and ironclad ships that were used almost exclusively to protect rivers and harbors.

The role of the U.S. Navy in the Civil War cannot be underestimated. Many people tend to forget that the navy was even involved in the conflict, but history shows that it played a decisive role in many battles and ultimately helped dislodge the Confederacy. Noted Abraham Lincoln during a tribute to Union servicemen late in the war: "It is hard to say that anything has been more bravely, and well done, than at Antietam, Murfreesboro, Gettysburg, and on many a field of lesser note. Nor must Uncle Sam's web-feet be forgotten. At all the watery margins they have been present. Not only on the deep sea, the broad bay, and the rapid river, but also up the narrow muddy bayou, and wherever the ground was a little damp. Thanks to all. For the great republic—for the principles it lives by, and keeps alive—for man's vast future—thanks to all."

CIVIL WAR FACTOID

The residents of New Orleans weren't particularly happy about the Union occupation of their city. To show her disapproval, one woman dumped the contents of a chamber pot on the head of David Farragut.

MAJOR NAVAL BATTLES

THE BATTLE OF NEW ORLEANS
APRIL 25, 1862

David Farragut's bold attack on New Orleans placed the city and its port under Union command, a striking defeat for the Confederacy. By taking New Orleans, located 100 miles above the mouth of the Mississippi River, the Union effectively controlled the very gateway to the Deep South.

New Orleans was an important Confederate city, vital to trade and commerce. However, military actions in other regions left it only lightly defended. Its greatest protection from Union invasion came from Fort Jackson and Fort St. Philip, which guarded the water approach 75 miles down river. Both forts were heavily fortified and armed with large cannons; a barricade of sunken ships in the river itself forced approaching craft to stop directly in front of their line of fire. Such a defense seemed insurmountable, and Confederate leaders were confident that the two forts could hold off any naval assault the Union might attempt.

But Union military leaders thought otherwise. Naval Commander David Porter believed that a strong mortar attack from boats on the river could disable the forts' firepower and allow a fleet to pass all the way to New Orleans; such an attack was readied in the early months of 1862.

To facilitate the invasion, Union General Benjamin Butler captured Ship Island, near the mouth of the Mississippi. Here, Squadron Captain David Farragut (Porter's adopted brother) assembled a fleet of 24 wooden sloops and gunboats, which were combined with Porter's 19 mortar schooners. The ships were renovated to make them lighter so that they could pass over the river's many sandbars, and the fleet began its long trip up the Mississippi in April 1862, supported by Butler's 15,000 troops for a possible land invasion.

On April 18, Porter put his plan into action, slamming the two forts with a six-day mortar attack. His 19 mortar ships lobbed more than 3,000 shells at the forts each day, but aside from making a horrible racket, they did little damage to the forts' defenses. The

bombardment did act as a distraction, however, and on the night of April 20, two Union gunboats approached the river barricade and cleared a small path for the rest of the fleet.

When it became evident that mortars were not having much of an impact, Farragut ordered his fleet to proceed past them anyway, hopeful that enough ships would survive the gauntlet to invade the city of New Orleans. The fleet began the treacherous run under cover of darkness early on the morning of April 24 and was quickly met with cannon fire. The mortar ships responded in kind, and the artillery duel lit up the sky over the Mississippi as if it were a July 4 fireworks display. In addition, Confederate officers tried to halt the invasion by sending out a small fleet of wooden ships to ram the approaching Union vessels. Several rafts that had been set on fire were also deployed in an attempt to slow the advance.

Farragut's flagship, the *Hartford*, caught fire and ran aground during the attack, but its crew quickly brought it around and back into the fray as the Union fleet methodically sank or disabled almost every Confederate ship in its path. The battle lasted about 90 minutes, and all but four of Farragut's fleet made it safely past the supposedly unpassable Confederate forts. Approximately 170 men were killed or injured during the assault.

Farragut sailed into New Orleans on April 25 and captured the city with little resistance, though the mayor of the city refused to officially surrender. The soldiers manning Forts Jackson and St. Philip laid down their guns on April 28, and Butler and his troops arrived the next day, quickly occupying the city of New Orleans despite a belligerent and antagonistic populace.

THE BATTLE OF MEMPHIS
JUNE 6, 1862

After a solid victory at Corinth, the Union army turned its attention to Memphis, Tennessee, the Confederacy's fifth largest city and a key port. But before Henry Halleck had a chance to invade, the city fell during one of the war's most impressive naval engagements.

In order to reach Memphis, Union forces had to take Island No. 10 and Fort Pillow, which stood just 50 miles above Memphis. The fort was armed with 40 guns, and Confederates had hedged their bet with a fleet of eight steamboats that had been converted into armed rams, a throwback to the days of the Roman galley. These rams surprised the Union fleet with a hit-and-run attack at Plum Run Bend, located just above Fort Pillow, and disabled two Union iron-clads by punching holes in them just below the waterline.

The Union navy vowed never to be caught unprepared again and fitted several steamboats of its own with sturdy rams. The brains behind the operation was Charles Ellet, a 57-year-old civil engineer from Pennsylvania who, having failed to convince the Union navy of the value of ram power, found a believer in Secretary of War Stanton. Ellet supervised the construction of nine steamboats, developing his own calculations for maximum strength. Ellet commanded the fleet's flagship and placed eight relatives aboard the others.

Ellet was eager to take on the Confederate fleet at Fort Pillow, but his plans changed when Beauregard ordered the evacuation of Fort Pillow after his withdrawal from Corinth. Instead, the Confederates decided to make a stand at Memphis, and early on June 6, the Southern ram fleet sailed out to take on five Union

AN IRONCLAD SHIP

ironclads and four of Ellet's self-designed ram ships. Thousands of Memphis residents lined the bluffs above the river to cheer the rebels.

However, there turned out to be little for them to cheer about. It took the Union ships less than two hours to reduce the Confederate vessels to driftwood. Charles Ellet charged the Union flagship toward the first ship in the Confederate fleet at 15 knots, ramming it with such force that the collision could be heard by the spectators high above. Ellet's ram knocked a huge hole in the bow of the Confederate ship, rendering it useless. At the same time, a ship commanded by Ellet's brother, Alfred, managed to squeeze between two Confederate rams that were converging on him, causing them to collide. Alfred then circled around and rammed the one Confederate boat that had survived the collision.

As the Ellet brothers proved the value of Charles Ellet's rams, the Union gunboats joined the battle. When the smoke cleared, they had taken out two crippled Confederate boats, sank another, and captured three others after they had been disabled. Only one Confederate boat escaped the battle. It was a devastating defeat for the Confederate river force and opened the door for the Union capture of Memphis. The residents who had so loudly cheered their side during the early minutes of the river battle stood silent as a four-man detachment led by Ellet's son, Charles junior, raised the American flag over the Memphis post office. Charles senior was wounded in the fighting and died two weeks later. Charles junior was promoted to colonel—at 19, the youngest person to hold that rank—and took command of his father's ram fleet. He was killed a year later in combat.

THE BATTLE OF MOBILE BAY
AUGUST 5, 1864

Alabama's Mobile Bay became increasingly important to the Confederacy as the war progressed. The Union blockade had effectively closed other ports, but Mobile Bay was still relatively free, making it the only open gulf port east of Texas and the primary site for the smuggling of arms and provisions from Europe. U.S.

THE MONITOR VERSUS THE MERRIMACK

One the best-known naval battles during the Civil War was the duel between the Union ironclad *Monitor* and the Confederate ironclad *Virginia*, formerly the *USS Merrimac*.

The Confederacy dredged up the *Merrimac*, which had been torched and scuttled by Union forces when the Confederacy took control of the Norfolk shipyards, and turned it into the first ironclad vessel to be built on American soil. News of the venture quickly reached Union officials, who immediately approved the development of ironclads for the Union navy. The first to be constructed (in a remarkable 101 days) was the *Monitor*. Like the *Virginia*, the *Monitor* was protected by 4-inch steel plates. However, it had two guns on a revolving turret, which provided more accurate firepower. It also was smaller, faster, and more maneuverable than the *Virginia*.

The *Virginia* sailed into Chesapeake Bay on March 5 and headed for Hampton Roads, a major Union blockading base. On March 8, at around 1 P.M., the ship confronted five wooden Union ships, which didn't know what to make of the bizarre vessel facing them. They fired all they had at the partially submerged craft but quickly found that their shells had little impact aside from making a horrific noise. The *Virginia* immediately set about its task, ramming and sinking the *Cumberland*, one of the Union's most impressive frigates; grounding and burning the 50-gun *Congress*; and knocking out of commission the flagship *Minnesota*. The only damage to the ironclad was a broken ram and injuries to its captain, Franklin Buchanan.

To the rescue sailed the *USS Monitor*, though it almost didn't make it. The ship nearly sank as it ponderously sailed to Hampton Roads, arriving around 1 A.M. on March 9. Officials in Washington feared the Union ironclad would be no match for the *Virginia,* but the *Monitor* soon proved otherwise. The two ships faced off, just 100 yards apart, at 9 A.M. on March 9 and began pounding each other with all they had. Shells bounced off their iron skins, and the two ships collided several times, sometimes by accident and sometimes not. The furious duel lasted for four hours, with neither ship gaining an advantage. The *Monitor* finally drew back when its captain, John L. Worden, was temporarily blinded by a shell blast, and the *Virginia*, which was slowly taking on water and experiencing engine difficulties, took that as its cue to withdraw. The battle ended in a draw, though it could be said that the Union was the real victor because its blockade of Hampton Roads survived.

Navy Rear Admiral David Farragut wanted to launch an assault on the port immediately following his success at New Orleans in April 1862, but circumstances forced him to wait until January 1864 to begin preparations. The attack itself wouldn't come for another seven months.

When the time came, however, Farragut had an impressive fleet behind him: 14 wooden boats and four ironclads. He began the assault early on the morning of August 5, easing the fleet into the bay, which was heavily mined with what were known back than as torpedoes. The fleet was met by heavy Confederate gunfire from Fort Morgan, the bay's main defense, as well as a Confederate fleet of three wooden gunboats and the South's largest ironclad, the *CSS Tennessee*, led by Confederate Admiral Franklin Buchanan.

As the battle commenced, Farragut tied himself high in the rigging of his flagship, the *Hartford*, so that he could better direct his ships. From his perch, he watched his lead ironclad, the *Tecumseh* strike a mine and sink with almost all hands in a matter of minutes. The rest of Farragut's ships stopped where they were, confused and fearful of other mines, as the cannons at Fort Morgan continued to roar. It was then that Farragut shouted the rallying words for which he is still remembered today: "Damn the torpedoes! Full speed ahead!" Moving the *Hartford* out in front, Farragut successfully led his fleet through the minefield and past the fort into Mobile Bay.

The *Tennessee*, commanded by Buchanan himself, tried to ram the Union ships, then engaged in a gun battle with them before slinking off to safe harbor at Fort Morgan. The Union crews took that quiet moment to have a quick breakfast, only to have their meal interrupted by the *Tennessee*, which had returned for another attack. The Confederate ironclad was a formidable ship, but Buchanan soon found himself surrounded by Union vessels, which rammed and fired upon his ship until it was a helpless hulk. Buchanan was injured during the battle and his ship surrendered at around 10. A.M. In just four hours, Mobile Bay had come under Union control. Fort Morgan, however, was not captured until August 23, and the city of Mobile would remain in Confederate hands until the following April.

6

The
Weapons
of War

THE TELEGRAPH

The telegraph had a remarkable influence on the Civil War and how it was fought. For the first time in history, field forces were able to talk with their superiors and fellow officers almost instantly, developing tactics, requesting reinforcements, coordinating attacks, and keeping all apprised of their progress. By 1864, the telegraph system had been perfected to the point where General Ulysses S. Grant was able to control the activities of units operating on very distant fronts from his post in the field with the Army of the Potomac.

Horse couriers and other means of communication

(continued)

The Civil War marked a dramatic turning point in the evolution of warfare. The years immediately preceding the war and the period of the conflict itself saw important advances in small arms, such as the rifle musket, the revolver, and the magazine rifle (also known as the repeater), as well as a huge array of innovations, including the use of balloons for reconnaissance, the first land mines and machine guns, and even the first military use of a primitive submarine. The telegraph, which had been invented by Samuel Morse just 17 years before the war began, also played an important role in the formation and implementation of combat strategy by allowing officers in the field to remain in close touch with their counterparts in other regions. It also allowed combat officers to relay important information to their superiors in Washington and Richmond.

The impact of advances in small arms can't be overestimated. The rifle musket, which replaced the smoothbore musket as the most commonly used infantry weapon in the 1850s, marked the first improvement in shoulder arms in nearly 150 years. Earlier smoothbore muskets, such as those used during the Revolutionary War, had limited accuracy (about 40 yards) and were effective to just 300 yards. They were also quite inefficient due to their reliance on the primitive flintlock mechanism that ignited the powder charge, resulting in a frustrating number of misfires. Because of their limitations, smoothbore muskets were most effective only in massed units.

The rifle musket, on the other hand, offered a number of improvements that resulted in greater accuracy, distance, and ease of use. The flintlock was replaced by the percussion lock, which ignited the propellant charge when the gun's hammer struck a copper cap coated on the inside with fulminate of mercury. And the use of the Minie bullet more than halved the rate of loading and firing.

In addition to the rifle musket, two entirely new types of firearms appeared during the Civil War: the breechloader and the magazine rifle. The breechloader had been around for quite a long time, but enjoyed limited use prior to the Civil War because manufacturers found it difficult to create a gas-tight seal at the breech. This problem was resolved with the introduction of metallic cartridges (another Civil War first), and breechloaders became safer and more effective than ever before, though they still saw limited use during the war because many ordnance officers thought the weapons were wasteful.

Today, small arms are fairly uniform, but the Civil War saw a huge number of different guns as well as variations on old standards. Some guns were manufactured within the United States, but the Union and the Confederacy also purchased weaponry from foreign countries. It would be impossible to discuss all of the different types of guns used in the war, but this chapter provides a general overview of the varied weapons, large and small, used on both sides. It also discusses the many other battlefield innovations developed and put to use by the North and the South, as well as naval weaponry, military uniforms, flags, and other identifying insignia.

SMALL ARMS

Small arms are any weapons smaller than a cannon and carried by a soldier. During the Civil War, the most common small arms included the following:

- Muskets—smoothbore, long-barreled shoulder arms
- Rifles—shoulder arms with spiral grooves cut into the inner surface of the barrel
- Carbines—short-barreled rifles, commonly used by the cavalry
- Handguns—pistols and revolvers

Small arms were commonly designated by their caliber, method of loading (breech or muzzle), and manufacturer. The most frequently used small arms in both the Union and Confederate armies were the .58 caliber Springfield musket and the .69 caliber Harpers Ferry rifle. Both were muzzleloaded weapons that fired the Minie ball, a revolutionary hollow-based bullet that greatly accelerated the loading and firing process.

The increased use of these weapons resulted in a remarkable change in infantry tactics. Smoothbore muskets were notoriously inaccurate and had a relatively short range; firing lines as close as

THE TELEGRAPH
(continued from previous page)

were still in common use, but by the end of the war, almost all strategic and tactical communications were handled by telegraph. This was especially true of Union forces because the telegraph system in the North was much more advanced than in the South. It also didn't hurt that Secretary of War Edwin Stanton, a former executive of the Atlantic and Ohio Telegraph Company, was able to secure the cooperation of several national firms to create the Federal Military Telegraph System.

CONFEDERATE GUN MANUFACTURERS

At the onset of the war, the South didn't have a single gun manufacturer within its borders. However, the Confederate government's offer of interest-free loans and lucrative contracts quickly changed that; within a year, several handgun factories had been established. Most folded soon after opening, the victims of a chronic lack of necessary materials. But a handful succeeded, most notably Griswold & Gunnison, Leech & Rigdon, and Spiller & Burr. These manufacturers were often forced to use inferior metals, such as brass and iron, due to a severe shortage of steel. Desperate for materials, it wasn't unusual for Southern gun manufacturers to melt down and use any metal that came their way, including metal from church bells.

100 yards inflicted little damage. For maximum effectiveness, soldiers usually had to run toward the enemy firing en masse and hoping they hit something, then use their bayonets for close-quarter fighting. The rifled musket introduced just prior to the Civil War was a completely different weapon, however. It offered accuracy at a considerable distance (skilled snipers could hit their target as far as a half mile away), which made a frontal assault especially hazardous. Unfortunately, many commanding officers failed to take these new weapons into consideration when formulating battle strategy, resulting in a huge number of casualties.

MUSKETS AND RIFLES

During the first weeks of the Civil War, as both sides scrambled to put together a fighting force, Union ordnance officials weren't too concerned about the state of the nation's arsenals. Secretary of War Simon Cameron and Chief of Ordnance James Ripley both believed that the number of guns readily available for service, though small, would be sufficient for a war everyone thought would last three months at best. After all, the number of troops necessary to bring the Southern rebellion under control was estimated at 250,000, and the federal weapons stores housed more than 400,000 rifles and muskets, which would also be supplemented with weapons brought by state militias.

However, the picture of the war changed dramatically after the first few battles, which demonstrated that the South was not going down without a long and costly fight. By July 1861, few weapons remained in the national arsenal except a number of very obsolete .69-caliber altered smoothbore muskets—long, awkward weapons that had their original flintlock ignition systems converted to percussion. Not surprisingly, the Union's entire supply of modern rifled weapons, which included 40,000 Model 1855 Harpers Ferry rifles, rifle muskets, and other weapons, were disbursed during the first six weeks of the war. Many of them went to influential politicians who gave them to favored regiments, rather than to the militia and three-year volunteers to whom they had originally been slated.

It wasn't until mid-1861 that the federal armory in Springfield, Massachusetts, started producing what would become the favored weapon during the war—the Model 1861 Springfield rifle musket. Before that, the average Union soldier had to make due with the traditional smoothbore musket, a weapon with a high-risk factor because of its inaccuracy and time-consuming loading procedure. Demand for the Model 1861 was tremendous. The Springfield Armory produced more than 250,000 of the weapons over two years, and the government still had to contract with 20 private manufacturers to make an additional 450,000. Each cost the U.S. Treasury between $15 and $20.

Some of the most impressive weapons in the federal arsenal were the .58-caliber rifled arms, most of them altered Mississippis and U.S. Model 1855s. Manufactured to conform to the new standards for arms established by Jefferson Davis, who was then secretary of war, in July 1855, the guns were designed to fire the .58-caliber Minie ball, which was easier to load and offered greater accuracy. The elimination of all calibers but the .58 from its muzzleloading regulation arms helped the government simplify weapons production.

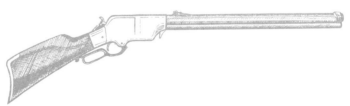

RIFLE MUSKET WITH MINIE BALL

Repeating rifles weren't readily available until the last two years of the war, but they had an incredible impact on the fighting. These weapons were decidedly different from single-shot musket rifles in that they were magazine fed and fired metallic cartridges, which were far superior to moisture sensitive paper or linen cartridges. The most popular brands of repeating rifles were the Spencers and Henrys, and though limited in number, they had a demoralizing effect on the Confederate soldiers

HENRY REPEATING RIFLE

SHARPS COMBINE

THE MINIE BALL

The half-inch lead rifle bullet commonly known as the Minie ball dramatically changed the face of warfare and resulted in a huge number of casualties on both sides during the Civil War, many the result of old-fashioned battle tactics that failed to take into consideration the new technology.

Prior to the introduction of the Minie ball (which was actually bullet shaped), the use of rifles in battle was considered impractical, due to the limitations of the weapons, and was usually reserved for specially skilled marksmen. The reason was simple: Rifles took a long time to load because tight-fitting projectiles had to be rammed into the grooves of the rifle's muzzle.

That changed in 1848, when French army Captain Claude F. Minie created a

(continued)

who faced them. Because they were multishot weapons, repeating rifles could make a handful of well-trained soldiers seem like a regiment. Unfortunately, the Federal Ordnance Department bought only 15,000 Spencer and Henry rifles for the entire Union army, making the weapons extremely coveted among the fighting forces.

For members of the cavalry, the weapon of choice was the carbine, a short-barreled rifle that was lightweight and easy to use, especially on horseback. As with many weapons, there was a shortage of these popular rifles at the onset of the war, but manufacturers soon corrected that, flooding the Union ordnance offices with a number of unique carbine designs. Realizing the value of the carbine to the soldier in the field, the government adopted nearly 17 different makes and models. The most advanced version was the magazine-fed metallic-cartridge breechloader, which could be mass-produced in volume. Other innovations included barrels that tipped up or hinged downward, cylinders that revolved, and breechblocks that slid vertically or swung to the side.

The Union suffered from a weapons shortage at the beginning of the war, but the Confederacy had it even worse. The new republic's arsenals contained just 296,000 shoulder arms, most of them outdated flintlock muskets and altered percussion smoothbores. When hostilities first broke out, the Confederate army had just 24,000 modern rifles to distribute among its troops.

The vast majority of Confederate infantrymen marched into battle armed with .69-caliber smoothbore muskets, which were quite effective at close range but wildly inaccurate at distances of more than 100 yards. The Union soldiers opposing them knew about this limitation and enjoyed taunting the rebels by dancing just out of range. Things changed dramatically in late 1862, when Confederate ordnance officials managed to finally bring the military arsenal up to date. Smoothbore muskets were replaced with much more accurate rifle muskets that extended the firing range up to 600 yards. Within just a few months, Northern soldiers stopped dancing and started ducking.

The individual states that comprised the Confederacy did their part by opening up state arsenals and requesting donations from private citizens. The call was met with enthusiasm, and a great

number of privately owned rifles, shotguns, and other firearms were donated to the Confederate cause. The Southern states also contracted with small-gun manufacturers and repair shops to alter muskets and rifles so that they would meet military specifications. Thomas Riggins, who owned a gun repair shop in Knoxville, Tennessee, employed 60 assistants, working night and day, to convert donated rifles and flintlocks into percussion carbines for a volunteer cavalry regiment known as the East Tennessee Squirrel Shooters. Riggins was a skilled craftsman, and the soldiers who came into possession of the weapons altered in his shop knew their guns would get the job done.

Additional weapons used by the Confederacy came from the North, primarily from federal arsenals that fell under Confederate control when the Southern states seceded. In 1859, a standing order was issued by the secretary of war to periodically supply Southern arsenals with weapons from Northern armories. As a result of that order, more than 18,000 percussion muskets, 11,000 altered muskets, and 2,000 rifles were shipped to the Baton Rouge Arsenal in 1860 and 1861—just in time to arm Confederate soldiers. And just a week into the war, the Confederacy captured the U.S. Armory at Harpers Ferry, Virginia. In addition to firearms, the raid also gave the South a tremendous amount of arms-producing machinery.

Weapons were also obtained from foreign manufacturers. In April 1861, for example, Captain Caleb Huse was sent to Europe by Confederate officials to purchase as many small arms as he possibly could. The result was a wide array of weapons that varied greatly in quality. British Enfield rifle muskets were greatly coveted by Confederate infantry, but others, such as the Austrian Lorenz rifle musket, proved to be shoddily made and fairly ineffectual in the battlefield.

Like their Northern counterparts, members of the Confederate cavalry preferred breechloading carbines above all other weapons because they were reliable, lightweight, and easy to use. However, only a few thousand Southern cavalry actually got to use breechloading carbines because they were in such short supply; Southern gun manufacturers couldn't meet the demand because of a lack of supplies, machinery, and technical know-how, and the

THE MINIE BALL
(continued from previous page)

smaller, hollow-based bullet that could quickly and easily be rammed into the bore. When the gun was fired, the bullet expanded, causing it to catch in the rifling and spin out of the barrel. This rifling action sent the bullet farther (up to a half mile) and made it far more accurate (a skilled marksman could hit a target with precision up to 250 yards away). It was also less expensive than traditional rifle ammunition.

Around 1855, James Burton, a worker at Harpers Ferry Armory, developed an even less expensive version of the Minie ball, which, along with the rifle itself, was soon widely used by the U.S. Army. This new version of the Minie ball became the standard bullet for both the North and the South.

How to Load a Rifle

The use of muzzleloaded musket rifles was anything but simple. In fact, the act required nine individual steps. Following is a wartime primer:

1. **LOAD:** Grasp the rifle with the left hand. Place the butt between the feet, the barrel toward the front. Seize the barrel with the left hand close to the muzzle, which should be held three inches from the body. Carry the right hand to the cartridge box on the belt.

2. **HANDLE CARTRIDGE/TEAR CARTRIDGE:** Seize the cartridge between the thumb and the next two fingers. Place it between the teeth. Tear the paper. Hold the cartridge upright between the thumb and the first two fingers in front of and near the muzzle.

3. **CHARGE CARTRIDGE:** Empty the powder into the barrel. Disengage the ball from the paper with the right hand and with the thumb and first two fingers of the left. Insert the ball, with its pointed end up, into the muzzle and press it down with the right thumb.

4. **DRAW RAMMER:** Draw the rammer out by extending the arm. Turn the rammer. Keeping the back of the hand toward the front, place the head of the rammer on the ball.

5. **RAM CARTRIDGE:** Insert the rammer. Steady it with the thumb of the left hand. Seize its small end with the thumb and forefinger of the right hand. Press the ball home, holding the elbows near the body.

6. **RETURN RAMMER:** Draw the rammer halfway out. Grasp it near the muzzle with the right hand. Clear it from the bore by extending the arm. Turn it and insert it in the carrying groove. Force the rammer home by placing the little finger of the right hand on the head.

7. **PRIME:** With the left hand, raise the piece until the hand is as high as the eye. Half-face to the right, with the right foot at right angles to the left. Half-cock the hammer with the thumb of the right hand. Remove the old percussion cap. Take the new cap from the pouch. Place it on the nipple. Press the cap down with the thumb.

8. **READY/AIM:** Fully cock the hammer and seize the small of the stock with the right hand. Place the butt against the right shoulder. Incline the head to align the right eye with the sight. Close the left eye.

9. **FIRE:** Press trigger with forefinger.

breechloading carbines they did produce were of poor quality. As a result, many cavalry soldiers were forced to use long, unwieldy, muzzleloading shoulder arms, which were next to impossible to load and shoot on a charging horse. Also popular among Southern cavalry were sawed-off shotguns, which were found to be extremely effective in close quarters. In fact, a regiment armed with 12-gauges was a force to be reckoned with.

HANDGUNS

Of the many weapons used during the Civil War, handguns proved to be the least desired. Rifles provided much greater accuracy and distance, and sabers and bayonets were much more effective during a charge or in close-quarters fighting. Noted Major Leonidas Scranton of the 2d Michigan Cavalry: "Pistols are useless. I have known regiments that have been in the field over two years that have never used their pistols in action."

For the average Union soldier, the issue was moot anyway. The government cheerfully handed out shoulder arms to all who needed them, but only cavalrymen and mounted light artillery were issued sidearms; everyone else had to provide their own.

According to government reports, the Union purchased just over 370,000 handguns over the course of the Civil War. The most preferred were the Colt and Remington .44 caliber (known as the Army) and .36 caliber (known as the Navy) six-shooters. They were well-made, reliable, and accurate weapons that packed a punch. A small number of foreign-made handguns were also purchased by Union ordnance officials, such as the Lefaucheux .41-caliber revolver, which was unique in that it was a nonpercussion firearm that required a self-exploding pinfire cartridge. The U.S. government bought about 12,000 Lefaucheux revolvers, most of which were used by soldiers in the western theater.

Because the government doled out handguns only to cavalrymen and mounted light artillery, the number of government-purchased sidearms was greatly exceeded by the number purchased privately by individual soldiers. A good sidearm set back the average soldier about $20, and at the beginning of the war, every well-armed soldier

CIVIL WAR FACTOID

Weapons fire on both sides was often wildly inaccurate, due to the limitations of the weapons and the hurried panic of the men who used them. As a result, some soldiers estimated that it took a man's weight in lead to kill a single enemy in battle. According to a Union munitions expert, each Confederate who was shot on the battlefield required 140 pounds of powder and 900 pounds of lead.

SOUTHERN SHARPSHOOTERS

The Union and the Confederacy both employed sharpshooters to pick off the enemy at a great distance, but the Southern snipers were particularly effective as a result of their incredibly accurate rifles. Only the best shots were recruited to become Confederate sharpshooters, and in many camps, their skills exempted them from most camp and guard duty. Instead, they spent up to six hours a day drilling on distance estimation and marksmanship. So skilled were these marksmen that the very best could hit a target nearly a half mile away, making them the bane of the infantry.

(continued)

had a handgun on his person to complement his shoulder arm. (Favored handguns included the Colt Model 1862 police revolver and the Smith and Wesson No. 2 army revolver.) However, as the war progressed, most soldiers found sidearms to be of little use (just as Major Leonidas Scranton noted) and to add unwanted weight. As a result, a great many sidearms were given away, sold, sent home, or merely tossed aside by Union soldiers, who found them more trouble than they were worth.

Confederate soldiers also found sidearms to be a real encumbrance on the battlefield, though Southern cavalrymen preferred them during the close quarters of a full cavalry attack because they were lightweight and extremely accurate at short range. But as with many other things, the South simply couldn't make or acquire enough of them to meet the demand, so one Confederate ordnance officer presented a simple solution to Secretary of War Benjamin: Take the handguns away from the infantry and give them to the cavalry, which needed them more. Benjamin agreed.

The handguns that were used to arm Confederate soldiers came from a multitude of sources, including Southern manufacturers, seized arsenals, fallen soldiers in the battlefield, foreign manufacturers, and private donations from Confederate citizens. Weapons of choice include the Colt "Army" revolver, the Colt "Navy" revolver, and the British-produced Adams and Deane revolver, a double-action .44-caliber sidearm greatly preferred by Confederate officers. The Adams and Deane and the Kerr revolvers were manufactured by the London Armoury Company, the largest single producer of handguns imported into the South. Over the course of the war, thousands of guns were purchased from the company, which was renowned for its quality craftsmanship, and smuggled past the Northern blockade.

SWORDS AND SABERS

Swords and sabers are traditional weapons of war and were an important part of every officer's dress uniform on both sides of the Civil War. Among the enlisted men in the Union army, however, only sergeants, cavalry members, select artillerymen, and musicians

were issued swords, and rather plain ones at that, since they were designed more for fighting than dress. The swords issued to officers tended to be much more ornate and served as a symbol of rank rather than a fighting weapon. Only the sabers carried by cavalry and light artillery officers were actual weapons, though they weren't used as often as rifles and sidearms.

The vast majority of regulation swords issued to Union soldiers were patterned on weapons of the French army and most were made by private firms or purchased from foreign manufacturers. European sword makers provided nearly all officers' blades, which were based on an 1850 pattern. It was also common for citizens and military subordinates to give specially made presentation swords to officers as tokens of appreciation for exceptional service or bravery, or as a symbol of esteem. Most of these very ornate swords, which were quite expensive, were for formal occasions rather than actual fighting.

Swords held much greater appeal among Confederate soldiers because they harkened back to an era of chivalry and romance, an era that was still in effect in the mid-century South. As in the North, swords were both a symbol of rank and a fighting weapon, though rarely used. Instead, cavalry and artillery forces came to rely on sidearms for self-defense because they were reliable and effective. Confederate infantry officers commonly wore swords but used them in combat only when absolutely necessary.

Most Confederate swords were variations of models used by the U.S. Army and were manufactured by Southern companies. A large number of Confederate officers, however, wore imported swords, cherished family heirlooms, or U.S. swords acquired during service in the prewar army.

In addition to their sidearms, many Confederate soldiers carried large bowie knives, named after James Bowie, one of the heroes of the Alamo, who was said to have originated the knife's design. The knives were large—blades ranged from 6 to 18 inches in length—and served a number of functions, including skinning wild animals, scaling fish, whittling branches, and self-defense. During man-to-man fighting, a well-honed bowie knife could take off a man's arm with a single swipe.

SOUTHERN SHARPSHOOTERS
(continued from previous page)

In one telling incident, Union General John Sedgwick and his corps were overseeing the placement of Union artillery at Spotsylvania when they were spotted by some Confederate sharpshooters nearly 800 yards away. As the snipers fired away, Sedgwick confidently walked over to a soldier who was cowering on the ground and said, "Why, what are you dodging for? They could not hit an elephant at that distance." The words had barely passed Sedgwick's lips when he was struck in the cheek by a sharpshooter's bullet. He died instantly.

ARTILLERY

All firearms larger than small arms are known collectively as artillery or cannon. Several dozen different types of artillery were used over the course of the Civil War, but they all fell into one of two distinct categories: smoothbore or rifled cannon. Artillery was further identified by the weight of their projectile, the caliber of their bore diameter, their method of loading (muzzle or breech), and sometimes the name of their inventor or manufacturer. Further distinction was made by the path of a weapon's trajectory (guns had a flat trajectory; mortars a high, arching shot; and how-itzers a trajectory that fell between the two) and its tactical deployment, such as seacoast, field, and siege artillery.

The most commonly used artillery on both sides was the Napoleon, a smoothbore, muzzleloaded, 12-pound howitzer. It was developed in France during the reign of Louis Napoleon and was first introduced in the United States in 1856. The Napoleon was a reliable, sturdy piece of machinery that worked equally well as an offensive and defensive weapon. Napoleons were first made of bronze, but Southern manufacturers were forced to make later ver-sions out of iron when bronze fell into short supply. The maximum range of the Napoleon was 1,000 yards, but the weapon proved most effective at shorter ranges—250 yards or less. It used both grape shot and canister ammunition and is believed to have killed more men on both sides than all other artillery weapons combined.

Second to the Napoleon were the 3-inch ordnance and Parrott guns, rifled cannon that had greater accuracy and range than smoothbore artillery. On a good day, a 3-incher could lob a shell up to 2,500 yards, but such long-range artillery proved ineffective during most battles because the gunner had to see what he was shooting at. Rifled cannon did have their valuable uses, however. They were very good at destroying fortifications and played an inte-gral role in the battles of Vicksburg and Atlanta. Most of the artillery used during the Civil War was muzzleloaded. Breechloading cannon was available, but most gunners found them unreliable and difficult to use.

Size played an important role in the use of artillery; the heavier guns were more difficult to transport, especially over hilly

or muddy terrain. The most portable artillery and thus some of the most widely used were the 6- and 12-pound mountain howitzers, which proved very effective during battles fought in the mountainous western theater. Naval and siege cannons were some of the heaviest and provided the greatest power. The 8- and 10-inch siege howitzers had ranges of more than 2,000 yards and could fire 45- and 90-pound shells, which inflicted tremendous damage on their targets.

The big guns fired an array of ammunition, including solid shot, grape, canister, shell, and chain shot, most of which came in any of the nine common artillery calibers. Solid shot and shell were used to destroy distant, fixed targets such as fortifications, while chain shot, which consisted of two balls connected by a short chain, was employed primarily against the masts and rigging of ships. Grape shot and canister were used most commonly in the field. Both were scattershot projectiles consisting of several iron balls in an iron casement. When fired, the casement would disintegrate, releasing the shot in a deadly spray very much like a giant sawed-off shotgun. At close range (250 yards or less), these weapons could inflict serious damage.

The Union had more and better artillery than the Confederacy, and its officers used the weapons to tremendous advantage in many, many battles. Typically, Confederate infantry would move forward against Union infantry, often through fields and woodlands, until they were within a specific range. At that point, the Union artillery would be moved into place, and iron death would rain down upon the hapless Confederate troops, breaking their charge and forcing them back. This tactic repeated itself throughout the war and enabled Union victories in such battles as Shiloh and Fredericksburg.

One of the biggest reasons the Union was able to maintain superiority in the area of artillery was its manufacturing might. The North contained far more manufacturing plants and skilled technicians than the South, as well as far greater access to the raw materials needed to build reliable weaponry. The South did its best to keep up but, in the long run, it was simply outmanufactured. Quite a bit of artillery was acquired from foreign manufacturers, but the Northern blockade of Southern ports played an important role in

HORSE ARTILLERY

Horse artillery consisted of various small but powerful cannons, usually howitzers, that could be easily disassembled, packed onto horses with special tack, and carried over rough terrain. Horse artillery was commonly used by the cavalry, and both Jeb Stuart and Nathan Bedford Forrest made excellent use of it during the Civil War.

The ease of assembly and transport of horse artillery allowed cavalry and other units to bring heavy cannon into regions that they otherwise could not have reached, surprising an unsuspecting enemy with devastating fire. The units could then be disassembled and quickly moved to another location. Horse artillery, in addition to causing heavy damage, often made opposing forces think they were facing a much larger foe.

CIVIL WAR
FACTOID

Firing artillery required the
efforts of several men
working in a sort of ballet.
Experienced gunners could
load and fire a fieldpiece
every 30 seconds, even in
the face of enemy fire. Not
surprisingly, gunnery teams
were a close-knit bunch
who treated their weapons
as a member of the family,
often giving them special
names.

keeping the Confederate army undersupplied. Noted General Henry Hunt, chief of artillery for the Army of the Potomac: "While the South had at the beginning of the war the better raw material for infantry and cavalry, the North had the best for artillery. A battery requires many mechanics, with their tools and stores, and also what are called handy men. No country furnishes better men for the artillery proper than our Northern, and particularly our New England, states."

Once the war began in earnest and it became apparent that hostilities would not be quickly concluded, foundries in the North worked almost around the clock to produce cannons and ammunition for the Union army. The greatest output was of 12-pounder smoothbore Napoleons and 3-inch ordnance rifles, which quickly became the muscle of the Union artillery because of their reliability, durability, and accuracy. A huge number of Parrott guns were also produced, primarily at the West Point Foundry. The Parrott came in various sizes, from 10- and 12-pounder field versions to huge cast-iron cannons that fired 100- and 200-pound shells. However, the larger cannons were greatly disliked by the Union soldiers because they had a nasty habit of exploding if they were fired repeatedly.

Aiding the Union effort greatly was the U.S. regular army artillery, a small but extremely well-trained corps of specialists who provided expert guidance in the art of field gunnery and tactics. These soldiers made sure their weapons hit their targets with deadly accuracy, and they played a crucial role in numerous battles. Sometimes, however, things didn't go as planned. In one famous incident, Brigadier General John Gibbon commanded the Iron Brigade during the Battle of Antietam on September 17, 1862. Gibbon placed six Napoleons of Battery B, 4th U.S. Artillery on a knoll overlooking a cornfield to protect his right flank but realized too late that his gunners had aimed the cannons' muzzles too high and were shooting over the heads of advancing enemy troops. Before too long, 40 of his battery's 100 men had fallen. As Confederate troops charged the Union battery, Gibbon leaped off his horse, ran to one of the guns, and quickly adjusted the elevating screw. On his orders, the crew fired several more volleys into the cornfield, blasting away a fence as well as a high number of

Confederate troops. Gibbon's daring saved Battery B from almost certain annihilation.

Artillery played an equally important role in the Battle of Malvern Hill, the last of the Seven Days' Battle. Almost the entire artillery arm of George McClellan's retreating army, approximately 250 cannon, was positioned on a bluff flanking the James River as Robert E. Lee's pursuing forces attacked. The big guns did extraordinary damage to the Confederate forces, cutting wide swaths within their ranks. Noted Confederate General D. H. Hill: "It was not war, it was murder." Other battles in which Union artillery inflicted extremely heavy casualties on Confederate forces include Antietam, Fredericksburg, Gettysburg, Stones River, and Nashville.

THE IRONCLADS

One of the most dramatic innovations in naval warfare was the ironclad ship, another Civil War first. These floating fortresses were almost impregnable and changed the face of ocean warfare forever.

At the beginning of the war, iron-armored vessels were still being tentatively explored. The British navy had two ironclad ships and the French had one, and that was all in the entire world. But that would change quickly as the Civil War progressed. Within a year, both sides were ravaging the wooden ships of the other with "floating tin cans" that, while unwieldy, proved to be extremely formidable vessels. Interestingly, it was the Confederate navy that first decided to give the new technology a try. The Union navy was confident its armada of heavily armed wooden ships would be sufficient and didn't follow suit until it became evident that it had no choice.

The idea of putting iron plating on a ship made tremendous sense, so much so that it's surprising it wasn't done earlier. Even iron plating a few inches thick provided sufficient protection from the most commonly used artillery shells, and no one at that time had invented an armor-piercing shell. With good reason, ironclads became the scourge of the waterways.

One of the very first ironclad vessels manufactured on American soil was the *Manassas*, a Confederate prototype that was

SPENCER RIFLE

Union ordnance men turned down the Spencer repeating breechloading rifle in 1860 with the explanation that soldiers would fire too quickly and waste ammunition. Smarter minds prevailed, and the Spencer eventually made its way to the battlefield, but not until near the end of the war.

CIVIL WAR
FACTOID

Confederate agents tried to buy ironclad ships from overseas, but Union diplomats were able to prevent delivery of all but one, a ship known as the *Stonewall*. The ship was built in France, sold to Denmark, then transferred to the Confederacy. However, the *Stonewall* never saw service; it arrived off the Southern coast too late to take part in the war and was surrendered and ultimately sold to Japan.

said to look like a turtle. The Confederates quickly realized the tremendous value of ironclad ships and set about manufacturing as many of them as they could.

The first Confederate ironclad was the *Virginia*, and its origins are fascinating. Before it was the *Virginia*, the ship was known as the *Merrimac*, a federal steam frigate. The ship's engines were in bad condition, and the ship was in drydock at the Norfolk Navy Yard when the war started. The navy yard quickly fell under Confederate control, and one of the last things the fleeing Union workers did was set fire to the *Merrimac* and scuttle her. However, Confederate engineers quickly raised the vessel and found it in fairly good shape; only the upper portion of the ship had been severely damaged by fire. This ship, they decided, would become the first serviceable ironclad.

The *Merrimac*'s hull was cut down to the berth deck, and a citadel with slanting sides was constructed on the midship section with ports for ten big guns. The walls of the citadel were made of pine and oak two feet thick, upon which was placed iron sheathing four inches thick. An open grating covered the top of the citadel so that air and sunlight could reach the gun deck. An armored pilot-house was placed toward the back of the ship, and a 4-foot iron beak was attached to the bow.

The *Merrimac*, rechristened the *CSS Virginia*, was one of the strangest looking vessels ever to be placed in the water. It floated awkwardly, sailed slowly, and was extremely difficult to steer, but it was also unbeatable. No wooden ship could touch it. Shots from naval cannons simply bounced off its metal shell, doing no more damage than a small dent. The Confederates had created the ultimate naval weapon.

The Union quickly learned of the Confederate plans to turn the scuttled *Merrimac* into an ironclad vessel, and in August 1861, the U.S. Congress authorized the development of ironclads for the Union navy. The first Union ironclad was the *USS Monitor*, which engaged in a two-hour duel with the *CSS Virginia* in Chesapeake Bay on March 9, 1862. It ended in a draw, but with that single engagement, the era of the wooden naval vessel came to an end.

CIVIL WAR CINEMA

A number of motion pictures have been made about the Civil War over the years, some more historically accurate than others. Here are just a few of them:

- *Birth of a Nation* (1915). This landmark silent film by D. W. Griffith demonstrated for the first time how powerful and evocative motion pictures could be. Its story of the Civil War and Reconstruction shows a strong Confederate bias (Griffith's grandfather was a deeply bred Southerner, hence the film's sympathetic portrayal of the Ku Klux Klan), but it's still an astounding piece of filmmaking. A ticket to its premiere in New York went for a whopping $2—a lot of money for a movie in those days.
- *The General* (1926). In this silent comedy classic, Buster Keaton plays a Southern train engineer named Johnnie Gray who finds himself embroiled in the Civil War. The title derives from Keaton's beloved railroad engine, "The General."
- *Gone with the Wind* (1939). This adaptation of Margaret Mitchell's best-selling novel is probably the most famous Civil War movie ever made, and it turned Clark Gable and Vivien Leigh into superstars. Though overly romantic in its portrayal of the conflict, it's still rousing entertainment, and the burning of Atlanta, for which the movie is justly famous, remains a stunning sequence.
- *Tennessee Johnson* (1942). Van Heflin stars in this relatively accurate film biography of President Andrew Johnson. The movie starts with his early political career and ends with his near impeachment, and is lots of fun once you know the background.

- *The Red Badge of Courage* (1951). Few books captured the terror of combat during the Civil War like Stephen Crane's *The Red Badge of Courage*, and this adaptation by John Huston, though flawed due to studio interference, still holds up pretty well. Audie Murphy stars, and James Whitmore narrates. A television version starring Richard Thomas was made in 1974.
- *The Horse Soldiers* (1959). This is the only feature-length movie director John Ford ever made about the Civil War, and while it's not his best movie, it's still quite entertaining. The film details a plan to help the Union take Vicksburg. It stars John Wayne, William Holden, and Hoot Gibson. Ford's one other Civil War-related film is *How the West Was Won* (1962).
- *Glory* (1989). One of the best films ever made about the Civil War, *Glory* tells the story of the 54th Massachusetts, the distinguished black regiment that took heavy losses trying to take Battery Wagner in South Carolina in the summer of 1863. Matthew Broderick stars as Colonel Robert Gould Shaw, ably assisted by Denzel Washington, Morgan Freeman, and Andre Braugher. Some historians have said the attack sequence in this film is the most realistic combat footage of any Civil War movie.
- *Gettysburg* (1993). This film version of the epic 3-day battle was first offered as a television miniseries, then released theatrically. While not perfect, it offers a very accurate portrayal of this pivotal fight, with some truly stunning combat sequences. Martin Sheen stars as Robert E. Lee and Tom Berenger as General James Longstreet. It's based on *The Killer Angels*, a Pulitzer Prize-winning novel by Michael Shaara.

Both sides immediately realized the tremendous advantage of ironclad vessels and raced to see which could build the largest ironclad navy, as well as improve on the basic design. By the end of the war, 58 ironclad warships had been launched or were in the process of being built by the Union navy. On the Confederate side, 21 armored ships had been launched or were close to release. Most were modeled after the *Monitor* and the *Virginia*, with important improvements that made them more effective in battle. But even with refinements, ironclads were difficult ships to sail; they were prone to flooding in rough waters. As a result, most of them saw duty protecting rivers and bays rather than the high seas (the one exception was a partially armored Union cruiser named *New Ironsides*, which played a pivotal role in the sea assault on Fort Fisher, North Carolina). Joining the traditional ironclads were flat-bottomed, armored paddlewheelers known as "Pook turtles," after their designer, Samuel Pook. These vessels became a major part of the Union's defense of the Mississippi River.

UNIFORMS

The Civil War is commonly known as the War of the Blue and the Gray, describing the colors of the uniforms worn by Union and Confederate soldiers. But in truth, there was very little conformity of dress on either side, at least during the first months of the war. The regular army had an established uniform, but the majority of participants were volunteers from state militias who often demonstrated their independence and esprit de corps by dressing in flamboyant (albeit impractical) uniforms of their own design. When these units got together, it looked more like a circus show than a fighting force.

The various units fighting for the Confederacy were even more independent in their attire, showing their disdain for the concept of a centralized government by dressing as colorfully and uniquely as they could. Again, when several different units gathered together, it looked like anything but an army going to war. Only later in the conflict would both sides establish a standard for military dress, though many units tenaciously continued to flaunt their independence by adding flourishes and various accouterments.

One of the biggest problems during the first months of the war was finding enough uniforms to dress the participants on both sides. In the North, a great many clothing manufacturers received lucrative government contracts to make military uniforms, but in the rush to meet quotas, factory-made uniforms were often of poor quality and design. The system also fostered corruption, which only made the situation worse. Eventually, the government cracked down on manufacturers who churned out inferior clothing while pocketing huge profits, and the quality of uniforms improved dramatically.

The U.S. Quartermaster Department was responsible for dressing the Union's fighting forces, having supervised the design and manufacture of clothing for enlisted men at the Schuylkill Arsenal since the War of 1812. However, the army was hard pressed to adequately dress the huge influx of new soldiers at the beginning of the war, so the War Department asked the various states to dress their own regiments—preferably in the traditional dark blue uniform—and apply to the government for reimbursement. But the states were also unable to supply adequate numbers of uniforms on such short notice, so many early volunteer regiments wore uniforms paid for by their local communities, with perhaps a little help from the state. Indeed, it wasn't unusual for communities to provide money and materials to outfit the men who volunteered for military service; most felt it was their patriotic duty, and they did so without complaint. Volunteer tailors and seamstresses also did their part, sewing uniforms as quickly as they could. Their efforts were greatly appreciated by the men who received the garments, though they weren't always a perfect fit. One Union soldier noted that half of his regiment's home-made coats were "two feet too large around the chest."

As odd as it may seem today, several regiments left for Washington without any uniforms at all. The 1st and 2d Ohio, for example, were sent to the nation's capital so soon after they were organized that their leaders decided to pick up uniforms during the trip rather than wait. However, their agent found the market in Pennsylvania overwhelmed by state purchasers, so he bought whole material instead and had the uniforms made by Pennsylvania tailors. The resulting uniforms could only be described as casual. In fact,

NEW YORK STATE
MILITIA COAT

Balloons and other Novelties

The Civil War saw a large number of innovations in warfare, many of which remain in common use today. One of the most amazing was the use of hot-air balloons for aerial reconnaissance. A small number of daring balloonists, led by Professor Thaddeus Lowe, chief aeronaut, Balloon Corps, Union army, made balloon reconnaissance a reality, observing enemy forces on the move and, in one case, telegraphically directing artillery fire onto Confederate positions. Balloons gave officers eyes where before they had none.

The Union had great hopes for balloon reconnaissance, and Lowe's fleet eventually grew to seven balloons. However, his force was mysteriously disbanded following the Battle of Chancellorsville. The Confederacy also toyed with balloons but abandoned the plan after their best balloon, nicknamed the "Silk Dress Balloon" (because it was made from strips of dresses donated by Southern women), was captured in 1862.

Balloons could give a fighting force a distinct advantage, so a number of antiballoon tactics and weapons were introduced, including camouflage and antiballoon artillery fire. The Confederates were especially adept at using camouflage to trick Union aerial observers, hiding weapons and painting logs black so that they looked like cannons (these nonweapons came to be known as "Quaker cannons"). More commonly, however, hidden batteries waited for balloons to draw near, then opened fire with artillery. Such attacks forced balloonists to retreat, but there is no record of a balloonist being killed in action during the war.

The war also saw the first use of water mines, which the Confederates used to protect rivers, harbors, and bays. These devices were very effective and resulted in the loss of 27 Union ships over the course of the conflict. Both sides also used spar torpedoes, which were bombs attached to long poles. They were driven to the target by a torpedo boat or submarine, then rammed home, causing a large hole at the waterline. The first sinking of a large surface ship by a submarine occurred on February 17, 1864, when the Confederate ship *Hunley*, a primitive submersible powered by a hand-cranked propeller, sank the *USS Housatonic* off Charleston. The *Hunley* had an unlucky history; it sank three times during trials, drowning 20 men, and was dragged down with the *Housatonic*, killing its crew of nine.

Other Civil War combat firsts include the rail gun, wire entanglements, land mines, flame throwers, and gas shells.

some didn't even have buttons! But these problems were quickly remedied, and the regiments marched into Washington looking almost like real soldiers.

Following the Union defeat at the First Battle of Bull Run, Congress immediately authorized a call for 500,000 volunteers to serve for three years, and the states started working overtime to clothe the new recruits. Some states wisely got the ball rolling before the call for volunteers went out. New York, for example, had decided in April to issue all of its new regiments a standard outfit that included a dark blue woolen jacket that closed in front with eight state-seal buttons, light blue pants and overcoat, and a dark blue fatigue cap. By the end of July, state officials had agreed to buy more than 30,000 jackets from nine individual contractors. Unfortunately, the quality of these garments left a lot to be desired. Many were made of cheap material, and the soldiers who received them complained bitterly of the poor workmanship. The jackets had a nasty habit of falling apart after minimal use, and the coarse material—which came to be known by the derogatory word *shoddy*—chafed the skin.

The uniform situation improved dramatically by the fall of 1861. The government purchased a large number of uniforms from foreign manufacturers, and the high quality of the garments forced American manufacturers to improve the quality of their own product, as well as increase production quotas. On September 13, 1861, the U.S. War Department, in a much needed attempt to stop Union soldiers from accidentally being killed by their own men, asked the officials of Northern states to stop furnishing gray uniforms to their soldiers. By mid-1862, gray uniforms had all but disappeared from Union regiments as Quartermaster General Montgomery Meigs assumed the job of contracting and distributing uniforms to Union troops. The blue uniform of the regular army became the standard for most units, though there were some regimental exceptions.

The Schuylkill Arsenal in Philadelphia could not keep up with the huge demand for uniforms, so additional manufacturing and purchasing depots were established in New York, Boston, Cincinnati, and elsewhere. Federal inspectors checked every piece of clothing

TRAINING SOLDIERS

Unlike soldiers today, most of whom can assemble their weapons blindfolded, many soldiers during the Civil War were sent into battle with weapons they barely knew how to use, a situation made worse by the terror of battle. On the field at Gettysburg, Union ordnance officers under General George Meade, commander of the Army of the Potomac, collected thousands of muskets loaded with 2 and up to 10 charges. In the fever of the fight, many of the soldiers had apparently loaded and reloaded without actually firing their weapons.

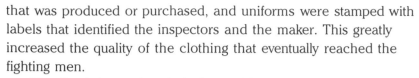

that was produced or purchased, and uniforms were stamped with labels that identified the inspectors and the maker. This greatly increased the quality of the clothing that eventually reached the fighting men.

The Confederacy faced similar problems in dressing its own fighting forces. The newly formed government struggled to find sufficient manufacturers to meet the demand for uniforms, and the civilian population often lent a hand by sewing uniforms for local soldiers before they went off to battle. Still, some Confederate soldiers had nothing to wear but the clothes they brought with them (at least for a while), and the situation only worsened; as the war dragged on, the South found itself running perilously low on manufacturing supplies. In some cases, entire units were forced to march from battle to battle lacking shoes and other garments.

But that's not to suggest that the entire Confederate army was ragtag in its dress. Many Southern units, in fact, were well attired through the duration of the war, impressing even their Northern foes. General Richard Taylor's Louisiana Brigade, for example, contained more than 3,000 soldiers, each of whom was perfectly uniformed, much to the marvel of all who saw them.

Few Southern states had dress regulations for their militia, which formed the backbone of the Confederate fighting force at the beginning of the war, and most found it easier to simply let the governor grant companies the right to choose their own style. Most of the time, the companies chose their uniforms first and then asked for permission, which all but a few governors granted. On the eve of the war, the sight of the various militias gathered together was nothing short of amazing. The troops included everything from Scottish highlanders and frontiersmen to French chasseurs and Zouaves, and many continued to wear their exotic dress even after they were made a part of the Confederate regular army.

By October 1862, an effective depot system had been established, and the Confederate government assumed the responsibility of supplying all clothing to its troops. The new issue system set annual allotments for articles of clothing as well as prices that were to be charged for items that exceeded the allotment. (If a soldier took less than he was allotted, he was paid the difference; if he

took more, the difference was taken out of his pay.) During the standard three-year enlistment, soldiers were supposed to receive four pairs of shoes a year, with additional pairs costing $6 each. They also were to receive two jackets the first year and one each for the following two years, plus one overcoat to last the full three years (replacements cost $25). All other clothes, down to socks and underwear, were similarly provided.

Of course, soldiers who participated in lengthy campaigns went through their allotted clothes in no time. Rather than spend their hard-earned money for replacements, many asked their friends and family to help by buying or making clothes for them. And those who were desperate enough took needed clothes off their fallen comrades in the battlefield.

As the war went on, Confederate officials found it increasingly difficult to meet the allotments they had imposed. Wool became a scarce commodity, resulting in smaller shipments of strong winter clothing such as coats and blankets. Cotton was in good supply during most of the war, so lightweight clothing such as underwear remained well stocked, but the new republic eventually found itself turning to foreign suppliers for the items it could no longer furnish. In September 1862, Confederate quartermaster purchasing agent J. B. Ferguson went to England to buy army shoes, bulk wool cloth, and other much needed items, but shortages still occurred. Whenever possible, the states themselves provided clothing to their own soldiers, often doing a better job than the government.

WHAT THE AVERAGE SOLDIER WORE

Exotic uniforms aside, the typical Union infantryman wore a dark blue, loose flannel sackcoat that hung at mid-thigh; blue trousers made of wool or jersey; a light blouse; heavy leather shoes that were derisively known as "gunboats"; and a blue forage cap, also known as a slouch cap. Additional clothing and protective gear included an overcoat with a blue cape; a thick wool blanket (which weighed approximately five pounds); a gum blanket that served as a tent floor (as well as a poncho, during inclement weather); a thick flannel pullover shirt, and a pair of wool socks.

MILITARY DRESS

The need for conformity in military dress was in part one of necessity. During the First Battle of Bull Run, soldiers on both sides dressed in a wide variety of colorful uniforms that sometimes made it difficult to differentiate between an enemy soldier and one of your own. Later on, Union uniforms were designated blue, and Confederate uniforms were designated gray, but during that first important battle, there were Southern units wearing blue and Northern soldiers decked out in gray. In the resulting confusion, more than one soldier was accidentally killed by friendly fire.

Affiliation with a specific branch of the service was indicated by stripes down the outer seam of the uniform—yellow for cavalry, red for artillery, light blue for infantry, emerald green for mounted rifleman, and crimson for ordnance and hospital personnel. Distinctions in rank were denoted by the type of frock coat worn— majors, lieutenant colonels, colonels, and all general officers wore double-breasted coats; lower ranking officers wore single-breasted coats. Additional rank distinctions included the number and place- ment of buttons and shoulder boards or sleeve chevrons—major generals' coats had nine buttons in each of three rows and wore two stars; brigadier generals wore four rows of two buttons each and one star; colonels, lieutenant colonels, and majors wore two rows of seven buttons. In addition, colonels also had an eagle emblazoned on their shoulder boards, lieutenant colonels had two silver embroidered leaves, majors had two gold embroidered leaves, captains had two groups of gold bars, first lieutenants had one gold bar, and a second lieutenant wore boards with no insignia.

Noncommissioned officers wore a single row of nine buttons. Sergeants wore three chevrons on their sleeves, and corporals wore two chevrons. Regular troops wore one stripe sewn on the lower sleeves for every five years of service.

The uniforms worn by Confederate troops were quite similar to their Union counterparts, except the color was gray or yellow-brown. The standard infantryman wore a gray or yellow-brown wool shell jacket; gray, yellow-brown, or blue pants; low-heeled leather shoes; and a gray or yellow-brown forage cap. Frock coats similar to those worn by Union infantry were also part of the uniform, but supplies were limited, and not all soldiers received them. Additional gar- ments traditionally included a homemade coverlet, a cotton shirt, a wool vest, and wool socks. All officers and enlisted men on both sides also received ankle-high boots.

In the Confederate army, affiliation with a particular branch of service was indicated by the colored facing on a man's coat— yellow for cavalry, red for artillery, light blue for infantry, and black for medical personnel. Variations in rank within each branch was designated by colored stripes on outer trouser seams—regi- mental officers had a $\frac{1}{4}$-inch stripe; generals wore a $2\frac{5}{8}$-inch

stripe; adjutant, quartermaster, commissary, and engineer officers wore one gold $\frac{1}{4}$-inch stripe. Noncommissioned officers wore a $\frac{1}{4}$-inch cotton stripe of colors appropriate to their branch of service.

Rank was also indicated by buttons and insignias. Generals, lieutenant generals, major generals, and brigadier generals wore three gold stars (the middle one larger than the other two) within a wreath on their collars. Colonels wore three stars of equal size, lieutenant colonels wore two stars, and majors wore one star. Captains and first lieutenants wore two gold bars, and second lieutenants wore one bar. Sergeants wore three chevrons on their sleeves, and corporals wore two chevrons. A brigadier general's coat had two rows of eight buttons, and a junior officer's coat had two rows of seven buttons each.

Soldiers on both sides were expected to carry all of their provisions, including clothing, equipment, personal effects, and weapons, on their backs, and a fully equipped infantryman might carry a load of 50 pounds or more. On long marches, the burden could be quite heavy.

THE ISSUE OF COMFORT

While the quality of the uniforms received by Union and Confederate soldiers gradually improved as the war progressed, their comfort did not. When the clothing arrived at training camps, it was placed in piles, and the soldiers lined up and took what was on top. The issue of fit was not a big concern, and it wasn't uncommon for soldiers to receive clothing that was much too big or small for them. The lucky ones were able to trade with someone else; others did the best they could under the circumstances. Men who were very tall or very short suffered the most.

Even if a soldier received a uniform that was a perfect fit, he still experienced great discomfort. Northern mills, following orders from the War Department, used wool to make almost everything—including underwear. The material was stiff, scratchy, and often unbearable against the skin, but unless a soldier had brought underclothes from home, he was stuck with what he got. One volunteer from Indiana wrote home to his family: "The shirts are rather

SPRINGFIELD RIFLE

The Springfield Model 1861 rifle musket was so popular that the U.S. government had to contract with private weapons manufacturers to meet the demand on the battlefield. Each rifle was examined by a government ordnance inspector, who fired a proof charge to test the barrel and removed the lock and fittings to check the components. Weapons that passed this rigorous inspection received a "VP" on the barrel (for "viewed and proved") as well as an eagle's head acceptance mark and the initials of the inspector.

coarse and the sox—well, I think I shall wear the ones I brought from home and have Mother knit me some more when they are worn out. As to the shoes, they are wide and big enough, goodness knows! No danger of cramped feet with them! They may be very good but surely they are not very stylish."

During the thick of the war, when soldiers were marching, skirmishing, and fighting for their lives, the majority of fighting men tried to lighten their load to the bare necessities. When spring broke and the temperatures rose to comfortable levels, many soldiers discarded their heavy winter coats and other clothing, knowing that the now efficient federal distribution system would provide them with more clothes when fall arrived. When soldiers were engaged in a major campaign, very often the only clothes they carried were those they were wearing. Speed on the battlefield meant much more than a wardrobe.

FLAGS OF THE NORTH AND SOUTH

The national flags of the Union and the Confederacy were more than colorful pieces of cloth; they quickly came to symbolize everything each side stood for, rallying troops and private citizens into a patriotic fervor unlike anything that had ever been seen before. In New York City, for example, an angry mob took over the offices of the *New York Herald*, which held a strong pro-Southern sentiment, and threatened to burn everything in sight if publisher James Gordon Bennett didn't display the Stars and Stripes. He quickly complied.

Indeed, it became quite fashionable to display the flag at one's home and office, and to wear the flag on one's person as a show of support for the Union cause. And the same was true for the Confederate "Stars and Bars." Failure to revere the flag of one's republic was viewed as extremely unpatriotic. Communities nationwide presented specially made flags—either traditional designs or variations thereof—to local militia units gearing up to go to war, hopeful that the colorful banners would inspire the troops to victory.

In 1861, U.S. Army regulations were revised to require infantry units to carry two silk flags, a national flag and a regimental flag, each nearly six feet square. The description of the national flag was very specific, requiring "13 horizontal stripes of equal breadth, alternately red and white, beginning with red. In the upper quarter, next to the staff, is the Union, composed of a number of white stars, equal to the number of States, on a blue field, one-third the length of the flag, extending to the lower edge of the fourth red stripe from the top." Flag makers tried to adhere to the requirements, which were somewhat awkward; others simply fashioned the dimensions as best they could. Interestingly, no pattern was set for the stars. Most prewar flags had the stars arranged in rows, but flag makers were free to arrange them any way they wanted. Some went with rows; others used a circular pattern.

Regulations also called for embroidered white stars and embroidered regimental designations on the center stripe of the national flag. The embroidery was to be in silver on infantry flags and gold on artillery flags, but a shortage of qualified embroiderers often forced quartermasters to have the designations painted on instead.

Regimental flags came in two basic patterns. Artillery units carried a yellow flag with two gold crossed cannons in the center; infantry flags were dark blue with a coat of arms of the United States in the middle. A red scroll beneath the central device displayed the unit designation on both flags, and each was fringed in yellow silk. a number of companies manufactured national and regimental flags. Most tried to adhere to the regulations, but it wasn't uncommon for similar flags from separate manufacturers to look decidedly different. The best presentation colors were made by Tiffany & Company of New York. Its flags, while expensive, were beautifully designed and wonderfully embroidered, and they came to be prized among the companies that possessed them.

Until 1862, the individual states were given responsibility for recruiting and outfitting the militias that came out of them, and they were usually responsible for their flags as well. The result was a plethora of colorful and creative patterns that helped distinguish one unit from another. Some states gave their militias flags that adhered fairly closely to army regulations; others went with a state motif. And a few combined the two, to interesting effect. Pennsylvania, for

CIVIL WAR FACTOID

At the Battle of Chickamauga, the 535 members of the 21st Ohio Infantry Regiment used their Colt revolving rifles to help prevent a Union rout. During five hours of fighting, the 21st Ohio fired off more than 43,500 rounds, proving the superiority of repeating rifles. Commented one captured Confederate soldier: "My God, we thought you had a division there!"

CONFEDERATE MUTINY

Early in the war, the majority of Confederate infantrymen found themselves armed with horribly inaccurate smoothbore rifles, which proved to be no match for the superior weapons used by most Union soldiers. In May 1861, several companies of the 28th Virginia mutinied, stating that they would no longer use smoothbore rifles. Jubal A. Early, colonel of volunteers, managed to bring the soldiers under control with threats of discharge and public disgrace. In the end, all but eight soldiers grudgingly accepted the smoothbore muskets. Those who refused were shouted out of camp.

example, placed the state's coat of arms on the traditional Stars and Stripes.

In early 1862, the federal government assumed responsibility for supplying all units raised by the states for military service. Prior to the war, the army's flags had been made at the U.S. Army clothing depot in Philadelphia (the Schuylkill Arsenal). But the huge influx of state volunteer regiments created more work than the facility could handle alone, so the Quartermaster Department created additional depots in New York and Cincinnati. Each depot adopted its own pattern, and the flags produced by the three facilities were noticeably different in style. The contractors to the three depots accounted for nearly 2,400 national flags and 2,300 regimental flags over the course of the war.

In the thick of battle, the regimental flag was often the only sign of a unit that was visible in the smoke and chaos, and thus it typically received a huge amount of enemy fire. As a result, casualties were usually the highest closest to the colors. To compensate for expected losses, the color guard of a Union regiment, whose sole job was to keep the colors flying, was fairly large, consisting of between six and nine men. If one man fell, another would quickly grab the flag and keep it aloft. To be a member of a regimental color guard was an esteemed honor and one that was assumed with great seriousness. The color guard of a cavalry regiment was much smaller, usually just a standard-bearer followed by a single corporal. Unlike infantry regiments, which carried two flags, cavalry color guards carried only the regimental standard.

THE FLAGS OF THE CONFEDERACY

Prior to the official formation of the Confederacy, many of the seceding states asserted their independence by abandoning the Stars and Stripes and adopting new flags that fell into three distinct categories. States with a strong colonial tradition, such as Virginia and South Carolina, chose symbols—typically a coat of arms—on a blue field. States with less of a colonial attachment, such as Alabama, proclaimed their independence by placing a single star (which represented them on the American flag) on a blue field.

And other states chose to symbolize their secession by displaying a single star as the prominent device. Louisiana, for example, adopted a flag that had a field of 13 alternating red, white, and blue stripes, with a single yellow star in its red canton.

Unlike the Union, which had just one national flag, the Confederate congress successively adopted three designs for the new republic's national flag. The first, adopted on March 4, 1861, looked very much like the Stars and Stripes, so much so that it was nicknamed the Stars and Bars. Designed by Nicola Marschall of Alabama, it consisted of a field of three equal horizontal bars of red, white, red. Its blue canton extended two-thirds the height of the flag and featured a circle of stars equal to the number of states in the Confederacy. The stars were usually white and had five points on them.

However, the Stars and Bars didn't last long. Citizens of the Confederacy felt it looked too much like the Stars and Stripes—a symbol they loathed—and after two years of debate, the national flag was officially changed. The new flag, nicknamed the Stainless Banner because it had a plain white field, featured a red canton crisscrossed by a white-edged, dark blue St. Andrew's Cross (also known as a saltire) emblazoned with 13 white stars. The flag was attractive, but in calm weather, its white field made it look like a flag of truce. So in March 1865, the Confederate congress changed the flag's proportions and added a wide red vertical bar to its fly edge. This decision was made just weeks before the war ended, however, and very few flags of the new Confederate design were made.

Because the Stars and Stripes and the Stars and Bars looked so much alike at the beginning of the war, it quickly became apparent that new battle flags would have to be designed for the Confederate armies to prevent the possibility of mistaken identity on the battle-field. In the eastern theater, the concept of a new battle flag was advocated by no less than General Pierre G. T. Beauregard, commander of the Confederate Army of the Potomac. He suggested a design by William Porcher Miles. It consisted of a rectangular red field crossed by a blue saltire with seven white stars—the number of states then represented in the Confederate congress. Beauregard discussed the issue with his departmental commander, General Joseph

CIVIL WAR FACTOID

Beginning in the winter of 1861–62, Union troops started marking their national and regimental flags with the names of battles in which they had participated, a practice that dated back to the 1830s in the regular army. The practice was officially sanctioned by the War Department on February 22, 1862.

Johnston, and the design was quickly adopted. The first of the new battle flags were made by Constance Cary Harrison, Hetty Cary, and Jennie Cary of Richmond. Two years later, Constance Cary Harrison received back the flag that had gone to General Earl Van Dorn, following his death in Tennessee. Between 1862 and 1865, the Richmond depot responsible for manufacturing the battle flags produced seven subvarieties, each with minor modifications. The most common changes were the sizes of the components, such as the width of the saltire or the size and spacing of the stars.

Individual unit flags were also important in that the linear deployment of troops required precise alignment when a unit was in battle formation. Very often, a unit's flag was a soldier's only guide to where he was supposed to be. The flag also acted as a guide for soldiers in the back during an assault, or as a rallying point for soldiers who were lost or in retreat.

Unit colors were identical when first issued, but they quickly took on unique characteristics that made them immediately identifiable to soldiers in the field. Sometimes an abbreviated unit designation was added to the flag; other flags featured the names and dates of battles in which the unit had participated.

MUSIC ON THE BATTLEFIELD

Music played an integral role in the Civil War. Bands performed during war rallies, they were used as a recruitment tool, and they helped inspire troops during battle engagements.

The U.S. War Department officially sanctioned regimental brass bands in May 1861. By decree, each infantry or artillery regiment was permitted one 24-man band, and cavalry regiments were allowed a 16-man ensemble. Regimental brass bands were so popular that a U.S. Sanitation Commission inspection of Union military camps in October 1861 found that nearly 75 percent of all regiments had one. Bands were very common within the Confederate army, too, and it wasn't unusual for musicians from both sides to jam together in the evening following a day of heavy combat.

The luckiest units on both sides were able to gather skilled, often professional musicians. Those not quite so lucky put together

CIVIL WAR FACTOID

Confederate General Thomas "Stonewall" Jackson drew his sword so infrequently that it actually rusted in its scabbard.

makeshift bands from volunteers, some more talented than others. Wrote Timothy Pendergast, an infantryman with the 2d Minnesota: "A wagonload, more or less, of brass instruments, varying in size from a dinner horn to a cartwheel, arrived for our band, and peace fled. For the next two weeks the braying of the horns from one side of the camp would be answered by the braying of the mules from the other side. The poor mules no doubt thought another wagon train was parking over there."

Most regiments, however, greatly appreciated their band members, who often helped them forget the labors of their day with a pleasant concert after dinner. Regimental bands also performed at dress parades, guard mount, formal reviews, and funerals, and they frequently led troops on long marches.

When not playing their instruments, band members performed a number of other functions, such as that of medical assistant. At Little Round Top during the Battle of Gettysburg, musicians from the 20th Maine aided surgeons performing fast and furious amputations—the medical procedure of choice on the battlefield. When not actually assisting doctors, band members often played their instruments to cheer up wounded soldiers in field hospitals.

Union and Confederate regiments without actual bands still had musicians, usually fife players or drummers for infantry units and buglers for cavalry units. Most of the daily aspects of camp life, such as reveille, were governed by these musicians, who also helped orchestrate with bugle blasts or drumrolls important tactical movements on the battlefield.

Sadly, the use of large brass bands was short lived within the Union army. In July 1862, the U.S. adjutant general ordered all volunteer regimental brass ensembles disbanded due to the high cost of their maintenance. Some unit leaders managed to keep their bands intact by having the members re-enlist as regular soldiers and then detailing them to serve as musicians. But ultimately, the majority of units were left with just their drum corps to keep them entertained.

7

The Horrors
of War

Throughout the ages, war has been called many things—thrilling, noble, romantic, character-building. Such descriptions are often tossed around by individuals who have never actually been to war, people who have no idea what it's like to face mortality as bullets fly, mortars explode, and other men die in shrieking agony. Any combat soldier will tell you that war may be necessary, but it's never fun or romantic. War is a curse upon humankind, a violent endeavor characterized by stark terror, bloodshed, and destruction, horrors of which the Civil War had more than its share.

Today's soldiers are highly trained individuals, skilled, prepared, and ready. But such was not the case during the Civil War. As noted earlier, this was a war led by professionals and fought primarily by amateurs, most of whom had received only a minimum of training (if any at all) and had little or no combat experience. The majority of combat instruction on both sides consisted primarily of the manual of arms (but with little actual target practice), company and regimental drill in basic maneuvers, and occasional skirmishing tactics.

For the most part, the typical soldier in the early days of the Civil War found himself on the battlefield woefully unprepared for the job he was sent to do. Some regiments were sent into battle less than three weeks after they had been organized, only to suffer heavy casualties due to their gross inexperience. European observers were shocked and dismayed at the lack of training the average soldier received, with one Prussian military official reportedly calling the armies of the North and South nothing more than "armed mobs chasing each other around the countryside." It was an insulting comment but, sadly, one that fit, at least in the beginning.

After the first year of the war, however, things changed dramatically. Raw recruits turned into battle-hardened veterans who were able to fight well. They learned how to survive the rigors of long campaigns, the elements, and unfamiliar territory. By 1863, European military observers had changed their tune regarding the condition and skill of the Confederate and Union soldier. Noted one British observer following the Battle of Antietam: "In about seven or eight

CIVIL WAR FACTOID

The average Civil War soldier was paid very little for laying his life on the line. Top pay for a Union infantry private was just $16 a month. His Confederate counterpart received $18 a month, but it was worth considerably less due to skyrocketing inflation.

acres of wood there is not a tree which is not full of bullets and bits of shell. It is impossible to understand how anyone could live in such a fire as there must have been here." The Civil War soldier, pushed to the very limits of human endurance, had finally come into his own.

CAMP LIFE

Combat during the Civil War was a nightmarish experience, as was camp life. The average soldier found himself battling a litany of camp problems, ranging from sheer boredom to disease and death. For many soldiers, camp was home for up to three years, and they coped as best they could.

Army regulations required camps to be laid out in a grid pattern, with officers' quarters at the front end of each street and enlisted men's quarters aligned to the rear. The camp was set up approximately along the same lines as the line of battle, and each company proudly displayed its colors on the outside of its tents. Military regulations also outlined where the mess tents, medical cabins, and other structures should be located, though the rules were often ignored when the terrain or situation made them difficult to follow.

Because soldiers were forced to bivouac in tents out in the open, the conditions at many camps were less than ideal. This was especially true in the Deep South, where wet weather in the spring and summer turned the ground into thick mud for weeks on end, and dry weather in the fall and winter turned it into suffocating dust.

During the summer months, most soldiers slept in canvas tents. At the onset of the war, both sides used what was known as the Sibley tent, named after its inventor, Henry H. Sibley, who eventually rose to the rank of brigadier general in the Confederate army. The Sibley tent was a large canvas cone about 18 feet in diameter, 12 feet tall, and supported by a center pole. It had a circular opening at the top for ventilation and was heated by a cone-shaped stove. The Sibley tent was designed to house 12 men comfortably, but a shortage of supplies often increased occupancy to up to 20

SUTLERS

Most of the armies on both sides of the war had "sutlers" attached to them. These were vendors who supplied goods—such as newspapers, candy, tobacco, tinned meats, shoelaces, and other items—not usually provided by the government. Most sutlers charged exorbitant prices for their often shoddy goods, but soldiers desperate for news from home, a cigar, or something sweet paid them without hesitation.

men per tent. As might be expected, the conditions within these tents often bordered on the intolerable. Bathing was a rare luxury for soldiers in the field, so the stench within the tents was suffocating during inclement weather when the flaps had to be lowered.

Overcrowding was alleviated somewhat when the Sibley tent was replaced by smaller, easier to carry tents. The Union army primarily used the wedge tent, a 6-foot length of canvas draped over a horizontal pole and staked to the ground at the sides, with flaps that closed over each end. The wedge tent also saw use in the South, but when canvas became scarce, many soldiers were forced to make open-air beds by piling leaves or straw between two logs and covering it with a blanket or poncho. During the winter, crude huts were made out of wood, when wood was available.

Soldiers in the Civil War did not see battle every day, or even every week. Most were inactive about 75 percent of the time, thanks to the hurry-up-and-wait nature of warfare. During these down periods, the typical day started at 5 A.M. during the spring and summer months and 6 A.M. during the fall and winter. Soldiers were awakened by reveille, roll call was taken by the first sergeant, and then everyone sat down to breakfast, which usually consisted of biscuits, some kind of cured meat, and coffee. If available, eggs and fruit were added to the menu.

During the rest of the day, soldiers engaged in as many as five drill sessions, during which they learned how to shoot their weapons with accuracy and perform various maneuvers. Drill sessions lasted about two hours each, and most soldiers found them extremely boring and tedious; they wanted to fight, not just practice, though they realized that when fighting actually occurred, the drills could mean the difference between life and death.

Between drill sessions, soldiers cleaned and readied the camp, built roads, dug latrines, gathered wood for cooking and heating, and sometimes foraged for food to supplement their meals. One of the biggest problems facing soldiers in the field was proper sanitation. Access to clean water for drinking and bathing was often limited, and illness from contaminated water or poor hygiene was rampant. Because army camps were tight-knit groups, a contagious disease such as measles or chickenpox could decimate a camp within days. Indeed, most soldiers had more to fear from illness than enemy bullets.

Food shortages became a serious problem for the Confederacy, and even for some Union forces during the later years of the war, but early on, soldiers on both sides were relatively well fed. By mandate, daily rations for Union soldiers in 1861 included a minimum of 20 ounces of fresh or salted beef, or 12 ounces of salt pork; more than a pound of flour; and a vegetable, usually beans. Soldiers also received regular allotments of coffee, salt, vinegar, and sugar.

In the field during long campaigns, however, mandated allotments often fell short. Quality meat and vegetables were in short supply, and soldiers were forced to subsist primarily on salt pork, dried beans, corn bread, and hardtack, a biscuit made of flour and water that more often than not was contaminated with weevils and other critters. The lack of fresh vegetables and fruit often led to outbreaks of scurvy, a disease caused by a vitamin C deficiency.

Back then, as today, the most coveted supply among soldiers was coffee. Most soldiers drank large amounts of the beverage and would readily trade other food items for raw beans, which they ground with stones or their rifle butts. Union soldiers were fairly well supplied with coffee over the course of the war, but Confederate forces often found themselves without and had to make a substitute out of peanuts, chicory, and other items.

As the war progressed and supply trains found themselves unable to reach forces in the field, soldiers on both sides often had to literally live off the land. Hunting helped provide meat, but sometimes armies on both sides were forced to take what they needed from nearby homes and businesses. Confederate soldiers, who usually found themselves fighting on the home field, did their best to control looting, preferring to request provisions from sympathetic citizens. But sometimes they stole supplies or took them by force, though pillaging was something most soldiers did only under the most dire of situations. There were some, however, who used the war as an excuse to line their pockets with ill-gotten gains.

Boredom was a chronic problem in most army camps. Drilling helped take up some of the day, but the soldiers had to

CIVIL WAR FACTOID

Numerous gastrointestinal complaints caused by poor sanitation and hygiene plagued the participants of the Civil War, enlisted men and officers alike. It's a little-known fact, for example, that Robert E. Lee suffered from severe diarrhea during the Battle at Gettysburg.

devise other forms of recreation to help them while away the rest of the hours. Those who were able wrote long letters home or read books, magazines, and newspapers (when they could get them). Others played cards or engaged in various sports, such as baseball, boxing, and cockfighting. Some camps, desperate for activity, even staged cockroach and lice races. Drinking and gambling were discouraged by military officials, but both activities were nearly impossible to control, especially after payday. Many soldiers lost their wages almost as quickly as they got them. Contact with prostitutes (known colloquially as "horizontal refreshment") also was strongly discouraged but, again, nearly impossible to stop. Soldiers on leave frequently visited brothels. And prostitutes were known to visit military camps in specially equipped wagons, especially around payday.

Alcohol was a huge problem on both sides. Soldiers on duty were prohibited by army regulations from buying liquor, and those who were caught were severely punished. But that didn't stop those who simply were determined to have a drink, and soldiers found a number of ingenious ways to smuggle alcohol into camp and keep it hidden from their commanding officers. The members of one clever Mississippi company managed to sneak a half-gallon of whiskey past guards by pouring it into a watermelon; they then kept the watermelon hidden by burying it beneath the floor of their tent and drinking from it through long straws. Homemade liquor was also readily accessible, though most of it could hardly be called quality drink.

Of all the hardships soldiers faced in camp, homesickness was probably the most rampant and difficult to cure. Soldiers wrote home as often as they could and desperately hoped for letters in return, but the nature of the war often made it difficult for mail from home

to reach its intended recipients. Furloughs were rarely given—both sides needed as many able bodies on the battlefield as they could muster—and often impractical, since most units were so distant that it would have taken soldiers days and even weeks to reach home. Many soldiers became so homesick that they deserted, sometimes for a short while, sometimes forever. Those who stayed may have cursed their runaway comrades, but they certainly understood. During the war, 141 Union soldiers were executed

SIBLEY TENT

for desertion, though Lincoln signed numerous pardons for the common offense. "I prefer to take the risk on the side of mercy," he explained.

Discipline was the key to a strong and efficient army, and officers on both sides weren't averse to punishing their troops when necessary. The type and severity of punishment was predicated on the offense and the whims of the officer in charge. For simple infractions, such as drunkenness or rowdiness, soldiers were given extra guard detail, or forced to dig latrines or stand at attention for hours at a time, but more serious offenses required more serious punishment, including some that would no doubt be illegal today. One popular military punishment of the era involved placing a knife or piece of wood between a man's teeth, keeping it in place with string tied around his ears. The punished man was then seated on the ground with his knees drawn up to his body. A sturdy stick was run through his legs, his arms placed under the stick on each side of his knees, and his hands tied in front of him. He was then forced to sit like that for hours.

BATTLEFIELD CONDITIONS

Many of the volunteers who joined the armies of the North and South did so more as a means of escape than because of patriotic pride. A great many had spent their lives on family farms and in small towns, and they saw the war as an opportunity to experience some excitement and see the rest of the country. In their fantasies, the war was a clean, bloodless affair that would be over in a matter of months with nary a bullet fired. The reality, unfortunately, was much different.

While camp life was filled with interminable boredom, the battlefield was filled with gut-wrenching terror. Once a battle commenced, the scene was usually one of chaos. The noise was deafening as cannons roared and hundreds and sometimes thousands of soldiers fired on each other. Officers would try desperately to rally and guide their troops in the throes of battle, but the smoke and the noise often made the task difficult, if not impossible. In addition, as many as half of the soldiers typically had little knowledge of the terrain, and it wasn't unusual for entire units to get lost.

Many soldiers, especially those experiencing their first battle, panicked at the first sounds of gunfire and fled to the rear. One common tactic was to help a wounded comrade to the medical tent and then not return to the fighting. Commanding officers quickly became wise to the ruse and ordered cavalry officers in the rear to challenge fleeing soldiers with the cry, "Show blood!" Those who could not were ordered to take up arms and return to the front.

(It's difficult to label the men who panicked cowards, however, considering the circumstances. Most of the soldiers on both sides were raw recruits, inexperienced young men barely out of their teens who had never been involved in a gunfight in their lives. In most cases, their only experience with firearms was hunting with friends. Now they were being ordered to face an often-unseen enemy and attack, knowing full well that many of them would not survive. Edward Edes, a private in the Union army, expressed his fear in a letter to his father prior to his first battle: "I have a mortal dread of the battle field, for I have never yet been nearer to one than to the hear the cannon roar & and have never seen a person die. I am afraid that the groans of the wounded & dying will make me shake, nevertheless I hope & trust that strength will be given me to stand up & do my duty.")

Every battle was different; the terrain changed, as did the weather, and even the number of men available to fight. Officers did the best they could under these ever-changing circumstances, and many of the most skilled officers managed to pull off some spectacular feats in the face of overwhelming odds.

Different too were the leadership styles of commanding officers. Some were skilled tacticians and strategists, others were exceptionally skilled at leading their men, and a few could do both. Generals tended to stay toward the rear lines during a battle, guiding the action with the aid of subordinates who would carry orders down to unit leaders. But a few reckless generals liked to lead by example and were out in the front of the charge. Sadly, both sides lost a great number of talented leaders as a result.

Those who have experienced battle say it heightens a man's senses. His clarity of vision increases dramatically in the heat of combat, and his sense of hearing and smell grow more vibrant than ever before. (Veteran soldiers say the odor of sweat produced by fear is noticeably different from the odor produced by labor.) it is said that a soldier stops thinking and acts by pure instinct, in a desperate attempt to survive for at least one more day. During major battles, it wasn't uncommon for soldiers to fight nonstop for hours, fueled by pure adrenaline and completely unaware of the passage of time. Only when the sun went down and the battle ceased did their rhythms return to normal, as did their need for food, drink, and sleep. This was the battlefield experience for hundreds of thousands of Civil War soldiers, sometimes for days on end, battle after battle. Those lucky enough to return home never forgot the sights, sounds, and smells of combat.

Amazingly, once the shooting stopped, opposing forces often put their differences aside in order to barter for various goods. There are innumerable examples of Union and Confederate soldiers meeting in a "truce zone" to swap food, coffee, tobacco, newspapers, and other goods, tell jokes, and maybe share a song. Occasionally, even the officers joined in. In one notable incident, a Union officer was invited by his Confederate counterparts to attend a country dance at a farmhouse near the area where both armies were camped. The officer accepted the invitation, enjoyed the dance, and was safely returned to his lines by his "hosts" before daybreak.

BATTLEFIELD DEATHS

Battlefield deaths weren't always the direct result of enemy bullets. Many wounded soldiers perished in raging brushfires that were ignited during heavy fighting in dry fields and forests. A number of battles were temporarily halted while both sides struggled to save their wounded from brushfires that threatened to engulf them.

CASUALTIES

Causes of death during the Civil War were many. Bullets and artillery took their share of lives on both sides, but soldiers also died from disease and other factors. In fact, more than twice as many men died from illness than from enemy fire.

P.O.W.s

Prisoner of war camps sprang up all over the North and the South. Some of the best-known prisons in the North were Point Lookout, Maryland; Johnson's Island, the Ohio State Penitentiary, and Camp Chase, Ohio; and Rock Island, Illinois. Captured Confederate officers were often housed at Fort Monroe, Virginia. In the South, the best known POW camps include Danville, Virginia; Camp Oglethorpe, Georgia; Mobile, Alabama; and Salisbury, North Carolina. POW camps were constructed wherever room could be found. The notorious Andersonville Prison was built on a vacant Georgia field, and Libby Prison in Richmond was nothing more than a converted tobacco warehouse.

The casualty statistics are staggering. According to an in-depth analysis of government records, slightly more than 350,000 Union soldiers died from various causes during the Civil War. The majority of deaths, as noted, were from disease. And nearly 25,000 men died from causes such as suicide, execution, sunstroke, and accidents. The Union navy lost nearly 5,000 men to illness, accidents, and battle injuries.

Records of Confederate deaths aren't nearly as comprehensive as those of Union casualties due to the destruction of military and government files during and after the war. However, a generally accepted estimate is 150,000 dead of disease and 95,000 killed or mortally wounded in combat. No statistics survive regarding deaths among Confederate naval personnel.

To put these figures in perspective, consider that more Americans died during the Civil War than all other American wars combined, from the Revolutionary War to Vietnam, including both World War I and II. In fact, the Battle of Antietam, on September 17, 1862, resulted in four times the casualties as the landing on Normandy Beach on June 6, 1944.

The high number of battlefield deaths during the Civil War is easy to understand. The weapons used caused massive physical damage when they hit their targets, and outdated battle tactics often put large numbers of soldiers in harm's way. But the number of deaths related to disease requires a little explanation.

The Civil War took place shortly before a number of important advances in human medicine. There were no vaccines for the most common of illnesses, and hygiene was poor, especially in mobile military camps. Young men who had lived their entire lives in relative seclusion in small towns and hamlets simply didn't have immunity to many types of illnesses, and they fell sick from the most innocuous of diseases.

One of the leading contributors to wartime illness was the latrine, usually a simple hole or trench used by all members of the camp. When the stench of the latrine became unbearable, it was covered over and a new one dug. As might be expected, camp latrines were veritable breeding grounds for every form of illness imaginable. They also attracted a lot of insects, particularly flies, which would deposit germs and bacteria on the food the men ate and the water they drank. The result was numerous outbreaks of diarrhea, as well as epidemics of cholera and other contagious diseases. Whooping cough, measles, scarlet fever, smallpox, dysentery, and other disorders also took a huge toll, as did environmental ailments such as sunstroke, frostbite, and tetanus. Every soldier came down with something at least once, and many suffered from gastrointestinal ailments and other complaints for almost the entire length of their enlistment.

Soldiers weren't the only ones to die during the Civil War. The conflict also took a huge toll on the civilian population, particularly in the South. While the number of Northern citizens who died as a direct result of the war is relatively small, some historians estimate that up to 50,000 Confederate citizens may have perished from various causes, including stray bullets from battles fought literally in their backyards and poor sanitation following the devastation of entire towns and cities.

PRISONERS OF WAR

For the most part, soldiers taken prisoner by both sides were relatively well treated. This was the Victorian era, after all, and chivalry still had its place during wartime. More importantly, however, the soldiers of the North and South weren't fighting some unknown, foreign enemy; they were fighting their own countrymen. To abuse another American, even a rebellious one, wasn't in the nature of most men (though, as with everything, there were exceptions). In addition, every soldier knew that there was a strong possibility he could be taken prisoner, so it behooved all to act with kindness toward captured enemy forces—today it was them; tomorrow it could be you.

At the beginning of the war, captured soldiers were expected to "give parole," or promise not to escape. If parole were offered and accepted, soldiers could expect to be sent back to their own lines under a flag of truce, at which time they would be sent home until an exchange was effected. (Union and Confederate military officials reached an agreement in 1862 that stipulated that all

THE GREAT ESCAPE

The largest mass escape from a Civil War POW camp occurred at a former cotton warehouse, in Richmond, Virginia. The Libby and Son Chandlers and Grocery was a small three-story structure that held nearly 1,200 men in eight crowded, filthy rooms.

Union Colonel Thomas E. Rose orchestrated the escape. The prisoners dug a long, crude tunnel from the prison's cellar. The rest of the prisoners held a musical show to occupy the prison staff while Rose and his men disappeared through the tunnel and into the city of Richmond. Roll call the next day showed 109 prisoners missing. A total of 59 managed to make it back to Union lines. Two drowned while crossing streams, and the rest—including Rose—were recaptured by Confederate forces.

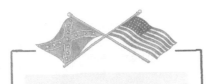

CIVIL WAR FACTOID

During the Civil War, Union forces captured between 215,000 and 220,000 prisoners, not including Confederate armies that surrendered at the end of the war. The Confederates captured between 200,000 and 211,000 federal soldiers. An estimated 26,500 Confederate soldiers and 22,600 Union soldiers perished in prison camps.

prisoners were to be exchanged within 10 days of capture.) After an official prisoner exchange, paroled soldiers could return to active duty. The fact that promises were made and kept demonstrates the gentlemanly nature of the Civil War during its first years—a man's word was his honor. However, if a soldier broke his promise by returning to the field unexchanged, he ran the risk of being shot or hanged.

The value of a prisoner depended on his rank. During prisoner exchanges, a general was worth up to 60 privates, a major general was worth up to 40 privates, and so forth. At the bottom end, a noncommissioned officer was worth two privates, and privates were traded one for one. Approximately 200,000 soldiers from both sides were freed through prisoner exchanges.

The concept of prisoner parole dates back many years. However, it was followed less and less as the Civil War progressed. In 1864, the Union ceased prisoner exchanges all together in an attempt to bring the Confederacy down by attrition. Prisoner exchanges did nothing but bolster an army's ability to fight, and Union officials finally realized that every Confederate soldier in a POW camp was one less rifle aimed at Union soldiers. The policy had a devastating effect on the South, where manpower shortages were rampant. Unfortunately, many POWs also suffered greatly as a result of the no-exchange policy.

The conditions at POW camps varied greatly. At the beginning of the war, when prisoner exchanges helped keep prisons relatively empty, conditions were fairly good on both sides. Prisoners were usually well treated, well fed, and adequately clothed. This remained true for most prisons in the North throughout the war, but the conditions of POW camps in the South deteriorated greatly as the Confederacy gradually found itself unable to feed and clothe even its own citizens and soldiers. The Georgia prison known as Andersonville is probably best known for the squalid and barbaric conditions in which Northern prisoners were housed, but it wasn't alone. Most prison officials did their best to maintain humane conditions, but they had less and less to work with during the final year of the war.

THE END OF THE PRISONER EXCHANGE

The exchange of prisoners between the North and the South lasted about 10 months. The end of the program came when black soldiers started serving in the Union army. The Confederacy was outraged at what it perceived to be the arming of escaped slaves, and in May 1863, the Confederate congress declared that black soldiers—fugitive slaves or not—would be re-enslaved and that white officers commanding black units would be subject to execution.

Union officials demanded that black soldiers be recognized as legitimate prisoners of war and included in formal prisoner exchanges. When Confederate officials refused, the Union canceled the prisoner exchange program, causing POW camps to fill quickly. The Confederacy later altered its policy by promising that only actual runaway slaves would be returned to slavery, but the Union refused to budge. Ulysses S. Grant restated the Union position in an order given in April 1864: "No distinction whatever will be made in the exchange between white and colored prisoners."

Many people felt that Grant had an ulterior motive for ceasing prisoner exchanges, which was to damage the Confederate war machine by keeping as many Southern soldiers as possible from returning to the front. Sadly, prisoners on both sides suffered greatly as a result. Starving Northern prisoners in Andersonville, one of the South's worst POW camps, sent desperate petitions to Lincoln begging him to reinstate the exchange program. The president was also lobbied by clergymen, doctors, and others who realized the dire straits of soldiers being kept in Southern prisons. However, Lincoln understood well how keeping Confederate prisoners from returning to battle would damage the Southern war effort, and he refused to give in.

By January 1865, the Confederacy was so short handed on the battlefield that it seriously contemplated conscripting slaves. Eager to bolster its dwindling military ranks, the Confederate congress finally agreed to include black soldiers in prisoner exchanges, and the program was resumed. The war ended three months later.

ANDERSONVILLE

No prisoner of war camp was more reviled than the Confederate prison constructed near the village of Andersonville in Sumter County, Georgia. Its name has become synonymous with barbarism and ill treatment.

Andersonville was opened in February 1864, after the high number of Northern prisoners started taking a heavy toll on the food supplies in Richmond, where prisoners had previously been housed. When the first prisoners arrived at the new camp, they were greeted by 16 acres of open land surrounded by a 15-foot-tall stockade. Originally designed to house 10,000 men, the facility soon contained more than three times that number and was expanded to 26 acres. Nearly 400 new prisoners arrived each day, straining the prison's meager resources to the breaking point. Almost from the start, rations were scarce and of poor quality, and few prisoners had adequate shelter from the summer sun and the winter cold. The only fresh water was what trickled through Stockade Creek, a small stream that flowed through the prison yard into Sweet Water Creek. Waste was often dumped into the water, and downstream, it was used as a latrine for all prisoners. The entire region was soon contaminated, but prisoners continued to drink from it. Health care was nonexistent.

The first commander of Andersonville was John Henry Winder, who oversaw all Confederate prisons. Winder died from exhaustion in February 1865 and was succeeded by Henry Wirz, a Swiss-born Confederate officer known for his hatred of the Union. According to reports, Wirz did little to alleviate the suffering of his inmates, and the prison's increasingly poor conditions took a heavy toll—approximately 13,000 prisoners died there, a mortality rate of about 29 percent.

At the end of the war, Henry Wirz became the only Confederate officer to be tried and convicted for war crimes. Numerous prisoners who suffered under his sadistic command testified against him, as did Clara Barton, who was outraged when she visited the prison site at the war's end to identify the dead and missing and see that they received a proper burial. Wirz was held accountable for the conditions at Andersonville, found guilty, and summarily executed. In his own defense, Wirz stated that he simply didn't have food, clothing, or medical supplies to give the prisoners and that his own staff suffered equally as the Confederacy began to crumble.

The North also had its share of less than ideal facilities. Point Lookout in Maryland, for example, was designed to house 10,000 men in tents, but it often contained 20,000 or more. Fort Jefferson in the Dry Tortugas, off the Florida Keys, was another prison known for its brutal conditions. An old fort converted into a military prison in 1861, Fort Jefferson housed Union army criminals. (One of Fort Jefferson's most infamous residents was Dr. Samuel Mudd, the doctor who set John Wilkes Booth's broken leg following the assassination of Abraham Lincoln.) The tropical climate at Fort Jefferson was stifling, and the work conditions unmerciful. Worse, unsanitary conditions promoted the spread of disease among the prison population, killing many.

Probably the worst Union POW camp, however, was located in the town of Elmira in New York State. More than 2,960 Confederate soldiers died there—almost a quarter of the prison population. According to government records, the death rate at Elmira was only slightly less than that of Andersonville and more than double that of other Union prisons. The most common cause of death was disease exacerbated by starvation and filthy living conditions. Many prisoners, denied warm clothing or even blankets, froze to death during the harsh winter months. Those who survived the camp referred to it as "Hellmira." It remains an indelible black mark on the conduct of the Union army.

In contrast to the brutality and horrifying conditions of some POW camps in the North and South are numerous reports of gallantry and kindness at others. Officers, for the most part, were especially well treated on both sides. They occasionally dined with the commanding officers of the camp and were often given new uniforms (minus their military buttons) when exchanged. In one example of unexpected chivalry, Union General Benjamin Butler, who was not particularly well known for his generosity, went to astounding lengths to find a special horse belonging to Confederate cavalry brigadier William H. F. Lee, the son of Confederate General Robert E. Lee. The horse had been stolen during the younger Lee's capture in 1863.

CIVIL WAR FACTOID

At its height, the Confederate POW camp near Andersonville, Georgia, contained more than 33,000 Union prisoners, making it the fifth largest city in the Confederacy.

Clara Barton

Clara Barton is well known as the founder of the American Red Cross, but it was her remarkable humanitarian efforts during the Civil War that established her reputation as the "Angel of the Battlefield." However, Barton's contributions to American society go much farther. She was also an ardent feminist, the first female diplomat, and an important advocate of health and education reform, as well as civil rights.

Barton was born in Massachusetts on Christmas Day 1821. She worked first as a schoolteacher and later took a job as a clerk in the U.S. Patent Office in Washington, D.C. It was there that Barton saw the first casualties of the Civil War and witnessed the often inadequate medical treatment they received. She also observed how the wounded frequently went without sufficient food or clothing, a situation she considered unconscionable. Working independently of other relief agencies, Barton—who had no formal medical training—started lobbying to change the horrific conditions of battlefield medicine. One of her first acts was to call on friends in Congress to help improve the health standards within the U.S. military.

In July 1862, Barton received permission from the U.S. surgeon general to take needed medical supplies directly to the front lines and field hospitals. She risked her life to help the soldiers on the front and made appearances during or immediately following a number of important battles, including Cedar Creek, Second Bull Run, Antietam, and Fredericksburg. She also provided medical aid during the Carolinas campaign and in Virginia during Grant's 1864 offensives, where she was granted an official position with the Army of the James under the command of General Benjamin Butler. At each stop, Barton prepared hot meals for the troops, helped army surgeons in their grisly duty, and assisted emergency medical procedures when there was no one else available.

As the war began to wind down, Barton was given a nearly overwhelming task by President Lincoln. He asked her to oversee the search for missing and captured Union soldiers, compile lists of the sick and wounded, and identify the Union dead buried in mass graves at Andersonville Prison and elsewhere. The endeavor took Barton four long years to complete, but her efforts went a long way toward ensuring that Union soldiers who died on the battlefield and in prison were given decent burials and, more importantly, were remembered for their sacrifice.

BATTLEFIELD MEDICINE

Medicine was still in its infancy during the Civil War, and the wounded and ill paid a horrible price for this lack of knowledge. Ironically, a number of important medical advances were made in the years immediately following the war, but they proved of little use to the poor wretches who found themselves under a battlefield doctor's care. In the eyes of many, those who died in battle were luckier than those who were wounded.

The Minie ball and other bullets and shells used during the Civil War wreaked havoc on the human body. In fact, head and gut wounds caused by Minie balls were almost always fatal. The treatment of choice for broken or lacerated limbs was immediate amputation. The majority of patients were anesthetized with chloroform, ether, nitrous oxide, or, at the very least, a glass of whiskey. When anesthesia was unavailable, a cloth or bullet was placed in the patient's mouth for him to bite on, and he was held down by several strong orderlies while the doctor attended to the damaged limb with a knife and saw. Field doctors quickly became adept at removing limbs with remarkable speed; many could amputate a leg in less than two minutes. But it was never fast enough for the poor patient, whose screams could be heard by all in the "waiting room." Following large battles with heavy casualties, doctors often worked nonstop for hours, tending to a seemingly endless stream of injured soldiers. Field hospital observers reported the all too common and grisly scene of severed limbs stacked like cordwood beside the operating table, waiting to be disposed of.

Amputation was only the beginning of a wounded soldier's troubles. If he survived the operation, he would then be transported via ambulance (usually nothing more than a rickety, overcrowded two-wheeled cart or four-wheeled wagon) to the closest army or city hospital. Though his wounds had been treated, chances were better than good that he would soon fall victim to infection or, worse, gangrene. Doctors in the mid-1800s had little understanding of the cause of infection; many thought it was the result of contaminated air, so they seldom did more to clean their surgical tools than wipe them off on a filthy apron before tending to the next patient. Many times, battlefield surgery was done in the open, with a door or wood plank serving as a table and tubs beneath to catch the blood.

PRISONER EXCHANGES

Following the fall of Vicksburg in 1863, General Ulysses S. Grant paroled 31,000 Confederate soldiers rather than go through the chore of sending them all to prison camps in the North. However, many of the Southern soldiers failed to live up to their parole promise and, much to Grant's chagrin, were captured again while fighting in Chattanooga. After taking command of all the Union armies, Grant ordered an end to prisoner exchanges until Confederate officials agreed to honor a one-for-one exchange.

WAR DOCTORS

One of the biggest medical problems during the Civil War was the inadequate training received by most doctors. Just prior to the war, the majority of physicians served as apprentices rather than attending medical school, which meant that many were woefully unprepared for what they encountered on the battlefield.

Even the doctors who attended the few medical schools in the United States at the time received a less than satisfactory education. In Europe, four-year medical schools were fairly common, and students received a great deal of laboratory training. As a result, European physicians had a far better understanding of the causes and treatments of disease and infection. By comparison, students in American medical schools trained for less than two years and received almost no clinical experience and very little laboratory instruction. Amazingly, Harvard University—one of the nation's finest universities—didn't own a single stethoscope or microscope until after the war.

At its onset, the Union army was surprised and shocked by the huge number of casualties the war produced. The federal army had fewer than 100 medical officers at the start of the conflict, and the Confederacy had only 24. By 1865, however, more than 13,000 Union doctors had served in the field and in hospitals. In the Confederacy, approximately 4,000 medical officers and a great many volunteers tended to the wounded. Doctors—almost all of whom were male—were assisted by a large force of volunteer nurses, who gave freely of their time. According to government records, approximately 4,000 women served as nurses in Union hospitals. The number of Southern women who acted as nurses in Confederate hospitals is unknown but believed to be almost as high.

Despite their lack of training and the horrible conditions under which they often worked, Civil War doctors did an astounding job of caring for the sick and wounded. More than 10 million cases of injury and disease were treated in just 48 months, and for the most part, doctors were compassionate and caring individuals who tried to put the concerns of their patients first.

As horrible as Civil War surgery was, it was often amazingly successful in saving a wounded soldier's life. According to U.S. Army records, of nearly 29,000 amputations performed during the war, only 7,000 or so patients died as a result. The most successful were those surgeries performed within 48 hours of injury; wounds tended later than that had a much poorer prognosis. The type of amputation also played a role; the smaller the limb, the less likely the chance of death. For example, of more than 8,000 finger amputations performed over the course of the war, fewer than 200 patients died. The deadliest type of amputation was that of the thigh; more than half of the patients receiving this procedure died within days, usually from massive blood loss and overwhelming infection.

AFRICAN-AMERICAN PARTICIPATION IN THE CIVIL WAR

A large number of black men saw battle during the Civil War—fighting for both the North and, as amazing as it sounds, the South. Bringing blacks into the military was an extraordinarily difficult task, but when they finally received their uniforms and guns, most proved to be exceptionally brave and skilled soldiers.

One might assume that the North would be eager to add black soldiers to its ranks, but such was the not the case. Even though blacks were free in the Northern states, they still faced a tremendous amount of prejudice and bigotry. Many white Northerners secretly—and some not so secretly—disliked blacks. They feared freed slaves would take jobs away from white laborers and drive down wages. Indeed, racial prejudice raised its ugly head in the North numerous times during the war years, and there were several violent and murderous race riots in 1862–63. These riots

Dorothea Dix

Dorothea Dix was a nurse of great renown during the Civil War. Prior to the war, Dix had fought to improve the treatment of the mentally ill and the conditions within the nation's prisons. When Fort Sumter was attacked in April 1861, the 59-year-old Dix volunteered her services to the Union, and was placed in charge of all female nurses working in army hospitals, a job she held for the duration of the war and for which she received no salary.

One of Dix's biggest jobs was convincing military officials that women could be competent nurses. To ensure that she would not be overwhelmed with young women who only wanted to find a husband, Dix accepted only women who were plain looking and over 30 years old. Those who were chosen were required to wear simple black or brown skirts and were forbidden to wear jewelry. Despite these restrictions, Dix successfully recruited more than three thousand women to serve as Union army nurses.

were sparked primarily by job competition but also by the fear that the emancipation promised by the Civil War would drastically alter everything they knew and held dear. There was a lot of talk in the North about the importance of abolition, and many people fought for it with their very souls, but bigotry still ran rampant.

Many Northerners were reluctant to advocate the enlistment of blacks because it was commonly believed that black people had been held in servitude for so long that they were too cowardly to make good soldiers. Of course, this was false, as evidenced by the fighting skill and bravery of the black regiments that were later formed, but many high-ranking politicians and military officials believed it. Even Abraham Lincoln, a strong advocate of abolition, felt the concept had merit. When a delegation from Indiana offered Lincoln two regiments of black men to aid the Union effort, Lincoln told them, "If we were to arm [the Negroes], I fear that in a few weeks the arms would be in the hands of the rebels." Lincoln also feared that recruiting black soldiers would turn those border states with strong Confederate sympathies against the Union, something he was loath to do.

Not all Union officers believed that blacks were inferior soldiers. Several officers, in defiance of the government, tried to enlist black men. General David Hunter, for example, organized a regiment of black soldiers on the South Carolina Sea Islands in 1862, but the War Department refused to sanction the regiment, and Hunter was eventually forced to disband all but one company. In Kansas, General James Lane successfully raised two regiments composed of fugitive slaves from Missouri and free blacks from the North. Lane's African-American soldiers were not officially recognized by the U.S. War Department until the early months of 1863, though they participated in several battles against Confederate sympathizers in Kansas and Missouri. And in New Orleans, General Benjamin Butler initially turned down a regiment of black soldiers who offered their services following the Union conquest of the city. However, Butler quickly changed his mind and recruited three regiments of black soldiers when he was threatened by a sizable Confederate attack in August 1862.

Sentiments regarding the recruitment of black soldiers slowly changed in the summer of 1862 as the North experienced a number of defeats and morale began to plunge. People were growing weary of the war, and the number of able-bodied white men who enlisted for military service saw a noticeable decline. This forced the government to seriously consider the idea of black recruitment, and in July 1862, Congress passed two acts that opened the door. The first was the Confiscation Act, which gave the president power to "employ as many persons of African descent as he may deem necessary and proper for the suppression of this rebellion." The second was an act that repealed the provisions of an 1792 law barring black men from joining a militia and authorized the active recruitment of free blacks as Union soldiers.

The passage of the two acts did little to quell Northern opposition to the recruitment of African-American soldiers, but on August 25, 1862, General Rufus Saxton, military governor of the South Carolina Sea Islands was authorized by the War Department to raise five regiments of black soldiers, to be commanded by white officers. Area blacks were somewhat reluctant to sign up at first, but the regiment, known as the First South Carolina Volunteers, was nearly filled by November. Several other regiments of African-American soldiers followed, all commanded by white officers. Aiding the recruitment effort were prominent Northern black leaders, who did all they could to rally their brothers and encourage them to sign up in support of their rights as free citizens.

It took tremendous courage for black men to join the Union army. Despite promises from the government, most knew that taking up arms against the Confederacy—where many had previously been held in bondage—placed them in tremendous jeopardy. Southern soldiers were more likely to kill black soldiers than take them prisoner, and those who were captured risked execution or being resold into slavery. The risks were high for the white commanders of black regiments as well. In May 1863, the Confederate congress authorized President Jefferson Davis to have captured officers of black regiments put to death or otherwise severely punished. History has shown that few white leaders of African-American regiments suffered at the hands of Confederate captors (though many died in battle with their troops), but there are several

> **CIVIL WAR FACTOID**
>
> An estimated 200,000 blacks served in the Union army over the course of the Civil War, and more than 37,000 perished in battle.

well-documented accounts of black POWs being horribly mistreated and even slaughtered by Southern soldiers.

Despite these concerns, black regiments for the most part fought well and with exceptional bravery, often in the face of overwhelming odds. During the Battle of Port Hudson, a heavily fortified Confederate stronghold on the lower Mississippi, two regiments of black soldiers fought for all they were worth in the face of blistering rifle and cannon fire. The attack failed, but the troops demonstrated incredible heroism as they fought across open ground. Noted General Nathaniel Banks in his official report of the battle: "Whatever doubt may have existed heretofore as to the efficiency of organizations of this character, the history of this day proves conclusively to those who were in a condition to observe the conduct of these regiments, that the Government will find in this class of troops effective supporters and defenders. The severe test to which they were subjected, and the determined manner in which they encountered the enemy, leaves upon my mind no doubt of their ultimate success."

Equally brave was the 54th Massachusetts, a black regiment commanded by Colonel Robert Gould Shaw. The regiment was decimated by Confederate fire while leading a Union assault on Battery Wagner, a fort protecting the entrance to Charleston, South Carolina, in July 1863. Sergeant William Carney became the first African-American to win the Congressional Medal of Honor as a result of his bravery in that ill-fated charge, though he didn't receive the honor until 1901. In fact, 23 black soldiers received the Congressional Medal of Honor for their bravery and service in the Civil War.

Black soldiers played an increasingly important role during the final year of the Civil War. Recruitment proved very successful, and by October 1864, there were 140 black regiments in the Union army containing a total of 101,950 men. Fifteen African-American regiments served in the Army of the James and 23 in the Army of the Potomac during the Union invasion of Virginia in the summer of 1864. In fact, black troops participated in every major military campaign in 1864–65 except William Sherman's invasion of Georgia and the Carolinas.

Blacks also served in the Confederate Army, especially during the latter part of the war, when fighting men were in desperately

THE 54TH MASSACHUSETTS REGIMENT

The 54th Massachusetts, made famous in the motion picture *Glory*, was one of the most distinguished black regiments to see combat in the Civil War. The regiment was organized by John Andrew, the abolitionist governor of Massachusetts, immediately following the Emancipation Proclamation, and was composed of 650 African-Americans from a number of Northern states.

Andrew was careful to make sure that all of the white officers in charge of the 54th Massachusetts were firm believers in black civil rights. Its commanding officer, Colonel Robert Gould Shaw, came from a vocal abolitionist Massachusetts family, and he worked hard to ensure that the men under his command were well trained and ready to fight.

After their training was complete, the 54th Massachusetts was assigned to the Department of the South and sent to the South Carolina coast in May 1863. Major General Quincy Gillmore had devised a very risky plan to take back Fort Sumter and capture Charleston. The biggest obstacle was Battery Wagner on the southern tip of Morris Island, which stood a little more

than a mile from Fort Sumter. The battery was small and fairly isolated, but it was well defended with 1,200 troops and much heavy artillery.

Gillmore successfully established a beachhead on the island on July 10, but the fort remained secure. Union forces bombarded the facility with cannon for almost a week, then Gillmore ordered a second assault by 6,000 infantry—with the 54th Massachusetts leading the way. The regiment fought a bloody hand-to-hand battle atop a palmetto parapet before being pushed back. Colonel Shaw was killed by a bullet through the heart, and nearly 40 percent of his regiment was slaughtered in the failed assault. The bodies of the dead, including Shaw, were buried on the beach in a mass grave.

Despite the failure of the assault on Battery Wagner, the noble efforts of the 54th Massachusetts contributed greatly to bolstering the image of black soldiers. The regiment's surviving members, under the command of Colonel Edward Hallowel, stayed in South Carolina for another year, then returned home to a hero's celebration.

short supply. Southern Negroes volunteered for a number of reasons. Some hoped that by volunteering, they would receive better treatment; others felt it was better to volunteer than to be forced into military service. And more than a few hoped that by fighting side by side with white soldiers, they could finally put to rest the common belief that blacks were inferior to whites.

But though the South needed the black soldier, its leaders felt that blacks couldn't be trusted, and most were treated just as harshly in the military as they had been while working on farms and plantations. Many Southern states enacted legislation that essentially kept freed blacks in bondage and prevented those still in servitude from tasting freedom. Black soldiers were untrustworthy, the Confederate thinking went, and if given the opportunity, they would almost certainly flee to the Union side.

Most free blacks and slaves pressed into Confederate military service were used as laborers, harvesting food and cotton and constructing fortifications and entrenchments. Some laborers, however, found themselves suddenly "recruited" as soldiers in the thick of battle, when the Southern army needed more armed bodies. Not surprisingly, a large number of blacks who found themselves in such a position deserted to Union lines the very first chance they got. Runaway slaves came to be known as "contraband," and in August 1861, the U.S. Congress passed a confiscation act that allowed the seizure of all property used to aid the Southern rebellion—including slaves who had worked on Confederate fortifications or other military efforts. The act did not emancipate runaway slaves, but it did go a long way toward making emancipation a reality.

ETHNIC MAKEUP OF THE CIVIL WAR

Soldiers from a wide variety of ethnic backgrounds participated in the Civil War. Of the approximately two million Union soldiers, nearly a quarter were foreign born. Approximately 175,000 were German, 150,000 were Irish, and 50,000 were English or Canadian. Native Americans also fought on both sides, as did a number of Hispanics and Scandinavians, as well as other nationalities. Immigration continued almost unabated in the North throughout the war, and many newcomers from foreign lands showed their gratitude by joining the Union army within months of their arrival.

Irish Americans, in particular, played an integral role in the war. The nation had seen an immigration boom between the 1830s and the 1850s, and New York and Boston both contained large Irish enclaves. According to the 1860 census, more than 1.5 million Americans claimed to be from Ireland. The number of soldiers of Irish descent in the Union army is well verified, but statistics regarding the Confederacy are almost unknown. Still, Southern songs of the era suggest a strong regional Irish influence. In the Union, some of the most notable regiments were Irish, such as Thomas Meagher's Irish Brigade, which went into battle with a green flag containing a large golden harp in its center.

The nation experienced severe economic problems prior to and following the war, and the Irish, in particular, were singled out for distrust and harassment. Many factories and businesses refused to hire people with Irish names, and placards reading "No Irish Need Apply" could be found in most large cities. One reason for this prejudice was that most Irish were Catholic, and there was growing opposition to the Catholic Church in the United States at that time. In July 1863, draft riots broke out in several large cities, and many of the troublemakers were Irish laborers who were frustrated over their inability to find work. They took out their wrath on draft officials as well as free blacks living and working in the North, a situation that didn't help their cause. After the war, many Irish veterans returned home to face the same bigotry and biases that had hounded them prior to military service.

A large number of Germans also immigrated to the United States in the decades preceding the war, and most of those who ended up in military service fought for the Union. Most German immigrants (as well as Austrians and Dutch) made their homes in areas that reminded them of their homeland, places such as Pennsylvania, Delaware, and Virginia. When the war broke out, they enlisted without hesitation, and

many German Americans rose to positions of great importance within the Union army. Carl Schurz, for example, became a confidante to Abraham Lincoln, who appointed him as minister to Spain. Schurz also served as an officer in the 11th Corps, which featured several German regiments. A number of German Americans also served in the Confederate army, including Major Johann August Heinrich Heros Von Borcke, who rose through the ranks to become an invaluable aide to Jeb Stuart.

Scandinavian Americans served primarily in the Union army because the vast majority of them had settled in the Northern states. In addition, most Swedes, Norwegians, and Danes were opposed to slavery and felt that they simply couldn't support a nation that promoted such an institution. In fact, a thorough genealogical search has uncovered fewer than 20 Confederate soldiers who were known to be of Scandinavian descent. Almost all others living in the Southern states at the time of the war were Union sympathizers.

A large percentage of the Scandinavian Americans who fought for the Union joined the navy. One of the most prominent was John Ericsson, a Swede who invented the propeller and designed the first Union ironclad ship, the *Monitor*. Two members of the *Monitor*'s crew, assistant engineer M. P. Sunstrum and seaman Hans Anderson, were also Swedish. Admiral John Adolph Dahlgren, the son of a Swedish immigrant, gained fame as the inventor of an artillery piece known as the Dahlgren Gun.

The participation of Native Americans in the Civil War cannot be overlooked. The war years were difficult for these indigenous people, most of whom were struggling for their own independence and autonomy. Some tribes, such as the Cherokee, participated directly in the war; others, especially those in the East, decided on an individual basis whether to get involved. In the West and elsewhere, many tribes realized that the war offered an opportunity for them to reclaim lands that had been taken from them, because it meant fewer federal soldiers overseeing their territories.

According to government records, approximately 3,600 Native Americans served in the Union army during the war. One of the

best known was Colonel Ely Parker, a Seneca who served as an aide to Ulysses S. Grant and held the unique distinction of transcribing the terms of Lee's surrender at Appomattox Court House. Statistics regarding Native American participation on the Confederate side are unavailable, but it is known that many did serve the Southern cause. Probably the best known is Brigadier General Chief Stand Watie, a three-quarter blood Cherokee who organized a regiment known as the First Cherokee Mounted Rifles. Watie and his men fought bravely in a number of battles, and Watie has the distinction of being the last Confederate officer to lay down arms—more than two months after Lee's surrender.

As Union forces did their best to defeat the Confederacy, they also found themselves battling various Native American tribes. According to government records, more than 90 engagements were fought by federal troops in the West during the war, most of them involving Native Americans. From January to May 1863, for example, there was almost continuous fighting in the New Mexico Territory as the government tried to control the Apache. There was also fighting against Native Americans in Minnesota in July 1864. Conflict with various Native American tribes continued long after the end of the Civil War.

CHRONICLING THE CIVIL WAR

The Civil War was one of the first wars to be extensively covered in the press on both sides. Newspaper and magazine journalists from the North, the South, and overseas were given amazing freedom to follow armies, observe battles, and talk with commanders. The resulting stories—while often showing a decided bias—have helped historians understand exactly what happened during the war and why.

Newspapers and magazines reported the war in two ways: through on-site coverage of battles and other important events and through editorials stating the publication's position on a particular subject. In the North, the majority of newspapers, but not all, shared the abolitionist sentiment expressed by the government.

PHOTOGRAPHY

Though a relatively new art form, photography helped put a human face on warfare for the very first time. People on the homefront were confronted with hundreds of images of war's inevitable death and destruction.

Mathew Brady is probably the most renowned photographer of the Civil War. Other famous photographers include George Barnard, Alexander and James Gardner, George Cook, and Timothy O'Sullivan.

Studio photographers, in cities and towns across the nation, captured the many emotions of families who found themselves thrown into conflict. Understandably, photographs of family and friends were cherished mementos among soldiers in the field.

Mathew Brady

Mathew Brady has been called the father of contemporary photojournalism, and with good reason; the photographs taken by him and his staff chronicled for the first time a war in progress and placed a human face on the horrible consequences of warfare.

Before discovering photography, Brady worked as a painter and a craftsman of jewelry boxes. His life changed, however, when he started experimenting with the daguerreotype photographic process, which was still in its infancy. He opened a portrait studio in New York in 1844, found great success photographing celebrities of the era, and opened a second studio in Washington, D.C., in 1858.

By the time the Civil War started, Brady was using a new wet-plate photographic process. Its mobility, he realized, would allow photographers to document the conflict at the scene, and he turned his back on studio portraits to follow Union troops, starting with the First Battle of Bull Run. Brady's photography wagon, which went with him to the battlefield, was a marvel. He started calling it his "What-is-it-wagon" because that's what people would ask wherever he went. Soon Brady and his staff became well known, and soldiers realized that at least one photographer would probably be present at every major battle.

The photographic process was extremely slow, and exposures were typically long, which explains why there are very few actual battle scenes—moving bodies photographed simply as blurs. Brady's cameras were set up next to his black wagon and aimed at the scene or persons to be photographed. An assistant would bring out a special 8-by-10-inch glass plate that had been stored in a dust-proof box and cleaned immediately before use. The plate would be inserted into the camera, exposed, then rushed into the wagon for development.

During this period, Brady's eyesight began to fail, so he hired a staff of photographers to continue his work. Few, however, received the credit due them, and Brady's name appeared on many photographs that he did not shoot. Several of the photographers under Brady's employ eventually went off on their own, seeking fame and fortune by covering the war for newspapers, magazines, and historical archives.

Brady and his staff managed to produce more than 3,500 photographs covering nearly every aspect of the war, including camp life, military portraits, and scenes of the aftermath of battle. Brady realized the importance of composition in a photograph and encouraged his staff to pose live soldiers as if they were going off to battle and to rearrange corpses for better visual effect.

Some papers sympathized with the Confederate cause and stated so vociferously. In the South, the vast majority of papers were proslavery and anti-Union. But again, there was a small number of dissenting voices. As might be expected, those who went against the common sentiment on either side risked retribution from angry mobs, and it was the brave publisher who continued to express an unpopular position in the face of overwhelming public opinion.

Modern newspapers frequently carry blistering attacks on public officials and government policy, and such was the case during the Civil War as well. Abraham Lincoln and Jefferson Davis were often pilloried in the press for their actions and policies, and their military leaders also found themselves subject to ridicule and attack, especially when they didn't win. Indeed, military success always seemed to play a role in whether the government was perceived positively or negatively. When things were going badly for the Union, for example, Lincoln was a scoundrel in the eyes of editorial-writing armchair quarterbacks. But when the Union started winning some decisive victories and it appeared that the Confederacy might crumble after all, Lincoln was suddenly a savior. Both Lincoln and Davis learned not to get into fights with men who bought ink by the barrel, yet the frequent editorial condemnation of their actions and policies disturbed them both.

As with combat journalists today, reporters covering field action risked their lives to get the story. Daily newspapers and weekly news magazines such as *Harper's Weekly* and *Leslie's* sent reporters, photographers, and artists out by the dozens to cover the action, and many lost their lives in the process. Photography was still in its infancy, so most newspapers and magazines relied on sketch artists to capture the essence of a particular event or scene in a drawing, which would be used to illustrate the reporters' words. It wasn't uncommon for artists to sit on hills overlooking violent battles, sketching as fast as they could, with the intent of fleshing out their illustrations afterward. Others captured the action in army camps, aboard ambulances, in hospitals, and on the streets. Afterward, the artists' sketches were redrawn on wood blocks for mass reproduction, though most engravers were unable to capture the energy and sheer power of the original artwork.

PRESS COVERAGE

The Civil War was covered at every angle by a literal army of journalists, artists, and photographers—nearly 500 by some estimates. So thorough was media coverage of the conflict that opposing generals sometimes learned more from enemy newspapers than from spy reports.

William T. Sherman, who found himself the frequent subject of journalistic ridicule, was not a fan of the press. He once noted: "Reporters print their limited and tainted observations as the history of events they neither see nor comprehend." Others, however, avidly followed the war in their favorite newspapers.

Thanks to these unsung heroes, no aspect of the Civil War was left unexamined and our understanding of this very unique conflict is probably better than in any previous American war.

ESPIONAGE DURING THE CIVIL WAR

Espionage has played an integral role in almost every war ever fought, and the Civil War was certainly no exception. Both sides had more than their share of spies—many of whom became both famous and infamous—as well as unique espionage technology. While glamorous in the eyes of many, spying was an extremely dangerous endeavor; if caught, a spy risked a lengthy prison term or death by hanging. Yet there was a constant stream of willing participants.

Both the North and the South had a network of spies in enemy territory whose job was to ferret out information on battle plans, the number of forces, as well as other information. Some spies were more effective than others. Rose O'Neal Greenhow, for example, was a member of Washington society, a friend of numerous Northern politicians—and a Confederate spy. She sent information on Union plans to Confederate military leaders via coded messages transported by women on horseback.

Even more famous was Confederate spy Belle Boyd, the Mata Hari of her time. According to lore, Boyd decided to become a spy for the Confederacy at age 17, after Union soldiers ransacked her family's Virginia home. Boyd operated from a Front Royal hotel owned by her father, and was especially helpful during Stonewall Jackson's Shenandoah Valley campaign in the spring of 1862. She provided important information regarding the movement of Union troops, as well as other secrets she managed to extract from Union officers by using her feminine wiles. Boyd delivered her reports via bold nighttime rides through enemy territory. She proved so helpful to the Confederate cause that Jackson named her an honorary aide-de-camp, and she became known throughout the South as "La Belle Rebelle."

Boyd eventually came to the attention of authorities in Washington and was arrested at least six times. In June 1862, Boyd was placed in a Washington jail after being betrayed by one of her lovers, but she continued to aid the Confederacy by tossing rubber balls containing detailed notes from her jail cell window to an operative on the street below. Boyd was released in a prisoner exchange after four weeks of incarceration but found herself behind bars yet again the following year, this time for five months. Boyd was released in December 1863 after contracting typhoid fever; she immediately went to Europe. She told people she was traveling abroad to recuperate from her illness, but in fact, she was delivering letters from Jefferson Davis to the British government.

Boyd tried to return to the South aboard a Confederate blockade runner, but the boat was stopped by a Union ship. The vessel's captain, Samuel Hardringe, fell in love with Boyd and helped her escape to Canada. They later married in England, but Hardringe, who had resigned his commission in the Union navy, died shortly after. When the war ended, Boyd published her autobiography and spent several decades entertaining lecture audiences in both the North and the South with tales of her adventures as a war spy. Belle Boyd died in 1900 while on tour.

Boyd's Union counterpart was Elizabeth Van Lew, a prominent Richmond citizen who loathed slavery and vowed to fight it in any way she could. She often lectured her neighbors on the evils of slavery, but her demeanor was mistaken for flightiness, and she was given the nickname "Crazy Bet." However, Van Lew was anything but crazy. She used her reputation as an eccentric to hide the many plans and schemes she concocted to aid the Union war effort from within Richmond, and she succeeded grandly.

Van Lew's first spy mission brought her to Libby Prison, a facility in downtown Richmond used to house Union POWs. She managed to get by the guards under the guise of bringing food, medicine, and books to the prisoners and came away with a wealth of information regarding Confederate troop movements and numbers. Van Lew visited the prison several times and even helped a number of prisoners escape. The prison personnel had no idea she was a spy; in fact, the guards and even the camp commandant, Lieutenant David Todd, provided Van Lew with invaluable information, which they unwittingly offered during friendly conversations. She was so crafty that she even infiltrated the home of Confederate

PROSTITUTION

Prostitution became a flourishing enterprise during the Civil War. Just one year after the war began, Washington, D.C., was home to more than 450 bordellos and an estimated 7,500 full-time prostitutes. The Confederate capital of Richmond boasted an equal number.

President Jefferson Davis by convincing one of her former servants to get a job on Davis's household staff.

Van Lew used a variety of means to send the information she gathered to federal authorities. In the beginning, she sent it by regular mail. But fear of discovery forced her to resort to more ingenious methods of acquisition and delivery. For example, she developed a code involving words and letters that prisoners would underline in the books she lent them. She also sent former servants into Northern territories carrying baskets of farm produce. Each basket contained eggs, many of which held coded messages in place of the yolk and white. Van Lew's courier system was fast and efficient; in fact, General Grant often received fresh flowers from Van Lew's garden via courier.

Following the war, President Grant showed his appreciation for Van Lew's services by making her postmistress of the Richmond post office, an office she held from 1869 to 1877. But while Van Lew was a hero to the North, her reputation was forever tarnished in the South, and she had few friends. "No one will walk with us on the street," she once noted. "No one will go with us anywhere; and it grows worse and worse as the years roll on." Van Lew died in 1900.

Yet another femme fatale was actress Pauline Cushman, a Unionist who gained the confidence of Southern officials by toasting the Confederacy from the stage following a performance in Kentucky. Cushman was eventually revealed to be a Union spy and was sentenced to death. However, the Confederacy crumbled before the sentence could be carried out, and Cushman was abandoned by her captors. Like Belle Boyd, she spent many years following the war entertaining audiences with stories of her daring activities.

WOMEN AND CHILDREN ON THE BATTLEFIELD

Contrary to popular belief, the Civil War was not fought only by adult males. Women and children also participated in the conflict in a variety of capacities, often giving their lives for a cause they deeply believed in.

Many women did their part by traveling with soldiers as members of the so-called "soapsuds brigade," whose sole job was to clean the clothes of military units. It was a difficult, physically challenging job, but the soldiers deeply appreciated and respected the women who kept them in clean uniforms. In most cases, members of the "soapsuds brigade" were the only women given official status in camp. Others, including officers' wives, were simply labeled "camp followers." In the Union army, each company was permitted four laundresses. Many washerwomen were married to soldiers and lived with their husbands in the area of camp commonly known as "suds row." If not married to a soldier, washerwomen were expected to be at least somehow related to a member of the unit. A washerwoman named Hannah O'Neil, for example, followed her son, who was a member of Company H of the 1st Minnesota Volunteer Infantry.

Far more rare were women who followed their loved ones into battle as more than washerwomen. A few military units "adopted" women as mascots or aides, and these women faced the same dangers as the male soldiers. One example is Kady Brownell, who was married to a member of the 1st Rhode Island (later the 5th Rhode Island). Brownell was made the official "daughter" of the regiment and followed her husband to the front. According to some accounts, Brownell showed tremendous heroism during a battle in New Berne, North Carolina, on March 14, 1862, when she saved the 5th Rhode Island from a friendly fire attack by rushing into the thick of battle and waving the flag. Brownell's husband was seriously wounded during that battle, and she spent the rest of her life caring for him.

Rarer still—but more common than many historians originally believed—were women who disguised their gender in order to enlist and fight at the front on equal standing with male soldiers. Pulling off such a feat was not easy, but many women did so successfully, slipping through the enlistment process and fooling their fellow soldiers for months and even years. The majority of women who are known to have done this fought with the same bravery and zeal as their male counterparts. Those exposed

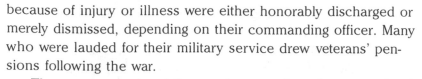

because of injury or illness were either honorably discharged or merely dismissed, depending on their commanding officer. Many who were lauded for their military service drew veterans' pensions following the war.

These women entered the war for a number of reasons. Sarah Emma Edmonds, for example, fled Canada to avoid an arranged marriage. She passed herself off as a male bookseller for a brief period, then enlisted in the Union army under the name Frank Thompson. Edmonds served in the 2nd Michigan Infantry until a bout of malaria threatened to expose her secret. She deserted her unit but was legally cleared years later, after she had wed and become a mother.

Jennie Hodgers was another famous imposter. She left Ireland as a stowaway, disguised herself as "Albert D. J. Cashier," and eventually saw service in the Illinois Volunteer Infantry, in which she served from 1862 to 1865. No one ever suspected that "Cashier" was really a woman, and Hodgers successfully kept her secret until age 66, when she was struck by a car. A doctor at the veterans' hospital where she was treated discovered her true gender, but he kept it secret at Hodgers's request so that she could continue to receive the veteran's pension to which she was entitled.

Probably the most amazing tale of hidden identity was that of Loreta Janeta Velazquez, the Cuban-born widow of a Confederate soldier, who raised and equipped at her own expense an infantry unit known as the Arkansas Grays. After her husband's death during the early months of the war, Velazquez left her home in Louisiana in search of adventure and found it serving in the Confederate army. She designed a unique wire shield to hide her breasts and passed herself off as Harry Buford. Velazquez traveled to Arkansas, where she was fairly sure she wouldn't be recognized, and enlisted recruits for her own unit.

She got her first taste of war at the First Battle of Bull Run, where she fought with bravery. She later served in Kentucky and Tennessee and was twice wounded and cited for gallantry. Velazquez was eventually stationed in Richmond, where her secret

was discovered. Arrested as a spy, she convinced Confederate officials of her allegiance to the South and began work as a secret agent. After the war, she wrote her autobiography. In that volume, she made a statement that applied to many other women who had seen battle disguised as men: "Notwithstanding the fact that I was a woman, I was as good a soldier as any man around me, and as willing as any to fight valiantly and to the bitter end before yielding."

Children—that is, boys under the age of 18—also saw quite a bit of military service. Many lied about their age when enlisting; others were adopted as mascots by various military units. The exact number of underage soldiers is unknown, but some historians say the figure could be as high as four hundred thousand. Many children were able to slip into the armed forces because recruiters were eager to fill quotas and usually didn't question boys who at looked at least 18 years old. However, even boys who were obviously underage succeeding in getting in; many were assigned as regimental musicians.

Probably the most famous child to participate in the war is Johnny Clem, who became a legend in the Northern press. Clem ran away from home in 1861 at age nine to join a Union army regiment that had traveled through his hometown in Ohio. He was turned away but later joined another unit and served as its drummer boy; he also performed other camp chores. The soldiers took a liking to Clem and chipped in to pay him a proper soldier's wage—$13 a month.

Clem was first immortalized in the press following the Battle of Shiloh in April 1862, during which his drum was apparently destroyed. The Union press started referring to Clem as "Johnny Shiloh" and identified him as the subject of a popular song and stage play. Officially enrolled in the army, complete with a miniature, hand-carved musket, Clem received additional press coverage as "The Drummer Boy of Chickamauga." During that battle, Clem allegedly shot and captured a Confederate soldier who tried to take him prisoner. Whether the story is true or not remains uncertain, but it helped make Clem a national hero.

BOYS AT WAR

A review of enlistment records suggests that between 10 and 20 percent of enlistees were underage. Many boys placed a piece of paper with the number 18 in their shoe so that they could state with a clear conscience that they were "over 18." According to U.S. military records, 127 Union soldiers were just 13 years old when they enlisted, 320 were 14 years old, nearly 800 were 15 years old, 2,758 were 16, and approximately 6,500 were 17. Statistics regarding the number of underage soldiers in the Confederate army are unknown, but most historians believe the numbers to be even higher.

Drummer Boy Johnny Clem

Despite his young age, Clem was captured once and wounded twice over the course of the war and rose to the rank of lance sergeant before his 14th birthday. A few years later, Clem tried to enroll in West Point but was denied admission because he lacked a formal education. As a result of a direct appeal from President Grant, he was then given a commission as second lieutenant and placed in command of a unit of black soldiers. He made the military his life career, retiring as a major general shortly before the start of World War I. Clem died in 1937.

Family Life During the Civil War

The Civil War was an all-encompassing event that touched the lives of almost every American. Whether you lived in the backwoods of Kentucky or a thriving eastern metropolis such as New York City, the effects of the war were pervasive and inescapable.

An astounding number of families on both sides of the conflict watched fathers, sons, and neighbors march off to battle, and many grieved when their loved ones and friends did not return. But even those families who didn't have members actively fighting in the war still felt its influence in myriad ways—raging battles only miles away, participation in the manufacture of products for the war machine, raucous debates over the causes of the conflict, or the pinch of increasingly higher taxes as the governments of the North and South struggled to finance their individual efforts. All Americans, whether Union or Confederate by sentiment, experienced the war every moment of every day.

Yet, while battles raged and lives were lost by the tens of thousands, life continued in relative normalcy for those outside its direct sphere of influence. Machinists worked, farmers tended their land, and families did their best to enjoy the simple pleasures. People went to plays and concerts, participated in sports such as baseball, entertained one another with fine parties and casual picnics, and lived each day in the desperate hope that night would fall without the bearing of bad news. Some families were luckier than others.

The Civil War is the largest military event ever fought on American soil, and the heaviest fighting occurred in the Southern states. Maintaining a semblance of normal daily living was much more difficult there than in the Northern states, which, for the most part, managed to get through the war without experiencing the devastating ravages of battle. Those living in the Confederacy were hopeful at the beginning that the war would be over quickly, that the Union would accept their proclamation of independence, and that they would soon be free to live their lives as they so wished. History, of course, shows that this was not the case. The war fell heavily upon the citizens of the Confederacy, and millions watched helplessly as family members perished, everything they worked for was destroyed, and the

normalcy of life became a distant memory. Indeed, during the final devastating year of the war, life was anything but ordinary within the Confederate States of America. Its army was in disarray, its soldiers and citizens were on the brink of starvation, and any hope of freedom seemed little more than a pipe dream. Yet its people persevered.

AMERICA ON THE EVE OF DESTRUCTION

As noted earlier, the United States of America was in the throes of remarkable growth and prosperity during the three decades prior to the onset of the Civil War. The nation's population, encouraged by seemingly endless expansion, multiplied by leaps and bounds. In fact, by 1860, the nation was home to nearly 32 million people (including four million slaves). Since 1810, the American population had grown four times faster than Europe's and almost six times the world average. And why not? There was plenty of room, plenty of food, and plenty of work for anyone who wanted it. America was, indeed, the land of opportunity.

In the decades preceding the war, as well as the war years themselves, most Americans continued to live in rural areas—that is, towns with fewer than 2,500 people. But the urban population was growing by leaps and bounds as people headed to burgeoning cities to seek their fortunes. The rate of urbanization during this period was the highest in American history, with the city population growing three times faster than the rural population in the five decades between 1810 and 1860. Industry flourished in the North while agriculture, particularly cotton, continued to dominate the Southern economy.

Americans witnessed a huge evolution in lifestyle in the decades prior to the Civil War. A network of canals, highways, and railroads made transportation faster and easier (and dramatically reduced the cost of shipping goods) throughout the Northern states and into the South and West, and the telegraph made transcontinental communication almost instantaneous.

CIVIL WAR FACTOID

Civil War memorabilia has become incredibly collectible today, especially hand-written letters from soldiers in the field. A family letter with interesting war-related content can sell for hundreds, even thousands, of dollars at auction.

Of equal importance was the rise of the middle class, which took advantage of dramatic advances in manufacturing. In the past, the manufacture of common goods relied for the most part on specialization. Talented craftsmen made everything by hand, from shoes to guns to farm equipment. But the American industrial revolution, with its emphasis on interchangeable parts and factory assembly, quickly changed the way Americans shopped. Craftsmen were still in high demand, especially in regions where the results of mass production had not yet reached in volume, but more and more Americans bought factory or premade goods simply because the price was so affordable.

A particularly good example of this phenomenon is housing. At the beginning of the nineteenth century, there were three different types of housing: rough-hewn log cabins, which tended to be drafty as well as austere; homes made from brick or stone; and homes made from fastened, heavy timbers cut to shape by carpenters. Log homes were the least expensive and easiest homes to make, but most middle- and upper-income families wanted something nicer. However, the craftsmen necessary to build stone or timber homes were in short supply, so the wait could be long.

The answer came in the form of balloon-frame houses, homes made from machine-sawed boards fastened together with industrial nails. Once the frame was up, factory-made siding, shingles, doors, and windows completed the structure. The construction of a balloon-frame home didn't take nearly as long or cost nearly as much as one made from stone or hand-hewn timber, and the resulting structure was both attractive and sturdy. The first balloon-frame homes were built in Chicago and Rochester, New York, in the 1830s and quickly revolutionized the housing industry in this country. Such advances greatly improved the lifestyle of many Americans.

In addition to the rapid expansion of industrialization, the growing use of mass production, and the rise of the middle class, the decades preceding the Civil War saw yet another positive social mark—the education of the American public. In years past, children often skipped a formal education in lieu of some sort of apprenticeship, which was designed to teach them a craft with which they could make a living upon reaching adulthood. But by the mid-1800s, a formal education was almost mandatory as increasingly affluent parents sought a better life for their children. According to historian James H. McPherson, New England led the world in educational facilities and literacy by the middle of the century. More than 95 percent of adults in the New England states could read and write, and three-fourths of the children between the ages of 5 and 19 were enrolled in school, which they attended for up to six months per year. And most of the other Northern states enjoyed almost as many educational opportunities.

Education in the South was not quite as commonplace as it was in the North. At mid-century, approximately 80 percent of the white population could read, write, and perform basic math, and one-third of white children attended school for an average of three months per year. The vast majority of slaves in the Southern states were denied a formal education; those who could read and write generally had learned to do so from members of the families that owned them. But even when slaves are factored into the equation, approximately four-fifths of all Americans were literate in the 1850s, compared to two-thirds in Britain and northwest Europe and one-fourth in southern and eastern Europe.

What does all this mean in regard to life during the Civil War? Only that the vast majority of Americans—North or South—were enjoying a fairly comfortable lifestyle as the dark clouds of dissent began to form on the horizon. It's true that there was still much poverty in the nation, especially in underdeveloped regions and over-crowded urban areas, but for the most part, things were good. Work was readily available, the majority of families enjoyed financial prosperity, and an increasingly wide variety of consumer goods was available at prices almost everyone could afford. It would be difficult to find a nation with more potential than the United States at mid-century, and its citizens were reaping the rewards.

This chapter looks at typical family life during the Civil War era, in cities and on farms and plantations. The daily activities people engaged in back then weren't that much different from the simple pleasures we pursue today. Like us, they worked, played, worshiped, and strived for a better life for their families. The biggest exception is that contemporary Americans don't have to contend with a civil war being fought on their very doorsteps.

> ### CIVIL WAR FACTOID
>
> Slaves were kept for their strong backs, not their brains, and the education of slaves was considered a very low priority by the majority of slave owners. As a result, only one-tenth of slaves could read and write with any fluency.

FAMILY LIFE

The Civil War was especially difficult on the family unit, which tended to be close knit and often extended. In most families, the husband and the eldest sons were the primary breadwinners, and it was a great loss when they had to go off to war. This was especially true among middle-class families, in which wives and mothers often had little experience providing for their families. A farmer's wife knew how to hold down the family stake in her husband's absence (though the labor issue was often a problem), but city women were in a much more difficult position.

Women of the era had an indomitable spirit, however, and they drew from deep reserves of strength and ingenuity when it came to supporting their families. Those who had been sheltered their entire lives, which was common, often found the transition traumatic, but they persevered as never before, falling back on whatever marketable skills they could muster and refusing to take no for an answer. In many ways, Civil War wives were the forbearers of World War II's "Rosie the Riveter" and the trend-setting feminists of the 1960s and 1970s.

While they may have disagreed on ideology, families on both sides of the war shared one common trait: the pain of personal loss. Husbands and fathers died by the hundreds of thousands in both the North and the South, and thousands more returned home wounded and maimed. Many men were so shattered by their wartime experiences that they were little more than emotional and physical invalids, a situation that placed a huge burden on their already struggling families.

In addition to the financial hardship, the families of wounded veterans often had to face tremendous psychological pain. Many soldiers returned home suffering from what today would be diagnosed as posttraumatic stress disorder, and they and their loved ones had few places to turn for help. Psychiatric therapy was unheard of back then, so most families turned to close friends and clergy for solace and guidance (which more often

CIVIL WAR
FACTOID

Lieutenant David H. Todd, commandant of the Confederate Libby Prison in Richmond, Virginia, was the half brother of Mary Todd Lincoln.

FAMILIES DIVIDED

The Civil War divided not only the nation but also individual families. School children have long been taught that the conflict pitted brother against brother, and this is absolutely true. In fact, the ideological rift at the center of the war went all the way to the White House; four of Lincoln's brothers-in-law served in the Confederate army. One of them, Ben Hardin Helm, turned down Lincoln's personal offer of a commission in the Union army so that he could fight for the Confederates. He eventually rose to the rank of general. Helm was killed in the Battle of Chickamauga.

Certainly the Lincolns weren't the only family to experience the pain of mixed loyalties. Many families, especially those from the border states, watched brothers march off in opposite directions, with the very real possibility that they would have to shoot at each other. Henry Clay of Kentucky, for example, had grandsons who served on both sides. And John J. Crittenden, the former governor and U.S. senator from Kentucky who tried to prevent the war in 1860 with a compromise known as the Crittenden Plan, had sons in both blue and gray.

Relatives rarely ended up actually facing each other in battle, though there are numerous tales of wartime encounters. One of the most touching stories is that of Major A. M. Lea, who was part of the Confederate force that captured the *USS Harriet Lane* during a naval battle off Galveston, Texas. When Lea's party boarded the Union ship, he found his son—a Union lieutenant—dying on its deck.

The duel between the Confederate ironclad *Virginia* and the Union ironclad *Monitor* also had a family connection. McKean Buchanan, the brother of *Virginia* commander Franklin Buchanan, was aboard a Union ship sunk during the battle.

than not consisted of the statement, "Just try to be patient"). Many women, initially ecstatic when their husbands returned home, watched their lives slowly crumble as they realized the rest of their years would be spent tending to their husbands' permanent wounds. More than one woman found that she couldn't tolerate her postwar family existence and fled for a better life elsewhere.

Soldiers in the field maintained a strong sense of family by bonding with their comrades through common experience and background. Many senior officers went even further by appointing actual family members to their staff. Unlike today, nepotism was a common practice in the military on both sides, and officers were often accompanied by close family relations. During the winter months, when the war all but came to a halt because to the weather, entire families often joined their husbands and fathers in camp, happy to have the time together despite the conditions. And during the summer months, wives and children occasionally made short camp visits when their husbands and fathers were close enough. Such respites made their time apart a little more bearable.

On the home front, many women participated in military assistance and relief efforts, such as sewing bees, food drives, and medical collections. Not only did these activities help provide soldiers with desperately appreciated items they probably wouldn't have been able to find elsewhere, but they gave the women a sense of unity and purpose. Weeks and months alone without their husbands plunged many women into severe depression; military relief efforts gave them something to do with their time and placed them in contact with others who understood their emotions. Families and soldiers also kept bonds strong by writing long letters back and forth. Nothing made a soldier's day like a letter from his loving wife, and vice versa. Thankfully, many of these letters have been passed down from generation to generation, creating a rich tapestry of information and opinion that has provided contemporary historians with deep insight into the war.

Northern families lost a great many loved ones over the course of the war and experienced their share of problems and grief, but it cannot be argued that Southern families suffered far more. In the North, only the Gettysburg and the Sharpsburg

campaigns brought the war to the doorstep of Union civilians. In the South, the threat of warfare was almost a daily occurrence. Numerous Southern towns and cities were destroyed over the course of the war, and the impact on the Confederate civilian population was enormous in virtually all areas. In many regions, it took all the coping skills families could muster to survive each day.

As the war progressed, the Northern blockade of Southern ports took a heavy toll on the general population. Items that Northerners took for granted became increasingly difficult to find in the South, and prices for basic necessities such as sugar and salt skyrocketed. Confederate money became almost worthless, and inflation reached staggering levels. For women who were the sole support of their families, it became a daily struggle to put together the most meager of meals.

Worse still for Confederate families were the indignities they were forced to endure when Union forces invaded their towns. Many watched in helpless horror as their livestock and produce was taken from them or simply destroyed on the spot by vengeful federal soldiers. Families risked having everything they owned stolen from them, and women whose husbands were off to war risked bodily harm at the hands of invaders. Rather than take their chances with the Yankees, many families simply fled, taking with them only what they could carry. Refugees in their own states, they wandered from area to area in search of food and shelter, often just one step ahead of conquering forces. This way of life was extremely hazardous, and the children suffered the most. An entire generation grew up hating the North, often justifiably.

Not all soldiers were ruthless bandits and marauders, of course. For the most part, the participants in both armies tried very hard not to harm civilians or civilian property. There are numerous examples of advancing Union forces giving food, water, and aid to refugees. For a great many soldiers, the horrors they had witnessed on the battlefield only increased their compassion for civilians caught in the middle. In addition, most soldiers had families back home, and they understood well the emotional trauma that the war had caused. A good deed on their part might result in a good deed by others later on.

CITY LIFE

When we talk about city life during the Civil War, we're talking primarily about the North. The vast majority of the nation's largest cities were located in the Northern states, with the South lagging far behind. One of the reasons for this was the huge influx of foreign immigrants—primarily from Ireland and Germany—who poured into the nation in the decades prior to the war. While many new arrivals spread out to settle in regions that reminded them of home, the majority stayed in the cities—New York, Chicago, Boston, and other metropolitan areas—in the hope of finding well-paying jobs in the many factories and businesses located there. This influx would continue as the war raged, making many American cities some of the most populous in the world.

What was city life like during the Civil War? In many respects, it wasn't that different from city life today. There were the very rich, the very poor, and the many in between. The poor tended to live in tenements; the rich lived in fine homes that often resembled palaces. The captains of industry, many of whom had grown rich off of the hard work of immigrant labor, usually lived in and around the cities in which their factories were located. That way, they could keep a close eye on their businesses without having to travel very far.

The streets of mid-century American cities were as busy and bustling as they are today. Illustrations of street life from that era offer grand images of people in buggies and carriages, on horseback and on foot, a veritable sea of humanity that would look very much like contemporary downtown New York or Chicago if you replaced the carriages with automobiles.

Entertainment was rich and diverse in cities of both the North and the South. Stage plays drew huge audiences. Operas, musical concerts, and lectures were also quite popular, as were ethnic stage shows that catered to a region's particular immigrant populations. If you had the money, there was seldom a lack of something to do. One of the most popular amusements in New York during the Civil War era was P. T. Barnum's curiosity museum in Lower Manhattan. The veteran showman sold a huge number of tickets as New

Yorkers flocked to see amazing animals and exhibits from around the world. In fact, the museum was so popular that people often refused to leave. Barnum, eager to get patrons in and out as quickly as possible, posted a sign by a door that read, "See the Egress." People who went through the door suddenly found them-selves outside.

Things were a bit more relaxed in the largest cities of the South, such as New Orleans, Richmond, Savannah, and Atlanta. The pace of the Southern states in general was much slower, a phenomenon that often baffled hard-working visiting Northerners before the war. One reason, of course, was that much of the region's hard labor was performed by slaves, giving its wealthier citizens plenty of free time in which to relax and indulge their personal passions.

Southern cities were bustling but not overly crowded. Just prior to the beginning of the Civil War, Charleston, Richmond, and Savannah each had fewer than 40,000 citizens. Only New Orleans was comparable to the largest Northern cities, with a population of around 150,000. People traveled by carriage, cart, or horseback and very often lived on the outskirts of the city itself. And as in the North, entertainment was ample and diverse, including stage produc-tions, musical concerts, and other shows.

The Civil War had a far greater impact on Southern cities than those in the North. As the war encroached farther and farther into the Confederacy, many Southern cities found themselves under assault and eventually under Union control. But even if Northern troops never actually invaded a particular city or town, the good life eventually stopped as supplies, both luxury and essential, became increasingly difficult to get and prices skyrocketed. (According to a report in the *Richmond Dispatch*, 10 pounds of bacon cost $1.25 in 1860. By 1863, the price had risen to $10. During the same period, five pounds of sugar rose from $.40 to $5.75.) Southern city dwellers did all they could to keep their spirits high, but every Confederate defeat made it more difficult.

Citizens of the Confederacy were also implored to give what they could to the military, which eventually ran desperately short on essential supplies. The situation was particularly dire during the winter months of 1863. In October of that year, Captain W. M.

POPULATION GROWTH

The population of many Northern cities exploded in the years prior to the war. The population of New York, for example, rose from 515,000 to more than 800,000 in the 1850s alone, and the pop-ulation of Chicago, which was just over 4,000 when the city was incorporated in 1837, rose to 112,000 by 1860.

IMMIGRATION

Immigration brought a strong, cheap labor force to the United States during the mid-1800s. However, many immigrant women were unable to find decent paying work and were forced into a life of prostitution. An estimated 1 in 20 women who had come to the United States from abroad was forced by circumstance to sell her body in order to survive.

Gillaspie, who was responsible for outfitting the army in Alabama, made an eloquent plea for supplies via the newspaper:

> I want all the blankets and carpets that can possibly be spared. I want them, ladies of Alabama, to shield your noble defenders against an enemy more to be dreaded than the Northern foe with musket in hand—the snows of coming winter. Do you know that thousands of our heroic soldiers of the West sleep on the cold, damp ground without tents? Perhaps not. You enjoy warm houses and comfortable beds . . . If the immortal matrons and maidens of heathen Rome could shear off and twist into bowstrings the hair of their heads to arm their husbands in repelling the invader, will not the Christian women of the Confederacy give the carpets off their floors to protect against the chilly blasts of winter those who are fighting with more than Roman heroism, for their lives, liberty, and more, their honor? Sufficient blankets cannot be had in time. Food and clothing failing the army, you and your children will belong to Lincoln.

By contrast, most Northern cities were overflowing with material goods and people with the money to buy them. The *New York Herald* reported in October 1863:

> All our theaters are open . . . and they are all crowded nightly. The kind of entertainment given seems to be of little account. Provided the prices are high and the place fashionable, nothing more is required. All the hotels are as crowded as the theaters; and it is noticeable that the most costly accommodations, in both hotels and theaters, are the first and most eagerly taken. Our merchants report the same phenomenon in their stores: the richest silks, laces, and jewelry are the soonest sold. At least five hundred new turnouts may be seen any fine afternoon in the park; and neither Rotten Row, London, nor the Bois de Boulogne, Paris, can show a more splendid sight. Before the golden days of Indian summer are over these five hundred new equipages will be increased to a thousand. Not to keep a carriage, not to wear diamonds, not to be attired in a robe which cost a small fortune, is now equivalent of being a nobody.

FARM LIFE

The life of farmers in both the North and the South was considerably different from that of their city-dwelling brothers. Farmers tended to live far from the city, often spending their entire lives in the small town of their birth, growing sufficient crops to feed their families and make a small profit.

Farm life in the middle of the nineteenth century was hard work, even with the many labor-saving devices that had become available as a result of the industrial revolution. Farmers typically rose with the sun, had a quick breakfast, then tended to their livestock. Even small farms usually had at least one cow and perhaps some hogs, chickens, and goats. All provided food for the family and perhaps a small amount to sell at market. Once the animals had been fed, the farmer would spend the rest of his day tending to his crops, which varied greatly from one region to another. In the Midwest, wheat, corn, potatoes, and other staples were common. In the South, cotton was king on most plantations, but smaller farms usually grew food crops such as corn, rice, and sugar, as well as indigo and tobacco, which even then were lucrative cash crops.

Farming communities in both regions tended to be fairly close knit, with farmers coming to the aid of others when necessary. Most farmers used hired help to tend the land, though smaller farms were typically family affairs, especially if the family included several strong boys. Despite the common notion regarding slavery in the South, most small- to middle-sized Southern farms did not use slaves, because of the high cost of purchase and maintenance; slaves were more a luxury for wealthy plantation owners.

As the war depleted the nation's male population, farmers' wives in both the North and the South suddenly found themselves the heads of their households. Unlike their overly protected city sisters, however, farm wives tended to be robust in nature and unafraid of hard labor. When their husbands went off to war, they picked up the hoe and plow and, without complaint, went to work. It was seldom a question of yes or no; for most farmers' wives, it was a simple issue of survival.

Many people were amazed at the ease with which women assumed male jobs during the war years, especially in the farm belt. Mary Livermore, a member of the U.S. Sanitation Commission, made the following observation following a tour of the Midwest:

> Women were in the field everywhere, driving the reapers, binding and shocking, and loading grain, until then an unusual sight. At first, it displeased me, and I turned away in aversion. By and by, I observed how skillfully they drove the horses around and around the wheat field, diminishing more and more its periphery at every circuit, the glittering blades of the reaper cutting wide swaths with a rapid, clicking sound that was pleasant to hear. Then I saw that when they followed the reapers, binding and shocking, although they did not keep up with the men, their work was done with more precision and nicety, and their sheaves had an artistic finish that those lacked made by the men. So I said to myself, "They are worthy women, and deserve praise: their husbands are probably too poor to hire help, and, like the 'helpmeets' God designed them to be, they have girt themselves to this work— and they are doing it superbly." Good wives! Good women!

Many farmers, especially those in the North, were European immigrants striving for a better life in the Land of Plenty. They brought their customs and traditions with them, including a strong worth ethic and a sense of family and religion. Church usually played a vital role in the life of the average farmer, and Sunday was commonly a day of rest, reflection, and prayer, except during harvesting season, when crops waited for no one. But even then, most farmers tried to attend church whenever possible.

Farmers often suffered greatly during the Civil War, especially in the South. They usually lived far from town, which made them easy targets for marauders and invading forces, especially those in desperate need of food. Hungry Confederate soldiers begged for whatever a farmer could spare, but Union soldiers were seldom as considerate. Pillaging was discouraged by most officers, but the rule was difficult to enforce, and Union soldiers often took whatever they wanted and destroyed crops and livestock simply to keep them from falling into Confederate hands. Sadly, many farmers were unjustly punished by this reasoning, and it wasn't uncommon for a fleeing farmer to return to his stead only to find it burned to the ground. This was especially true during Sherman's march to the sea and his campaign through the Carolinas.

PLANTATION LIFE

Contrary to popular belief, which has been fueled by movies such as *Gone with the Wind*, the South was not one huge collection of large plantations. In truth, there were far more small- and middle-sized farms—most of which were tended without slaves. However, it's the easy lifestyle of the landed gentry that has become so firmly embedded in the public consciousness.

The Deep South was home to the majority of plantations, as they are recalled today—large, almost palatial homes overseeing hundreds and often thousands of acres of prime farmland, tended by slaves. Louisiana and Virginia both contained a large number of plantations, most of which grew cotton, tobacco, indigo, and rice. But plantations could be found in almost all of the Confederate states. Indeed, the plantation embodied the Southern sensibility and lifestyle in the eyes of most Northerners, even if they had never seen one.

Plantation owners were, for the most part, wealthy individuals with a taste for the finer things in life. They typically left the daily maintenance of their estates and farms to their staff, which allowed them plenty of time to indulge their particular hobbies. Hunting was a favorite pastime among wealthy plantation owners, and most Southern men—rich and poor—learned to ride and shoot at a very young age. Horse racing was another popular activity, and one that usually resulted in sizable bets between local plantation owners; many brought surplus slaves to the races to back large wagers.

Wealthy Southern planters, like the Northern rich, also enjoyed entertaining. Large, lavish house parties, balls, and banquets were held quite frequently. Attire was often formal, and the women reveled in showing off their best dresses, including the hoop skirts that have come to typify the classic "Southern belle." Anyone who has viewed the scene in *Gone with the Wind* in which Scarlett

WHAT IS A PLANTATION?

A functioning plantation usually consisted of a large family home, slave quarters, smokehouses, gardens, a stockyard, and the farmland itself, which could be quite expansive. Many large plantations contained everything necessary for daily maintenance and were virtually self-sufficient. The slaves worked the fields, occasionally assisted by paid white laborers, and their owners considered it a good year if each field slave produced a profit of $250 or more.

O'Hara is stuffed into a corset and then a hoop skirt will understand the pains to which Southern women went in order to be fashionable.

Most planters were doted on by a house staff that included one or more butlers, maids, and cooks, as well as nannies for the planter's children. Like the farmhands and plantation overseers, the majority of plantation house staff were slaves. The nannies, commonly referred to as mammies, played an especially important role in the daily running of the household, and the children of a plantation often grew up with a closer bond to her than to their own mother. It was the responsibility of the nanny to care for the children—to see that they were fed, went to school, and behaved themselves. When they misbehaved, it was usually the nanny who punished them as well; it was one of the few instances in which a slave was allowed to lay a hand on a white person.

The treatment of slaves varied greatly among plantation owners. Some were strict to the point of brutality, administering severe punishment for the slightest infraction and running the home more by fear than respect. But for the most part, planters took relatively good care of their slaves, who were viewed as an expensive investment (a capable farmhand could cost more than $1,000 at auction). Punishment was doled out where appropriate, but minor infractions were often ignored. Many plantation owners also gave their slaves a small piece of land to farm for themselves and sometimes even paid them a small wage or allowance with which they could buy personal items. Of course, that's not to infer that the life of a slave was pleasant. Even under the best circumstances, slaves were still considered nothing more than property, and even the best-treated slave still dreamed of freedom.

As with small- and medium-sized farms, many large plantations were hard hit as the Civil War went on. Even the wealthiest land baron had little purchasing power when all he had in the bank were worthless Confederate notes, and many planters found themselves scrimping to survive during the later months of the war. Plantation owners also faced the wrath of invading Union forces, many of whom saw the Southern plantation as the embod-

CIVIL WAR FACTOID

Jefferson Davis's plantation in Mississippi was turned into a home for freed slaves at the end of the war.

iment of Southern evil. It wasn't uncommon for Union forces to vandalize and even destroy plantation homes, steal personal belongings, set free the slaves, and harass or attack the owners if they were home.

RELIGION

Nineteenth-century America found itself in the midst of a religious upheaval. Prior to 1830, the majority of white Americans were of British heritage and Protestant in their beliefs. By 1830, however, the floodgates of immigration had been thrown wide open and tens of thousands of Irish and German immigrants made their way across the Atlantic. More than two-thirds of these new settlers were Catholic, a situation that greatly alarmed many Protestant Americans and resulted in an increase in nativist organizations. Sadly, this anti-Catholic bias would last for decades.

Americans, for the most part, were a deeply religious people. The Protestant work ethic was alive and well during the Civil War era, and it was the rare individual in either the North or the South who didn't attend church on a regular basis. In addition, evangelists traveled the countryside preaching fire and brimstone at every stop. The sins of alcohol was an especially popular subject of sermons, and many regions experienced a noticeable drop in alcohol consumption and an increase in productivity after a visit by a particularly eloquent preacher.

In the North, the evil inherent in slavery was also a popular subject, and abolitionist preachers used the pulpit to stir up anti-slavery sentiment. Southerners countered by quoting scripture they felt actually condoned slavery. Genesis 9:25-27, for example, was often used as justification for enslaving blacks. The passage quotes Noah, who has been angered by his son Ham, cursing all of Ham's descendants: "a slave shall he be to his brothers." According to the Bible, Ham fathered four sons, who gave rise to the southern tribes of the earth, including all of the people of Africa. Many Southerners also defended the institution with the argument that slavery was actually good for blacks because it enabled them to be converted to Christianity and thus go to heaven.

THE ROLE OF QUAKERS

Some of the very first abolitionists in the United States were the Quakers. In 1688, a group of vocal Quakers made the first organized protest against slavery and the slave trade in Germantown, Pennsylvania.

The issue went to the core of Quaker religious beliefs. They felt that holding another man in servitude was a sin, and many Southern Quakers migrated West rather than live in a society that promoted the institution.

One of the most important contributions Quakers made to the cause of abolition was their efforts to educate free blacks and instill in them a passion to see slavery abolished. During the 1700s and 1800s, free black Quakers such as James Forten, Absalom Jones, and Richard Allen used their own funds to promote various abolitionist causes.

The End
of the
Civil War

Conspiracy Theory

Abraham Lincoln's assassination was initially believed to be a conspiracy enacted by agents of Confederate President Jefferson Davis. Union Secretary of War Edwin Stanton even announced as much to the press, despite having absolutely no proof. The claim turned out to be completely false and only served to inflame Union animosity against the South.

The Civil War ended almost four years to the day after it started—sort of. Most people assume that hostilities between the North and the South concluded immediately with Robert E. Lee's surrender to Ulysses S. Grant on April 9, 1865, but sporadic fighting continued on various fronts for another two and a half months.

Nonetheless, Lee's surrender truly did signal the final defeat of the Confederacy. It was the last of a long line of falling dominoes that included Grant's hard-fought triumph at Petersburg; the fall of Richmond; Sherman's victories at Atlanta, Savannah, and through the Carolinas; and Philip Sheridan's lengthy Shenandoah Valley campaign. All of these events took a huge toll on the Confederacy's already weakened fighting force, which had been hit hard by a lack of necessary supplies and the plummeting morale of its soldiers, a growing number of whom deserted during the war's waning days.

Amazingly, Confederate President Jefferson Davis had plans to continue the war even as he and his cabinet fled Richmond to the din of approaching Union forces echoing behind them. An angry Confederate to the bitter end, Davis carried with him up to the moment of his capture the belief that the Confederacy would prevail if given enough time, but he was pretty much alone in that sentiment. By April 1865, the Confederacy had clearly lost its ability to fight, and no amount of rally cries could revive it. Most of Davis's closest advisors and associates knew the cause had been lost months before, but none could convince Davis to bargain for peace.

A number of diverse factors contributed to the Confederacy's ultimate demise. Foremost was the combined forces of Grant and Sherman, who brought down the South with a divide-and-conquer strategy. While Grant forced Lee's hand at Petersburg, Sherman took Atlanta then effectively split the South in half with his march to the sea and into the Carolinas. The combined attacks pushed the already battered and much smaller Confederate army to the point where it could no longer defend itself, ensuring a Union victory.

The state of the Southern economy was also a contributing factor. The gravity of the situation became evident more than a year before the war officially ended, and it only got worse as the conflict progressed. Its economy close to ruin, the fledgling nation had neither the credit nor the cash to buy foreign goods for its army or its people. As a result, consumer goods became increasingly scarce and outrageously expensive, and the army was finally forced to literally beg the civilian populace—most of whom had long grown tired of the war—for food, clothing, and other essential items. Of course, this situation did little to instill confidence in the Confederacy.

Able-bodied men also grew short in numbers as the war went on, forcing the military to take almost anyone willing to fight, including underage boys and old men. At the beginning, prisoner exchanges allowed both sides to maintain strong numbers, but the Union cessation of the program in 1863 hit the Confederacy hard; all of a sudden, tens of thousands of Southern soldiers were languishing in Union prisons. The manpower situation grew so dire toward the end that Confederate officials started conscripting slaves, a concept viewed with derision just a couple of years earlier. The huge number of casualties in many of the major battles also severely depleted Confederate forces. In many cases, the actual number of Union casualties was higher, but the overall percentage was smaller. In other words, the South lost fewer men on average but took a harder hit with the number it did lose. Not surprisingly, Confederate recruitment drives during the final year of the war provided fewer and fewer soldiers willing to lay down their lives for a cause many were starting to believe was hopeless.

Another factor in the defeat of the Confederacy was its inability to receive formal international recognition, particularly from England and France. These and other countries assisted the Confederacy in a number of ways, but they ultimately refused to grant it official status as an independent nation. This meant that the Confederacy was unable to get much-needed loans with which to buy supplies to maintain its war machine. This, compounded with the Union blockade of Southern ports, dealt the Confederacy a serious blow.

The international eye was on the Confederacy from the very beginning of the war, and early Confederate victories suggested that recognition might be forthcoming. After all, the South had a lot to offer the international market by way of food, textiles, and other

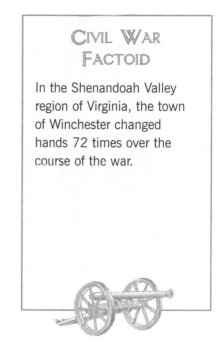

CIVIL WAR FACTOID

In the Shenandoah Valley region of Virginia, the town of Winchester changed hands 72 times over the course of the war.

EXCERPT FROM ABRAHAM LINCOLN'S SECOND INAUGURAL ADDRESS

With malice toward none, with charity for all, with firmness in the right as God gives us to see the right, let us strive on to finish the work we are in, to bind up the nation's wounds, to care for him who shall have borne the battle and for his widow and his orphan, to do all which may achieve and cherish a just and a lasting peace among ourselves and with all nations.

goods. However, the Confederacy was unable to maintain its momentum, and the foreign powers finally sided with the sure thing—the Union. Of course, the Confederacy's ill-fated 1861 European cotton embargo didn't help matters.

THE FINAL BATTLES

Historians could easily spend years trying to determine which specific battle or event was the loosened lynchpin that brought down the South. But for all intents and purposes, the death of the Confederacy started at Petersburg, Virginia, in June 1864.

Petersburg was an important city. It contained communication and supply lines that were vital to the Confederate capital of Richmond, which was just 20 miles away. This made it an important target for Grant, who knew that when Petersburg fell, Richmond would be next. And with Richmond—the heart of the Confederacy—would go the war.

However, as noted earlier, Petersburg was not an easy Union victory. Defending Confederate forces under Lee, though relatively small, were well entrenched. Despite Grant's larger numbers, it took a grueling 10-month siege to bring the city under Union control.

The length of time Lee's forces held their position is as much a tribute to Lee's skills as a leader and strategist as it is to the willpower and tenacity of the Confederate soldiers. But ultimately, it was a doomed endeavor. Lee knew he was outnumbered. He also knew that Grant would press his advantage inch by inch until Petersburg fell. By this late date in the war, Lee and Joseph Johnston, whose small army was doing its best to stop Sherman's assault through Georgia and the Carolinas, were the Confederacy's sole protectors. When they finally fell, as Lee surely knew they would, the Confederacy would be no more. So bleak was the future at this juncture in the war that Lee warned the Confederate secretary of war: "You must not be surprised if calamity befalls us."

For Lee, calamity came in late March 1865. Realizing that Petersburg was a lost cause, Lee developed a daring plan that called for him and his troops to flee the city, hook up with

THE HAMPTON ROADS CONFERENCE

The Civil War almost ended two months before it actually did. On February 3, 1865, President Abraham Lincoln and Secretary of State William Seward met with representatives of the Confederate government aboard a steamboat in Hampton Roads, Virginia, at the mouth of the James River.

The peace conference was conceived by newspaper editor Francis P. Blair Sr., who hoped that the two sides would be willing to settle their differences and join forces to secure American interests in Mexico, which was under the control of Austrian emperor Maximillian. Blair first consulted Jefferson Davis with the idea and then, after receiving permission from Lincoln, set the meeting in motion.

Davis knew that the chances of hammering out an actual peace treaty were slim, but he felt that standing up to the North would help rally the Confederacy during this especially dire time. Lincoln agreed to the meeting in the hope that a peace treaty would help avoid the punitive Reconstruction that was sure to come in the wake of a decisive Confederate defeat.

Lincoln and Seward spent several hours negotiating with the Confederate representatives, who included Vice President Alexander Hamilton Stephens, ex-Supreme Court Justice John Campbell, and former Secretary of State Robert Hunter. However, the talks fell apart when the Confederacy refused to consider Lincoln's demand for complete restoration of the Union and the abolition of slavery.

Davis used the meeting to his advantage, printing up Lincoln's demands and distributing them throughout the South as a way of stimulating Confederate patriotism and rallying the fledgling nation's flagging spirits. At the same time, radical Republicans were outraged at Lincoln's plans for a mild Reconstruction and immediately started the groundwork for far more severe punishments for the rebellious South.

Johnston to stop Sherman's assault, then return to take on Grant. It was a bold ploy that might actually have worked had Lee a sufficient number of men, though even with his small army, he had no other choice.

Just before daylight on March 25, 1865, Confederate forces under General John Gordon attacked Union-held Fort Stedman, which lay directly east of Petersburg. The surprise assault was a success, and the rebel forces pushed on to the Union secondary line. If they could break the line and hold it, Lee's army could push through and on to North Carolina, where Johnston continued to nip at Sherman's heels. Unfortunately for Lee, the Union forces rallied with a mighty counterattack that destroyed the Confederate front. My midmorning, Lee's forces had been pushed back at a loss of nearly five thousand men. With that, Grant—assisted by Philip Sheridan's cavalry—made a major push against Lee's right flank in the hope of preventing Lee's escape to the south. On March 29, a full corps attacked Lee's right while Sheridan led a corps of cavalry and infantry in a wide sweep toward the small town of Five Forks on the Confederate right. Sheridan knew that if he could get behind Lee's army, he could stop it in its tracks and effectively end the war that day.

But Lee wasn't about to go down without a fight. He quickly realized what was happening and sent troops under George Pickett to oppose Sheridan's assault. Pickett managed to stop Sheridan at Dinwiddie Courthouse, just short of Five Forks, on March 31. But Sheridan wasn't defeated; he merely waited for reinforcements. Grant sent him a corps, under General Gouverneur Kemble Warren; it arrived shortly.

The ensuing battle was hard fought, with Sheridan, atop his horse, loudly rallying his troops, hell-bent on stopping Lee at all costs. He was almost a man possessed, pushing and prodding his men with all the strength and vehemence he could muster. During an early skirmish, a soldier beside him was struck in the throat by a Confederate sniper. "I'm killed!" the soldier said, blood gushing from his neck. "You're not hurt a bit!" Sheridan raged. "Pick up your gun, man, and move right on!" The soldier dutifully picked up his rifle, walked a few steps, then fell over dead.

Sheridan's goal was the Southside Railway, a Confederate central supply line. It wouldn't happen on that first day of fighting, but Sheridan's forces did manage to all but annihilate Pickett's army and take the town of Five Forks. Grant cabled Lincoln that Five Forks was under Union control and that Petersburg was next. Lincoln contacted the press, which carried the news under huge headlines. The end of the war was within the Union's grasp.

On April 2, Grant launched an all-out assault along the Confederate line defending Petersburg. Artillery battered the rebel forces, softening the line and killing many. Then the guns stopped, and Union infantry attacked in a huge wave that eventually tore a hole in the middle of the Confederate line. The rebels fought with all they had, but they were simply outnumbered and outgunned. Lee knew that Petersburg was lost and made plans to abandon the city. He wired Jefferson Davis that Richmond could no longer be protected and encouraged Davis and his cabinet to flee the capital as quickly as possible. Then Lee took his remaining army of hungry, ill-equipped men and headed west, with the intention of joining Joseph Johnston's army.

News that the Confederate government was abandoning Richmond spread quickly, and soon the city's civilian population was fighting with government and military officials for all available vehicles. Those who were able to joined Davis and his staff in flight. Those who couldn't leave took to their homes, locking doors and shuttering windows, unsure of what to expect as Union forces advanced upon them.

Fires were set and buildings destroyed in an attempt to keep anything useful out of Union hands. Before long, the city was engulfed in a blaze that could be seen for miles away. The citizens of Richmond, having suffered for so long, began looting the city, looking for food and anything of value. Many got drunk on whiskey that had been left undestroyed. Chaos reigned as the once proud Confederate capital literally collapsed upon itself.

Grant's forces marched into Richmond on April 3, the day after the fall of Petersburg. The Crown of the Confederacy was finally under Union control.

THE HOMES OF WILMER MCLEAN

Wilmer McLean witnessed firsthand both the beginning and the end of the Civil War. McLean's family estate was located near Manassas, Virginia, directly in the path of the Battle of Bull Run.

McLean was so shaken by the incident that he decided to move as far away from the war as possible, settling his family in Appomattox, a quiet town southwest of Richmond. The McLeans lived in relative peace for almost the entire war, only to find the conflict knocking on their door once again on April 9, 1865. McLean was asked about possible locations in which Lee could meet with Grant to discuss surrender terms. McLean reluctantly offered his own home.

The Lingering War

Lee's surrender at Appomattox Court House on April 9, 1865, effectively brought the Civil War to an end. However, Lee's surrender was not the conclusion of hostilities; three other Confederate commanders continued to do battle with the Union for another two and a half months.

General Joseph E. Johnston, for example, followed William Sherman's march northward through North Carolina even after receiving news of the fall of Richmond and Lee's surrender. He finally agreed to discuss surrender terms with Sherman on April 17, 1865. Sherman offered his foe a very generous surrender agreement, which was rejected by the federal government. A second agreement was accepted by both parties on April 26, and Johnston's troops formally surrendered on May 3.

In Mobile, Alabama, Confederate Lieutenant Richard Taylor, the son of former President Zachary Taylor, also continued to fight, with a force of 15,000 troops, after hearing of Lee's surrender and the dissolution of the Confederate government. Taylor finally surrendered to E. R. S. Canby on May 4.

On May 12 and 13, Lieutenant General E. Kirby Smith, unaware of Lee's surrender, waged the last land battle of the war in west Texas. Smith's force of 300 rebels won a surprising victory at Palmito Ranch over more than 800 Union soldiers under Theodore Barrett. Smith's men disbanded after hearing that Richmond had been taken, but Smith refused to give up the fight and went to Houston to rally more troops. His plan never saw fruition, however, because Lieutenant Simon Buckner, acting in Smith's name, surrendered the Trans-Mississippi Department in New Orleans on May 25.

And then there was Stand Watie, leader of the Cherokee Nation and commander of the largest Native American force in the Confederate Army. Watie continued to wage war against the North until he was finally convinced to surrender to Lieutenant Colonel Asa C. Matthews on June 23, 1865.

Equally devastating to the Confederacy was Sherman's march to the sea and through the Carolinas, a campaign discussed earlier at length. This amazing assault sliced the Confederacy in half, captured a large number of essential Southern supply lines, and destroyed anything that might be useful to the Southern war machine. History has questioned the degree of devastation Sherman left in his wake, but to the Union general, it was necessary to bring the war to a quick conclusion. In his mind, he was just a soldier doing his job, though he fully understood the ramifications of his actions. "War is cruelty and you cannot refine it," Sherman told the mayor of Atlanta after ordering the civilian population evacuated from the city. "But when peace does come, you may call on me for anything. Then will I share with you the last cracker."

The third front that helped the North get the foothold it needed to bring down the Confederacy was Philip Sheridan's Shenandoah Valley campaign, which began in August 1864 and ended in early March 1865. The goal of the seven-month assault was to stop Confederate General Jubal Anderson Early, whose forces had wreaked havoc in areas much too close for Lincoln's comfort to Washington, D.C. Sheridan also took it upon himself to ravage the Virginia valley countryside in the process. Like Sherman, he wanted to keep anything of use out of Confederate hands, including food crops and other materials.

With nearly 40,000 cavalry and infantry troops at his disposal, Sheridan began his Shenandoah Valley campaign rather slowly, engaging in a number of small skirmishes with Early's forces in August and September. But after Sherman captured Atlanta, Sheridan felt confident enough to take his campaign to a new level, and he began attacking Early with all he had.

On September 19, Sheridan's forces met Early's on a field near the small town of Winchester. The day-long battle was merciless, taking the lives of nearly 8,500 men. It concluded with a Confederate retreat to nearby Fisher's Hill. Three days later, Sheridan sent three divisions under George Crook to attack Early's left while he led his remaining forces on a frontal assault of the Confederate line at Fisher's Hill. Again, the Confederates were routed.

ARLINGTON NATIONAL CEMETERY

One of Confederate General Robert E. Lee's greatest contributions to the United States—albeit unwillingly—was the land that currently serves as the nation's most famous military burial ground, Arlington National Cemetery.

Lee's family home, located just across the Potomac River from Washington, D.C., was seized by the Union army shortly after Lee resigned his commission to fight for the Confederacy. The mansion house was turned into headquarters for officers supervising the defense of Washington, D.C., and the fields were used as campgrounds for Union troops. Shortly after the Battle of Gettysburg in July 1863,

(continued)

Sheridan then decided to return to Winchester to reinforce Grant while Early retreated to Mount Jackson, near the Blue Ridge Mountains. Sheridan regrouped his forces at Harrisonburg, then headed through the valley to Winchester, laying waste to everything in his path. Following Sherman's example, he burned homes and destroyed crops and livestock. The people of the region were left with next to nothing, and Sheridan proudly boasted, "A crow would have had to carry its rations if it had flown across the Valley."

Confederate cavalry dogged Sheridan's withdrawal, harassing his forces to such a degree that Sheridan finally ordered commander Alfred Torbert to "either whip the enemy or get whipped yourself." On October 9, Torbert met the Confederate cavalry at Tom's Brook, where he won a decisive victory.

In mid-October, Sheridan's army was camped at Cedar Creek while Sheridan traveled to Washington to meet with Secretary of War Stanton. During Sheridan's absence, a tenacious Jubal Early decided to once again take on the Army of the Shenandoah. He launched a surprise attack on Sheridan's forces early on October 19 and drove the federals back from several successive positions during the morning and early afternoon. However, Sheridan made it back from Washington in time to rally his troops and effect a successful counterattack that all but crushed Early's army.

The two generals met one last time on March 2, 1865, at Waynesborough. Despite his best efforts, Early couldn't match Sheridan's firepower and the Union once again emerged triumphant. That battle marked the end of major military action in the Shenandoah Valley, which remained under complete Union control for the short duration of the war. Having conquered Jubal Early, Sheridan joined Grant in his ongoing campaign against Robert E. Lee.

THE SURRENDER OF ROBERT E. LEE

Robert E. Lee's army got a one-day jump on Ulysses S. Grant's pursuing forces, abandoning Petersburg for Danville, Virginia, where Jefferson Davis hoped to reinstate the Confederate government and keep the war going. Lee knew the continuation of hostilities was futile, but as a professional soldier, he couldn't bring himself to question his commander-in-chief.

On the night of April 3, 1865, Lee's army found itself in Amelia Courthouse, a little more than 20 miles from Petersburg. Lee had hoped to find rations for his starving men, but there wasn't a single morsel to be had. Desperate to move on, he had no choice but to remain an extra day while scouts foraged the countryside in search of food. This cost Lee his one-day head start and placed him and his men in great jeopardy.

The area was swarming with Union troops. Following very close behind were three corps of Union infantry, marching a few miles south of Lee on a parallel course. And on the night of April 4, some of Sheridan's cavalry made a tentative move into Amelia Courthouse. Lee knew he couldn't stay; to do so would be folly.

The forage wagons upon which Lee had pinned his hopes returned nearly empty on April 5. This meant that his men would have to march on empty stomachs, something they had been forced to do for far too long. After another brief delay so that additional Confederate forces under General George Thomas Anderson and General Richard Ewell could join him, Lee ordered his army to move out—only to find his path blocked by Union infantry and cavalry.

Rather than directly face the larger Federal force, Lee shifted west toward Farmville, where he hoped to receive food and provisions for his men from nearby Lynchburg. The night march there took a heavy toll on Lee's hungry, exhausted men, many of whom stumbled out of the walking columns and were never seen again. And as always, Federal forces continued to harass the Confederates as they slowly made their way. Grant dogged Lee with unflagging determination, pressing closer and closer, unwilling to let his esteemed foe escape yet again. The end was close, and both men knew it.

On April 6, Union forces overwhelmed John Gordon's army, which was covering the Confederate trains, at the small town of Sayler's Creek. During that battle, federal soldiers captured the majority of Lee's supply wagons and, even more heartbreaking, decimated the corps led by Anderson and Ewell. Lee's army took a huge hit during the battle, losing more than 7,000 men and

ARLINGTON NATIONAL CEMETERY

(continued from previous page)

the U.S. government officially confiscated the land because Lee had not shown up in person, as required by law, to pay a property tax of $92.02.

In the spring of 1864, Secretary of War Edwin Stanton instructed Quartermaster General Montgomery Meigs to find a suitable location for a new military cemetery. Meigs chose the Lee estate, which offered expansive land and a fitting view of the nation's capital. Meigs also enjoyed the irony of using the home of one of the Confederacy's most famous generals as a final resting place for Union dead.

reducing his force to just 15,000 soldiers armed with only muskets and sabers. Opposing them was 80,000 Union infantry and cavalry.

The following day, Lee's army stumbled into Farmville, where they received food for the first time in many days. Once his men had eaten their fill, Lee pressed on, crossing the Appomattox River and burning the bridges behind him. But even that failed to hold back Grant's forces, and Lee continued to feel the Union commander's presence just miles behind him. That evening, Lee received an invitation from Grant to surrender, an offer he quickly refused. A tiny ray of hope remained: If Lee could get his men to Appomattox Station, he could feed them from supply trains from Lynchville and then swing south to Danville.

On April 8, Grant's army forced Lee into another rear-guard action to protect his remaining wagons. As Lee's men fought for their very survival, Sheridan's cavalry and infantry under E. O. C. Ord quickly moved past Lee's southern flank and drove into Appomattox Station, where they captured Lee's supply trains and placed themselves across his line of march. That evening, Lee's army entered Appomattox Court House and saw the extent of Sheridan's force. The Confederates were greatly outnumbered by heavily armed Union cavalry and infantry, far too many for them to engage. An assault would have been sheer suicide, and all knew it. The end had finally come for Lee's Army of Northern Virginia.

The following day, April 9—Palm Sunday—Lee put on his very best dress uniform, including a red silk sash, a jeweled sword given to him by some women in England, red-stitched spurred boots, and long gray gloves, known as gauntlets. He planned to meet with Grant to discuss surrender terms and wanted to look his best if Grant took him prisoner. It was an agonizing decision for Lee, who told Gordon he would rather "die a thousand deaths." But he had no choice. If he didn't surrender, thousands more would needlessly die.

Sheridan was about to launch one final attack on Lee's army when a single man in gray rode out from the opposing ranks carrying a white flag of truce. He

LEE'S FINAL ORDER

On April 10, 1865, General Robert E. Lee issued his final order—one of farewell—to the soldiers of the Army of Northern Virginia. It read:

After four years of arduous service marked by unsurpassed courage and fortitude, the Army of Northern Virginia has been compelled to yield to overwhelming numbers and resources. I need not tell the brave survivors of so many hard fought battles, who have remained steadfast to the last, that I have consented to this result from no distrust of them; but, feeling that valor and devotion could accomplish nothing that could compensate for the loss that must have attended the continuance of the contest, I have determined to avoid the useless sacrifice of those whose past services have endeared them to their countrymen.

By the terms of the agreement, officers and men can return to their homes and remain there until exchanged. You will take with you the satisfaction that proceeds from the consciousness of duty faithfully performed; and I earnestly pray that a Merciful God will extend to you his blessing and protection.

With an unceasing admiration of your constancy and devotion to your Country, and grateful remembrance of your kind and generous consideration of myself, I bid you all an affectionate farewell.

R. E. Lee, Genl.

THE CIVIL WAR CONTINUES

Karen Storer of Chaffin's Bluff, Virginia, which is 10 miles south of Richmond, was nearly struck on the head by a Civil War cannonball in late November 1999. The ball had apparently been lodged in an old tree in Storer's backyard since 1864; it came crashing to the ground when a large branch broke as Storer was washing her car. The ball now resides on the mantle of former country singer Jimmy Dean, for whom Storer works as a gardener. "It was a close call," Storer laughs. "And I'm a Yankee!"

told Sheridan that Lee was waiting to meet with Grant at the nearby home of a man named Wilmer McLean. Sheridan was at first skeptical, but he quickly ordered a cease-fire, and for a long moment, the two armies simply stood there staring at each other. Grant then rode up to Sheridan and was told that Lee was expecting him at the house below. "Well then," Grant said, "let's go up."

Grant and Lee were an exercise in contrast when they shook hands in Wilmer McLean's parlor. Lee looked resplendent in his finest dress uniform, and Grant, who had been nursing a severe headache that morning and hadn't had time to clean up, rode up mud spattered and disheveled. Grant arrived alone and found Lee standing with two aides. He removed his gloves and extended his hand to the man he had pursued for so long. The two officers then sat down as six of Grant's generals entered the room and stood behind their commander.

Grant made a gesture at small talk, mentioning a time he and Lee had met while serving in Mexico years before. They discussed better times for a few moments, then Lee, who was anxious to get on with the sad business at hand, said: "I suppose, General Grant, that the object of our present meeting is fully understood. I asked to see you to ascertain upon what terms you would receive the surrender of my army."

Realizing the gravity of the situation and the pain his adversary must have felt, Grant did no gloating that day. Though he had won, he was in no mood to celebrate. He told Lee that his officers and men would have to surrender, then be paroled and disqualified from taking up arms again until properly exchanged, and that all arms, ammunition, and supplies were to be delivered up as captured property. The terms were written down, then reviewed by Lee, who quietly corrected an unintentional oversight before agreeing to them. He then asked whether his cavalrymen and artillerists could keep their horses, most of which were private property. Grant noted at first that only officers would be allowed to keep their horses, but he quickly realized how much the issue meant to Lee. Changing his mind, he promised to "let all the men who claim to own a horse or mule take the animals home with them to work their little farms." Grant also authorized all of the provisions Lee needed to feed his starving men. Lee was very appreciative of Grant's kind gesture, noting, "This will have the best possible effect on the men. It will be very gratifying and will do much toward conciliating our people."

After signing the declaration of surrender, Lee stood up and shook Grant's hand one more time. He bowed to the other men in the room, all of whom knew they were witnessing history in the making, and walked silently out the door. On the porch, Lee put his riding gloves on and gazed for a moment toward the hill-side where his ragtag army awaited his return. He absently drove his right fist into his left hand three times, then mounted his beloved horse Traveller and rode away to deliver the difficult news to his men.

Three days later, on April 12, what was left of Lee's Army of Northern Virginia relinquished their weapons and received their paroles, which allowed them to return home. Though a handful of minor battles would be fought in the weeks ahead, the war was finally over, and the Confederate States of America, so eager to prove its independence, no longer existed. On April 14, General Robert Anderson raised the American flag over Fort Sumter—the same flag he had been forced to lower exactly four years earlier. Later that evening, Lincoln was killed at Ford's Theatre by John Wilkes Booth. Others would die in skirmishes over the next few weeks, but in many ways, Lincoln was the final casualty in a war that took so many.

ARLINGTON CEMETERY FACTS

The first soldier to be buried at Arlington National Cemetery was a Confederate prisoner of war who died in a local hospital. Over the course of the war and after, more than two hundred other Southerners would also be interred there. Most of the early plots were located in what had been Mary Lee's rose garden; one such area includes a mass grave containing the bodies of more than two thousand unidentified Union soldiers.

THE THIRTEENTH AMENDMENT: THE END OF SLAVERY

The Thirteenth Amendment, ratified at the end of 1865, officially abolished slavery. It reads as follows:

Section 1—Neither slavery nor involuntary servitude, except as a punishment for crime whereof the party shall have been duly convicted, shall exist within the United States, or any place subject to their jurisdiction.

Section 2—Congress shall have power to enforce this article by appropriate legislation.

Its ratification freed approximately four million blacks who had not otherwise been freed over the course of the Civil War and ended the institution of forced servitude forever.

However, had things gone differently, the Thirteenth Amendment would have continued slavery rather than abolished it. In 1861, an amendment to that effect was proposed in a desperate attempt to avoid a civil war and keep the Union whole. It was supported by nearly half of the congressional Republicans and the vast majority of Democrats and had passed both the House and the Senate by the required two-thirds majority. However, the war erupted before the amendment could be ratified by three-quarters of the states.

Lincoln's Emancipation Proclamation officially made the abolition of slavery a goal of the war, but because it was a wartime edict, it freed only slaves from states in armed rebellion against the Union. There was a very good chance that it wouldn't apply once the war was over, and many believed the Supreme Court would rule the proclamation unconstitutional.

In an attempt to end slavery in the United States once and for all, Lincoln laid the groundwork for a Constitutional amendment abolishing the institution in 1864. The Democratic Party opposed ratification of the amendment, even though Lincoln tried to sweeten the pot by promoting financial compensation from the federal government to all slaveholders. But despite objections from the Democrats, the Republican-dominated Senate quickly passed the proposed amendment in April by a vote of 38 to 6. However, the House, which had far more Democrats than Republicans, failed to give it the necessary two-thirds support. Lincoln called for a second vote after his re-election suggested national backing for emancipation, and the amendment passed in January 1865 by a close vote of 119 to 56. Lincoln signed the amendment in a symbolic gesture the very next day, and eight states ratified it within a week. The passage of the Thirteenth Amendment was celebrated with a one-hundred-gun salute from artillery batteries on Capitol Hill. However, it took eight months for the rest of the states to follow suit. The amendment was officially ratified on December 18, 1865.

RECONSTRUCTION

Reconstruction—the process of rebuilding the war-torn South—began shortly after the fall of the Confederacy and would continue for approximately 12 years. The many policies enacted during this period by the U.S. Congress and Presidents Andrew Johnson and Ulysses S. Grant were designed to bring the seceded states back into the Union and aid displaced individuals, especially freed slaves. But many of the policies were also punitive; radical Republicans within Congress wanted to make sure that the rebellious South was sufficiently penalized for putting the nation through four years of war, and to ensure that such a thing would never happen again.

Abraham Lincoln tentatively began the process of Reconstruction in 1863 with the announcement of a policy for the reconstruction of Southerners who denounced the Confederacy. Lincoln was eager to extend a compassionate hand to the South, despite the trials and tribulations it had wrought, and this policy was one of his first endeavors in that direction.

On December 8, 1863, Lincoln issued a proclamation in which he offered a full pardon and amnesty to any recanting Confederate who took an oath of allegiance to the United States and to all of its laws and proclamations regarding the institution of slavery. The only exemptions to this offer of amnesty were Confederate government officials and high-ranking military officers.

In addition, the proclamation provided for the formation of a state government that would be recognized by the president when the number of persons taking the oath of allegiance reached 10 percent of the number of voters in 1860. Congress retained the right to decide whether to seat the senators and representatives elected from such states.

Lincoln based the proclamation on his unwavering belief that secession was illegal and, thus, that all of the Southern states had remained in the Union; their governments had only temporarily been taken over by rebels, and the key role of Reconstruction was to return loyal officials to power. It was Lincoln's hope that the offer of amnesty would result in a snowball effect in which the

CIVIL WAR FACTOID

Civil rights for freed slaves was not an easy accomplishment. Many Southerners did all they could to keep blacks down following the war, often resorting to mayhem. And not all violence against blacks was at the hands of civilians. In New Orleans, 48 African-Americans were killed when police viciously put down a peaceful demonstration promoting black suffrage.

CARPETBAGGERS

Carpetbaggers were Northerners who moved to the South following the war to take advantage of the ensuing social and political turmoil. The disparaging name came from the luggage they typically carried, called carpetbags.

Carpetbaggers were unwelcome and feared by most Southerners because of the way they twisted issues and situations for personal financial gain. One common tactic was to use the chaos of Reconstruction to secure local and state political positions, primarily on the shoulders of easily manipulated black voters. Once in, carpetbaggers lined their pockets through graft and bribery with seldom a glance toward their constituencies.

(continued)

leaders of the South would defect back to the Union, and the seceded states would return one by one.

However, many in Congress were fearful that Lincoln's early program, which was quite moderate in tone, would leave intact the political and economic framework that made slavery a driving force in the South. Even though slaves may have become free citizens as a result of the war, there was nothing to help them establish themselves as self-sufficient and contributing individuals after the fact; rather than slaves in chains, they would simply become landless serfs forced to labor under nearly the same conditions that had kept them in servitude for so long. Many Congressmen believed Reconstruction should be more of a revolution in which the South was dismantled and rebuilt with more Northern sensibilities. Only then could freed slaves enjoy all of the benefits of citizenship, including the right to vote and to walk the streets without fear of persecution.

The first response to Lincoln's plan came from radical Republicans in the form of the Wade-Davis Bill, which offered more stringent criteria for rejoining the Union. Lincoln killed the bill with a pocket veto (meaning he didn't sign or return the bill to Congress before it adjourned for the year). By the end of the war, Congress had passed the Thirteenth Amendment, which abolished slavery throughout the Union and gave Congress the power and authority to enforce abolition with the proper legislation. Shortly after the passage of the Thirteenth Amendment, Congress established the Freedman's Bureau, which was a federally funded agency designed to distribute food, clothing, and other provisions to impoverished freedmen and to oversee "all subjects" relating to their condition and treatment in the South.

President Andrew Johnson tried to continue Lincoln's moderate Reconstruction policies following Lincoln's assassination in April 1865. In May of that year, he granted amnesty and pardon, including the restoration of all property rights except for slaves, on all former Confederates who took an oath of loyalty to the Union and accepted emancipation. Johnson also appointed provisional governors to lead the Southern states in drafting new constitutions that would allow them to rejoin the Union.

However, what Johnson did not do, other than emancipation, was provide for the millions of slaves who suddenly found themselves free men and women. Johnson believed that the Southern states should decide for themselves the future of freedmen, a short-sighted position that led to the institution of numerous Black Codes—states laws designed to keep African-Americans out of politics and "in their place."

Johnson tried to make the restoration of the Union as painless as possible by appointing men loyal to the Union to lead the readmitted states. However, radical Republicans took a different tack. They felt that since the seceded states had been defeated in the war, they no longer had any rights and should be treated as conquered territories. In their eyes, black suffrage and equal rights were the most important goals of Reconstruction, followed by the rebuilding of the ravaged South.

Many Southern whites felt extreme anger and frustration at the abolition of slavery and often expressed their hatred for blacks with violence. Between 1865 and 1866, more than five thousand African-Americans were killed or severely beaten because of the color of their skin. So vehement was this racial hatred that the federal government quickly realized military control would be necessary to slowly bring Southern blacks into the national mainstream.

Johnson faced other problems as well. Many in Congress felt that Reconstruction should be the responsibility of the legislative branch of government and that Johnson had overstepped his authority as president in instituting certain Reconstruction policies. In order to maintain control, Congress enacted the Reconstruction Act of 1867, which dramatically affected Johnson's moderate plans for the rebuilding of the war-ravaged South. The 11 Confederate states were divided into five military districts under commanders who had the authority to use the army to protect the lives and property of all citizens—especially blacks. New state constitutions were required to include a promise to ratify the Fourteenth Amendment (which granted citizenship to newly freed slaves and directed the federal government to protect citizens from arbitrary state actions, including Black Codes), a loyalty oath swearing allegiance to the Union, and a ban that prohibited former Confederate leaders from holding political office.

CARPETBAGGERS
(continued from previous page)

However, not all Northerners who moved to the South were immoral. Many kindhearted Northerners arrived eager to help the region get back on its feet. These included teachers, doctors, industrialists, clergymen, and agents of the Freedman's Bureau. In addition, a large number of Union soldiers who had been sent to the South during the war decided to settle there afterward because they fell in love with the natural beauty of the region. But even these innocent men and women were viewed with skepticism by Southerners of both races, and the term *carpetbagger* was used as a pejorative term for any Northerner for generations after the war.

THE FREEDMAN'S BUREAU

The Bureau of Refugees, Freedmen, and Abandoned Lands was established by Congress on March 4, 1865, in an attempt to aid the more than four million former slaves who lived in the South at the end of the Civil War. In existence for only one year and hobbled by allegations of corruption as well as a lack of funds and manpower, the bureau still managed to do much for the uneducated and poverty-stricken African-Americans who suddenly found themselves without homes, jobs, or money.

Congress created the Freedman's Bureau and gave it just one year to do its job. Its primary goal was to distribute food, clothing, fuel, and medical care to impoverished former slaves, as well as oversee their well-being and treatment. General Oliver O. Howard, a well-respected Civil War veteran, was chosen to head the Bureau's nine hundred agents.

One of the agency's most difficult tasks was creating a judicial system that was fair to both blacks and whites. Not surprisingly, most Southerners weren't particularly eager to treat freed slaves fairly, so the bureau first established its own judicial authority with local agents setting up temporary three-man courts to hear disputes.

The Freedman's Bureau also worked diligently to bring former slaves into a free labor economy. Plantations were still integral to the Southern economy, and the agency strived to bring African-Americans into that workforce with fair wages and the opportunity for advancement. One way in which that was accomplished was through the distribution of land that had been confiscated or abandoned during the war. The initial pledge was "40 acres and a mule" to every freed slave, but only about 2,000 South Carolina and 1,500 Georgia freedmen actually received the land as promised.

Another important agency concern was health care. The agency tried to strengthen existing health care facilities such as hospitals, as well as establish a series of rural health clinics. During its operation, the bureau helped nearly 500,000 freed slaves to receive medical attention.

Reconstructionist policies enacted by Congress achieved quite a bit, including the first public, tax-supported school systems in most Southern states. There were also strong attempts to broaden and strengthen the Southern economy through aid to railroads and other industries. Most important of all, blacks were finally given a voice in local, state, and federal government.

However, things were far from perfect in the New South. The region's economy continued to be dominated by agriculture, despite attempts to lure industry (a situation that would continue into the twentieth century), and many Southerners did all they could to keep African-Americans from assuming their rightful place in society. For example, many Southern states made it extremely difficult for blacks to vote by enacting deliberately prohibitive laws such as the poll tax. Most blacks also received far lower wages than white workers, which prevented them from buying land and otherwise becoming financially independent. Southern African-Americans may have found themselves out of bondage, but they were far from free. It wasn't until the civil rights movement of the 1960s that many of their invisible shackles were finally removed.

BLACK CODES

Black Codes were special laws passed by many Southern state governments during the first year of Reconstruction to prevent former slaves from enjoying the benefits of their freedom. They restricted blacks' rights to buy, own, and sell property; make legally binding contracts; serve on juries; own weapons; and vote or run for political office. Black Codes also restricted African-Americans from working in various professions, enforced apprenticeship prerequisites, required blacks to carry travel passes and proof of residence, and denied them their Constitutional right to free assembly.

Between 1866 and 1877, Congress tried to eliminate Black Codes by appointing Northern governors to head Southern states. However, after Reconstruction ended and politicians were replaced by Southerners, versions of Black Codes—known as Jim Crow laws after a popular minstrel song of the era— once again became commonplace.

Appendix A
The Civil War Time Line

1860

November 6: Abraham Lincoln is elected president.

December 20: A state convention in South Carolina votes to secede from the Union.

December 27: South Carolina troops seize Fort Moultrie and the federal arsenal in Charleston.

1861

January: Florida, Alabama, Georgia, Mississippi, and Louisiana join South Carolina in seceding from the Union.

January 29: Kansas is admitted to the Union as a free state.

February 4: The six seceded states form a provisional government as the Confederate States of America (CSA).

February 9: Jefferson Davis is chosen president of the CSA by the Provisional Congress. Alexander Stephens is chosen as vice president.

February 23: Texas secedes from the Union.

March 4: Abraham Lincoln is inaugurated as the 16th president.

March 16: The Confederate congress adopts a constitution similar to the U.S. Constitution but with one very important difference: It prohibits any law that interferes with slavery.

April 12: South Carolina troops bombard Fort Sumter in Charleston Harbor. Major Robert Anderson surrenders the fort the next day.

April 15: Lincoln proclaims a state of insurrection following the capture of Fort Sumter. He calls for 75,000 volunteers to serve for three months.

April 17: Virginia secedes from the Union. A month later, Richmond is designated the capital of the CSA.

April 19: Union troops marching through Baltimore on their way to Washington, D.C., are attacked by Confederate sympathizers; 12 civilians and 4 soldiers die in the riot. That same day, Lincoln calls for a blockade of Southern ports.

May 6: Arkansas and Tennessee secede from the Union and join the Confederacy.

May 13: Britain announces it will remain neutral regarding the Civil War. The Confederacy is granted "belligerent status."

May 20: North Carolina secedes from the Union and joins the Confederacy.

July 21: The First Battle of Bull Run is fought. Union forces are routed, signaling a long, drawn-out fight.

July 27: General George B. McClellan replaces General Irvin McDowell as head of the Army of the Potomac.

October 21: The Union is handed another defeat at the Battle of Ball's Bluff, near Leesburg, Virginia.

November 1: Lincoln retires General-in-Chief Winfield Scott and replaces him with General George B. McClellan.

November 8: The *Trent* Affair occurs. Confederate agents are removed from the British ship *Trent* by Union forces, sparking a diplomatic crisis between the United States and Great Britain that comes close to war.

1862

January 11: Edwin Stanton replaces Simon Cameron as secretary of war.

February 16: Ulysses S. Grant takes Fort Donelson in Tennessee.

February 25: Nashville, Tennessee, falls to the Union without a fight.

March 9: The Union ironclad *Monitor* and Confederate ironclad *Virginia* (formerly the *Merrimac*) engage in a lengthy duel at Hampton Roads, Virginia. The battle ends in a draw but proves the superiority of armored vessels.

March 11: Lincoln, frustrated by McClellan's unwillingness to engage the enemy, demotes him from general-in-chief to commander of the Army of the Potomac.

April 4: The Peninsular campaign begins with a Union advance toward Yorktown, Virginia, located on the peninsula between the James and York Rivers. Yorktown falls to the Union on May 4, and Williamsburg falls on May 5.

April 6–7: The Battle of Shiloh results in a Confederate withdrawal from Pittsburg Landing, Tennessee. Ulysses S. Grant commands the Union forces, Pierre G. T. Beauregard the Confederate forces.

April 7: A Confederate fortress on the Mississippi River known as Island No. 10 falls after being attacked by combined Union land and naval forces. The victory places the Mississippi River under Union control all the way to Memphis.

April 10: Lincoln signs a congressional resolution calling for gradual emancipation and the compensation of slave owners. Slavery is also abolished in Washington, D.C.

April 25: New Orleans is taken by Union Flag Officer David Farragut.

May 12: Natchez, Mississippi, also falls to Farragut.

June 1: Joseph Johnston is wounded in battle. He is replaced by Robert E. Lee as leader of the Confederacy's Virginia forces.

June 6: Union forces take Memphis, Tennessee.

June 25–July 2: The Seven Days' Battle results in a Union retreat and temporarily ends the Union threat to Richmond. Lee commands the Confederate forces, McClellan the Union. Casualties are extremely high on both sides.

July: Congress authorizes the acceptance of African-Americans into military service and passes a second Confiscation Act that frees slaves belonging to all rebels.

July 11: Lincoln names Henry Halleck as general-in-chief.

August 28–30: The Second Battle of Bull Run ends pretty much as the first one did—that is, with a Union defeat. General John Pope, who led the Union forces, is replaced by McClellan.

September 17: The Battle of Antietam, Maryland, becomes the single bloodiest day of the war, with a huge number of casualties on both sides. Though technically a draw, the battle forces Lee to abort his planned invasion of the North.

September 27: The First Regiment Louisiana Native Guards becomes the first officially recognized black regiment.

October 8: The Battle of Perryville, Kentucky, stops a second Confederate invasion of the North, under Braxton Bragg. Don Carlos Buell leads the victorious Union forces.

November 5: Lincoln dismisses McClellan a second time after McClellan fails to pursue Lee's forces following the Battle of Antietam. McClellan is replaced with Ambrose Burnside.

December 13: The Battle of Fredericksburg, Virginia, results in a Union rout with numerous casualties.

December 31: The Battle of Murfreesboro, Tennessee (also known as the Battle of Stones River), begins. It ends inconclusively with a Confederate retreat on January 2, 1863. More than 25,000 men are killed or wounded.

1863

January 1: Lincoln formerly issues the Emancipation Proclamation.

January 25: Lincoln replaces Ambrose Burnside with General Joseph Hooker as commander of the Army of the Potomac.

March 3: Lincoln signs the first Conscription Act.

May: The Bureau of Colored Troops is established by the U.S. War Department, signaling the active recruitment of blacks.

May 1–4: The Battle of Chancellorsville, Virginia, results in a solid Confederate victory over Hooker's Army of the Potomac. The win is tempered by the loss of Thomas "Stonewall" Jackson.

May 22: Grant attacks Vicksburg, Mississippi. Experiencing heavy losses, he begins a lengthy siege of the city.

June 22: West Virginia, formed out of several pro-Union counties in western Virginia, is admitted to the Union as a free state.

June 27: Lincoln replaces Joseph Hooker with General George Meade as commander of the Army of the Potomac.

July 1–3: The Battle of Gettysburg, Pennsylvania, results in a Union victory, but the cost is extremely high with a combined total of nearly 50,000 casualties. Lee begins a retreat to Virginia; Meade fails to pursue him. The battle signals the beginning of the end for the Confederacy.

July 4: Vicksburg finally surrenders to Grant after a lengthy siege, resulting in Union control of the Mississippi River.

July 13–16: Crowds in several Northern cities riot in response to the Conscription Act.

July 17: Jackson, Mississippi, is abandoned by Confederate troops.

September 19–20: The Battle of Chickamauga, Georgia, results in a Union retreat back to Chattanooga, Tennessee.

October 3: Lincoln issues a proclamation making the last Thursday in November a national day of Thanksgiving.

October 16: Lincoln appoints Grant commander of the united western armies.

November 19: Lincoln delivers his famous Gettysburg Address.

November 23–25: Grant comes to the rescue of Union-held Chattanooga, which had been besieged by Confederate forces. The Confederates later abandon Knoxville, bringing Tennessee under complete Union control.

December 8: Lincoln offers amnesty to all Confederates willing to take an oath of allegiance.

1864

January 19: Arkansas, a Union slave state, adopts a new antislavery constitution.

February 3–14: General William Tecumseh Sherman captures Meridian, Mississippi, and begins his policy of "total warfare," destroying anything that could be used to aid the Confederacy.

March 10: As a result of his victory at Chattanooga, Grant is named commander of all the Union armies.

April 12: Confederate soldiers under General Nathan Bedford Forrest capture Fort Pillow in Tennessee and slaughter hundreds of black soldiers in the aftermath. More than 50 white Union soldiers are also murdered.

May 3: Grant, commanding 120,000 troops, begins his campaign to take the Confederate capital of Richmond. Waiting for him are 60,000 Confederate troops under Robert E. Lee.

May 4: Sherman begins his march toward Atlanta with an army of 110,000 men.

May 5–6: The Battle of the Wilderness, a tangle of briars and close woods in Virginia's Rapidan basin, ends in a draw between Grant and Lee. Casualties are high, with many wounded soldiers perishing in brushfires sparked by the fighting.

May 8–12: The Battle of Spotsylvania, Virginia, ends in a draw between the two forces.

May 15: Confederate General Jubal Anderson Early puts the brakes on a Union offensive by defeating federal troops entering the Shenandoah Valley region of Virginia.

June 1–3: The Battle of Cold Harbor, Virginia, results in a victory for Lee after Grant makes several crucial errors in judgment. However, Grant realizes his superior numbers can eventually wear down the Confederate army.

June 7: The Republican Party nominates Lincoln for a second term as president despite growing public dissatisfaction with the way Lincoln has handled the war.

June 15–18: Grant assaults Petersburg, Virginia, but is repelled by Lee. Realizing a frontal assault would be futile, Grant lays siege to the city.

June 27: The Battle of Kennesaw Mountain, Georgia, results in a Confederate victory over William T. Sherman. More than 2,000 Union soldiers are killed or wounded in the fighting.

July 14: Confederate General Jubal Anderson Early reaches the outskirts of Washington, D.C., before being halted by Union General Lew Wallace. Early withdraws from the region when Wallace receives reinforcements.

July 17: Jefferson Davis replaces Joseph Johnston who, with John B. Hood, was attempting to halt Sherman's assault on Atlanta.

July 20–28: Hood attempts a direct assault on Sherman's army, resulting in high casualties. Sherman spends most of August severing connections to all roads and railroads leading into Atlanta.

August 5: Mobile, Alabama, falls to Admiral David Farragut. It's during this daring battle that Farragut utters the now famous words, "Damn the torpedoes! Full speed ahead!"

September 2: Sherman captures Atlanta. Two days later, he orders the evacuation of all civilians.

September 19–October 19: Union General Philip Sheridan drives Confederate General Jubal Anderson Early from Virginia's Shenandoah Valley, eliminating one of the last supply sources for the Confederate army.

October 13: Maryland adopts a new state constitution that abolishes slavery.

October 31: Nevada is admitted to the Union as the 36th state.

November 8: Lincoln, buoyed by recent Union victories, is elected to a second term as president. His primary opponent is George B. McClellan.

November 16: Sherman begins his march to the sea, from Atlanta to Savannah.

November 30: The Battle of Franklin, Tennessee, proves a costly victory for Hood's Army of the Tennessee, which experiences nearly 6,300 casualties, including the deaths of six generals. Union General John Schofield retreats from Franklin to Nashville to hook up with General George Thomas.

December 15–17: The Battle of Nashville gives General George Thomas a solid Union victory. John Hood's much smaller army loses nearly 4,500 men.

December 22: Sherman marches unopposed into Savannah, Georgia. He presents the city to Lincoln as a Christmas gift.

1865

January 11: Missouri adopts a resolution abolishing slavery.

January 15: Fort Fisher, which protects Wilmington, North Carolina, is captured by a combination of Union army and navy forces.

January 31: The House passes the Thirteenth Amendment abolishing slavery. It then goes to the states for ratification. Lincoln's home state of Illinois is the first to do so on February 1.

February 22: Wilmington, North Carolina, is the last Confederate port to be taken by Union forces.

March 3: Congress establishes the Bureau of Refugees, Freedmen, and Abandoned Lands to aid former slaves and white refugees.

March 4: Lincoln is inaugurated for a second term.

March 13: Jefferson Davis signs a bill allowing blacks to join the Confederate army. Those who do so will be freed. Few take up the offer.

April 1: The Battle of Five Forks, Virginia, results in a sound victory for Union General Philip Sheridan.

April 2: Lee withdraws from Petersburg after 10 months of fighting that includes a grueling siege. He wires Jefferson Davis that Richmond will soon fall.

April 3: Union troops march into Petersburg and Richmond. Lincoln tours Richmond two days later.

April 6: The Army of Northern Virginia and the Army of the Potomac engage in their last battle at Sayler's Creek, Virginia.

April 9: Confederate General Robert E. Lee formally surrenders to Union General Ulysses S. Grant at Appomattox Court House, Virginia.

April 14: President Abraham Lincoln is shot in the head by John Wilkes Booth while attending a performance at Ford's Theatre in downtown Washington, D.C. Lincoln dies the next morning.

April 15: Vice President Andrew Johnson is sworn in as the nation's 17th president.

April 18: Confederate General Joseph Johnston surrenders to General William Sherman, signaling the formal end to Confederate resistance. Aside from a few Confederate holdouts, the Civil War is over.

Appendix B
Resources

If you would like additional information regarding the Civil War, check out The Civil War Trust's Web site at *www.civilwar.org*. The Civil War Trust is the largest battlefield preservation organization in the United States, and its Web site contains links to dozens of other Civil War–related sites, including the National Park Service Home Page (which includes separate pages for 22 Civil War battlefield sites, parks, and memorials), the United States Civil War Center, the Library of Congress American Memory Page, and the American Battlefield Protection Program.

The following books may also be of interest:

- *Battle Cry of Freedom: The Civil War Era* by James M. McPherson (Ballantine Books)
- *The American Heritage Picture History of the Civil War* by Bruce Catton (American Heritage/Wings Books)
- *A Stillness at Appomattox* by Bruce Catton (Pocket Books)
- *The Life of Johnny Reb: The Common Soldier of the Confederacy* by Bell Irvin Wiley (Louisiana State University Press)
- *The Life of Billy Yank: The Common Soldier of the Union* by Bell Irvin Wiley (Louisiana State University Press)
- *Divided We Fought: A Pictorial History of the Civil War, 1861–1865*, edited by David Donald (The MacMillan Company)
- *Annals of the War* (The Blue & Grey Press)
- *The Civil War* by Robert Paul Jordan (National Geographic Society)
- *The Civil War Almanac* John Bowman, executive editor (World Almanac Publications)
- *The Civil War and Reconstruction: An Eyewitness History* by Joe H. Kirchberger (Facts on File)
- *Don't Know Much about the Civil War* by Kenneth C. Davis (William Morrow & Company)
- *The Negro's Civil War* by James M. McPherson (Ballantine Books)
- *Mr. Lincoln's Camera Man: Mathew B. Brady* by Roy Meredith (Dover Publications)

Many of these books are, sadly, out of print, but they and a wealth of other volumes on the Civil War can be found in almost any used bookstore, especially one with an extensive history section. Most major bookstores also feature large Civil War sections.

Appendix C
A Comprehensive List of
National Civil War Sites and Memorials

The National Park Service maintains numerous Civil War battlefields, sites, and memorials, all of which are available to the general public. Most offer a variety of exhibits, activities, and anniversary/seasonal programs. Call the individual sites for complete visitor information or visit the National Park Service Web site at *www.nps.gov*.

Andersonville National Historic Site, Andersonville, Georgia. Phone: 912-924-0343. Operating hours: Park grounds—daily 8 A.M. to 5 P.M.; National Prisoner of War Museum/ Visitor Center—daily 8:30 a.m. to 5 p.m. Grounds only are open Christmas Day and New Year's Day. Admission: Free. A driving tour audiocassette is available for a $1 rental fee.

☆☆☆

Antietam National Battlefield, Sharpsburg, Maryland. Phone: 301-432-5124 (Programs and Information); 301-432-7672 (Superintendent and Administration). Operating hours: Summer 8:30 A.M. to 6 P.M. daily; winter 8:30 A.M. to 5 P.M. daily. Closed Thanksgiving, Christmas Day, and New Year's Day. Admission: $2 per adult, $4 per family. Children 16 and under are admitted free.

☆☆☆

Appomattox Court House National Historic Park, Appomattox, Virginia. Phone: 804-352-8987. Operating Hours: The Visitor Center is open daily in winter, 8:30 A.M. to 5 P.M., and summer, 9 A.M. to 5:30 P.M. The Visitor Center is closed on federal holidays, November–February. Admission: The entrance fee is on a seasonal schedule based on services offered. From Memorial Day until Labor Day, the National Park offers a full schedule of daily programs, including Living History, ranger talks, and audiovisual programs and charges $4 per person, or a $10 maximum per vehicle. Children 16 and younger are admitted free. During the off-season, only audiovisual programs are available, and fees are $2 per person, or $5 maximum per vehicle.

☆☆☆

Brices Crossroads National Battlefield Site, Baldwyn, Mississippi. Phone: 800-305-7417 or 662-680-4025. Operating hours: The Natchez Trace Parkway—daily during daylight hours; the Brices Cross Roads National Battlefield and Visitor Center—Tuesday–Saturday 9 A.M. to 5 P.M., Sunday 12:30 P.M. to 5 P.M. Admission: The Natchez Trace Parkway is free. Admission to the Visitor/Interpretive Center is $2 for adults, $1 for children.

☆☆☆

Chickamauga and Chattanooga National Military Park, Fort Oglethorpe, Georgia, and Chattanooga, Tennessee. Phone: 706-866-9241. Operating hours: Visitors Center—summer 8 A.M. to 5:45 P.M. daily; winter 8 A.M. to 4:45 P.M. daily. Closed Christmas Day. The Cravens House—open summer 9 A.M. to 5 P.M. daily; weekends, spring, and autumn 9 A.M. to 4 P.M. Check with the Point Park Visitors Center (423-821-7786) for current schedules. Admission: $2 for ages 18 to 61 for tours of the Cravens House. The Chickamauga Battlefield Visitor Center offers a 26-minute multimedia presentation. Admission is $1.50 for visitors 6 to 16 and 62 and older, and $3 for visitors 17 to 61. Point Park at Lookout Mountain has instituted a $2 per day user fee.

☆☆☆

Fort Donelson National Battlefield, Dover, Tennessee. Phone: 931-232-5348 (Administration); 931-232-5706 (Interpretive

Services). Operating hours: Visitor Center—daily 8 A.M. to 4:30 P.M., closed Christmas Day. Dover Hotel (Surrender House)—June–September, noon to 4 p.m., closed October–May. Admission: Free.

☆☆☆

Fort Pulaski National Monument, Savannah, Georgia. Phone: 912-786-5787. Operating hours: 8:30 A.M. to 5:15 P.M. daily; closed Christmas Day. Hours may be extended in the summer—call for information. Admission: Park entrance fee is $2 per person age 17 and older, or $4 maximum per immediate family. A 17-minute film, *The Battle for Fort Pulaski*, is shown on demand in the Visitor Center.

☆☆☆

Fort Sumter National Monument, Sullivan's Island, South Carolina. Phone: 843-883-3123. Operating hours: 10 A.M. to 5:30 P.M. daily April–Labor Day; 10 A.M. to 4 P.M. September–November and March. Closed Christmas Day. Hours vary so call for information. Admission: Concession fee for the boat ride is $10.50, the fee for children under 12 is $5.50, children under 6 are admitted free. This fee is subject to change. For more information, call Fort Sumter Tours at 843-772-2628. A history tape is played during the tour boat ride to Fort Sumter.

☆ ☆ ☆

Frederick Douglass National Historic Site, Washington, D.C. Phone: 202-426-5961. Operating hours: Summer 9 A.M. to 5 P.M. daily; fall and winter 9 A.M. to 4 P.M. daily. Closed Thanksgiving, Christmas Day, and New Year's Day. Admission: Home tours are $3 for adults and children 6 and older, $1.50 for seniors 62 and older, children under 6 are admitted free.

☆ ☆ ☆

Fredericksburg and Spotsylvania National Military Park, Fredericksburg, Virginia. Phone: Fredericksburg Battlefield Visitor Center 540-373-6122, Chancellorsville

Visitor Center 540-786-2880, Chatham Manor 540-654-5121, Jackson Shrine 804-633-6076. Operating hours: Grounds are open from sunrise to sunset. Fredericksburg Battlefield Visitor Center and Chancellorsville Visitor Center—9 A.M. to 5 P.M., with extended hours in the summer and weekends in the spring and fall. Chatham Manor—9 A.M. to 5 P.M. year round. Jackson Shrine—daily in the summer, Friday–Tuesday in the spring and fall, Saturday–Monday in the winter. Call the park for operating hours on the day of your visit. Closed Christmas Day and New Year's Day. Admission: $3 entrance fee (good for one week). An annual park pass is $20.

☆ ☆ ☆

Gettysburg National Military Park, Gettysburg, Pennsylvania. Phone: 717-334-1124. Operating hours: Park grounds and roads—daily 6 A.M. to 10 p.m. Visitor Center—daily 8 A.M. to 5 P.M., summer 8 A.M. to 6 P.M. Contact the park for exact dates and times. The Cyclorama Center is open daily 9 A.M. to 5 P.M. Buildings are closed Thanksgiving, Christmas Day, and New Year's Day. The National Cemetery is open at dawn and closes at sunset. Admission: The park is free. Admission for the Electric Map and Cyclorama program is $3 for adults 17 and older, $2 for children 6 to 16, $2.50 for seniors 62 and older. Children under 6 are admitted free. Group rates are available at $2.50 per adult.

☆ ☆ ☆

Harpers Ferry National Historic Park, Harpers Ferry, West Virginia. Phone: 304-535-6298. Operating hours: Summer 8 A.M. to

6 P.M. daily; winter 8 A.M. to 5 P.M. daily. Closed Christmas Day. Admission: A three-day entrance pass is $5 per vehicle or $3 per person (cyclists and walk-ins). Commercial tour fees are available upon request. Call 304-535-6029 for information on seasonal programs and exhibits.

☆☆☆

Kennesaw Mountain National Battlefield Park, Kennesaw, Georgia. Phone: 770-427-4686. Operating hours: 8:30 A.M. to 5 P.M. daily, with some extended hours in the summer—call for specifics. Closed Christmas Day. Admission: Free. The Visitor Center contains a small exhibit area with Civil War uniforms, guns, cannons, and a medical kit. A 10-minute historical slide program is also provided.

☆☆☆

Lincoln Boyhood National Memorial, Lincoln City, Indiana. Phone: 812-937-4541. Operating hours: Summer 8 A.M. to 6 P.M. daily; winter 8 A.M. to 5 P.M. daily. Closed Thanksgiving, Christmas Day, and New Year's Day. Admission: $2 per person age 17 and older, or $4 maximum per family. (The entrance fee is good for seven days after the date of purchase.) The Memorial Visitor Center features a museum and two memorial halls: the Abraham Lincoln Hall and the Nancy Hanks Lincoln Hall. Exhibits focus on the story of the Lincolns as pioneers in the Indiana wilderness.

☆☆☆

Lincoln Home National Historic Site, Springfield, Illinois. Phone: 217-492-4241, ext. 221 (Visitor Center). Operating hours: Daily 8:30 A.M. to 5 P.M., with extended spring, summer, and fall hours. Closed Thanksgiving, Christmas Day, and New Year's Day. Free ranger-conducted tours of the Lincoln Home occur daily, with the last tour beginning a half hour before closing. Admission: There is no admission fee to the Lincoln Home National Historic Site, but a free tour ticket is required to tour the Lincoln Home. Tickets are distributed at the Visitor Center on a first-come, first-serve basis the day of the tour.

☆☆☆

Manassas National Battlefield Park, Manassas, Virginia. Phone: 703-754-1861 (Headquarters), 703-361-1339 (Visitor Center). Operating hours: Park—daily, sunrise to sunset; Visitor Center—daily 8:30 A.M. to 5 P.M. Closed Thanksgiving and Christmas Day. Admission: $2 per person 17 and older (good for three days). An annual park pass is available for $15. Guided tours and other programs are scheduled on a regular basis during the summer season and on the weekends during the remainder of the year. Call for details. A 13-minute orientation slide program is shown in the Visitor Center on the hour and the half hour.

☆☆☆

Monocacy National Battlefield, Frederick, Maryland. Phone: 301-662-3515. Operating hours: Gambrill Mill Visitor Center—daily April 1–October 31 from 8 A.M. to 4:30 P.M. (extended to 5:30 P.M. on weekends, Memorial Day–Labor Day). Open Wednesday–Sunday, November 1–March 31, from 8 A.M. to 4:30 P.M. Closed Thanksgiving, Christmas Day, and New Year's Day. Admission: Free.

☆☆☆

Pea Ridge National Military Park, Pea Ridge, Arkansas. Phone: 501-451-8122. Operating hours: 8 A.M. to 5 P.M. daily. Closed Thanksgiving, Christmas Day, and New Year's Day. The 7-mile tour road is open from 8 A.M. to 4:30 P.M. The park is subject to closure during snowy or icy conditions. Admission: $2 for adults 17 to 61 or $4 maximum per car. Park headquarters houses a Visitor Center and museum.

☆☆☆

Petersburg National Battlefield, Petersburg, Virginia. Phone: 804-732-3531. Operating hours: Visitor Center and museum—8 A.M. to 5 P.M. daily, with extended summer hours. Closed Christmas Day and New Year's Day. The Park Tour Road closes at dusk. Admission: $3 per person or $5 maximum per vehicle, September–May; $5 per person or $10 maximum per vehicle, June–August at the Main Unit. This also covers the City Point Manor entry. City Point grounds are free. There is a $1 per person fee to enter Appomattox Manor. There is no fee at the Five Forks Unit. A 17-minute relief map presentation is offered in the Visitor Center on the hour and the half hour. Mid-June through mid-August, costumed interpreters demonstrate mortar and cannon firings and soldier life.

☆☆☆

Richmond National Battlefield Park, Richmond, Virginia. Phone: 804-226-1981. Operating hours: 9 A.M. to 5 P.M. daily. The Visitor Center is closed Thanksgiving, Christmas Day, and New Year's Day. Admission: Free. Activities include ranger-guided walking and van tours and a living history program.

☆☆☆

Shiloh National Military Park, Shiloh, Tennessee. Phone: 901-689-5696 (Visitor Center). Operating hours: 8 A.M. to 5 P.M. daily. Closed Christmas Day. Admission: $2 per person, with a $4 maximum per family. The Visitor Center offers a historical film and museum exhibits from the Shiloh battlefield. Ranger interpretative programs are located on-site daily from Memorial Day through Labor Day.

☆☆☆

Stones River National Battlefield, Murfreesboro, Tennessee. Phone: 615-893-9501. Operating hours: 8 A.M. to 5 P.M. daily. Closed Christmas Day. Admission: Free. The Visitor Center offers a slide show and museum. On summer and occasional spring weekends, living history programs are presented.

Tupelo National Battlefield, Tupelo, Mississippi. Phone: 800-305-7417 or 662-680-4025. Operating hours: Call for details. Admission: Free. No site-specific parking.

Ulysses S. Grant National Historic Site, St. Louis, Missouri. Phone: 314-842-3298. Operating hours: 9 A.M. to 5 P.M. daily. Closed Thanksgiving, Christmas Day, and New Year's Day. Admission: Free. The site, also known as White Haven, holds five historic structures (main house, stone building, barn, chicken house, and ice house). A temporary Visitor Center with exhibits is located in the historic barn. Future restoration includes modern Visitor Center facilities in a fully restored barn.

Vicksburg National Military Park, Vicksburg, Mississippi. Phone: 601-636-0583 (Visitor Center); 601-636-2199 (Cairo Museum). Operating hours: Visitor Center—8 A.M. to 5 P.M. daily. Cairo Museum—8:30 A.M. to 5 P.M. November–March, and 9:30 A.M. to 6 P.M. April–October. Closed Christmas Day. Admission: $4 per vehicle, $2 per noncommercial bus passenger. An annual park pass is available for $10. The park features more than 1,300 monuments and markers; reconstructed trenches and earthworks; one antebellum structure; more than 125 emplaced cannon; the *USS Cairo*, a restored Union

gunboat; and the Vicksburg National Cemetery. Guided tours of the battlefield are available with licensed park guides. Availability information and reservations can be made by calling 601-636-0583, ext. 8028.

Wilson's Creek National Battlefield, Republic, Missouri. Phone: 417-732-2662. Operating hours: Visitor Center—8 A.M. to 5 P.M. daily; park hours—8 A.M. to 9 P.M. Memorial Day–Labor Day; 8 A.M. to 7 P.M. April 1–October 31; 8 A.M. to 5 P.M. November–March. Closed Christmas Day and New Year's Day. Admission: $2 per person or $4 maximum per vehicle. Children 16 and under are admitted free. An annual park pass is available for $10. The Visitor Center offers battle-related exhibits, a 13-minute historical video, and a 6-minute fiber-optic lighted map program illustrating battle tactics. A Civil War research library is available to visitors on an advanced reservation basis.

INDEX

We Have

EVERYTHING!

Everything® **After College Book**
$12.95, 1-55850-847-3

Everything® **American History Book**
$12.95, 1-58062-531-2

Everything® **Angels Book**
$12.95, 1-58062-398-0

Everything® **Anti-Aging Book**
$12.95, 1-58062-565-7

Everything® **Astrology Book**
$12.95, 1-58062-062-0

Everything® **Baby Names Book**
$12.95, 1-55850-655-1

Everything® **Baby Shower Book**
$12.95, 1-58062-305-0

Everything® **Baby's First Food Book**
$12.95, 1-58062-512-6

Everything® **Baby's First Year Book**
$12.95, 1-58062-581-9

Everything® **Barbeque Cookbook**
$12.95, 1-58062-316-6

Everything® **Bartender's Book**
$9.95, 1-55850-536-9

Everything® **Bedtime Story Book**
$12.95, 1-58062-147-3

Everything® **Bicycle Book**
$12.00, 1-55850-706-X

Everything® **Build Your Own Home Page**
$12.95, 1-58062-339-5

Everything® **Business Planning Book**
$12.95, 1-58062-491-X

Everything® **Casino Gambling Book**
$12.95, 1-55850-762-0

Everything® **Cat Book**
$12.95, 1-55850-710-8

Everything® **Chocolate Cookbook**
$12.95, 1-58062-405-7

Everything® **Christmas Book**
$15.00, 1-55850-697-7

Everything® **Civil War Book**
$12.95, 1-58062-366-2

Everything® **College Survival Book**
$12.95, 1-55850-720-5

Everything® **Computer Book**
$12.95, 1-58062-401-4

Everything® **Cookbook**
$14.95, 1-58062-400-6

Everything® **Cover Letter Book**
$12.95, 1-58062-312-3

Everything® **Crossword and Puzzle Book**
$12.95, 1-55850-764-7

Everything® **Dating Book**
$12.95, 1-58062-185-6

Everything® **Dessert Book**
$12.95, 1-55850-717-5

Everything® **Digital Photography Book**
$12.95, 1-58062-574-6

Everything® **Dog Book**
$12.95, 1-58062-144-9

Everything® **Dreams Book**
$12.95, 1-55850-806-6

Everything® **Etiquette Book**
$12.95, 1-55850-807-4

Everything® **Fairy Tales Book**
$12.95, 1-58062-546-0

Everything® **Family Tree Book**
$12.95, 1-55850-763-9

Everything® **Fly-Fishing Book**
$12.95, 1-58062-148-1

Everything® **Games Book**
$12.95, 1-55850-643-8

Everything® **Get-A-Job Book**
$12.95, 1-58062-223-2

Everything® **Get Published Book**
$12.95, 1-58062-315-8

Everything® **Get Ready for Baby Book**
$12.95, 1-55850-844-9

Everything® **Ghost Book**
$12.95, 1-58062-533-9

Everything® **Golf Book**
$12.95, 1-55850-814-7

Everything® **Grammar and Style Book**
$12.95, 1-58062-573-8

Everything® **Guide to Las Vegas**
$12.95, 1-58062-438-3

Everything® **Guide to New York City**
$12.95, 1-58062-314-X

Everything® **Guide to Walt Disney World®, Universal Studios®, and Greater Orlando, 2nd Edition**
$12.95, 1-58062-404-9

Everything® **Guide to Washington, D.C.**
$12.95, 1-58062-313-1

Everything® **Guitar Book**
$12.95, 1-58062-555-X

Everything® **Herbal Remedies Book**
$12.95, 1-58062-331-X

Everything® **Home-Based Business Book**
$12.95, 1-58062-364-6

Everything® **Homebuying Book**
$12.95, 1-58062-074-4

Everything® **Homeselling Book**
$12.95, 1-58062-304-2

For more information, or to order, call 800-872-5627
or visit everything.com
Adams Media Corporation, 57 Littlefield Street, Avon, MA 02322

Available wherever books are sold!
Visit us at everything.com

Everything® **Home Improvement Book**
$12.95, 1-55850-718-3

Everything® **Horse Book**
$12.95, 1-58062-564-9

Everything® **Hot Careers Book**
$12.95, 1-58062-486-3

Everything® **Internet Book**
$12.95, 1-58062-073-6

Everything® **Investing Book**
$12.95, 1-58062-149-X

Everything® **Jewish Wedding Book**
$12.95, 1-55850-801-5

Everything® **Job Interviews Book**
$12.95, 1-58062-493-6

Everything® **Lawn Care Book**
$12.95, 1-58062-487-1

Everything® **Leadership Book**
$12.95, 1-58062-513-4

Everything® **Learning Spanish Book**
$12.95, 1-58062-575-4

Everything® **Low-Fat High-Flavor Cookbook**
$12.95, 1-55850-802-3

Everything® **Magic Book**
$12.95, 1-58062-418-9

Everything® **Managing People Book**
$12.95, 1-58062-577-0

Everything® **Microsoft® Word 2000 Book**
$12.95, 1-58062-306-9

Everything® **Money Book**
$12.95, 1-58062-145-7

Everything® **Mother Goose Book**
$12.95, 1-58062-490-1

Everything® **Mutual Funds Book**
$12.95, 1-58062-419-7

Everything® **One-Pot Cookbook**
$12.95, 1-58062-186-4

Everything® **Online Business Book**
$12.95, 1-58062-320-4

Everything® **Online Genealogy Book**
$12.95, 1-58062-402-2

Everything® **Online Investing Book**
$12.95, 1-58062-338-7

Everything® **Online Job Search Book**
$12.95, 1-58062-365-4

Everything® **Pasta Book**
$12.95, 1-55850-719-1

Everything® **Pregnancy Book**
$12.95, 1-58062-146-5

Everything® **Pregnancy Organizer**
$15.00, 1-58062-336-0

Everything® **Project Management Book**
$12.95, 1-58062-583-5

Everything® **Puppy Book**
$12.95, 1-58062-576-2

Everything® **Quick Meals Cookbook**
$12.95, 1-58062-488-X

Everything® **Resume Book**
$12.95, 1-58062-311-5

Everything® **Romance Book**
$12.95, 1-58062-566-5

Everything® **Sailing Book**
$12.95, 1-58062-187-2

Everything® **Saints Book**
$12.95, 1-58062-534-7

Everything® **Selling Book**
$12.95, 1-58062-319-0

Everything® **Spells and Charms Book**
$12.95, 1-58062-532-0

Everything® **Stress Management Book**
$12.95, 1-58062-578-9

Everything® **Study Book**
$12.95, 1-55850-615-2

Everything® **Tall Tales, Legends, and Outrageous Lies Book**
$12.95, 1-58062-514-2

Everything® **Tarot Book**
$12.95, 1-58062-191-0

Everything® **Time Management Book**
$12.95, 1-58062-492-8

Everything® **Toasts Book**
$12.95, 1-58062-189-9

Everything® **Total Fitness Book**
$12.95, 1-58062-318-2

Everything® **Trivia Book**
$12.95, 1-58062-143-0

Everything® **Tropical Fish Book**
$12.95, 1-58062-343-3

Everything® **Vitamins, Minerals, and Nutritional Supplements Book**
$12.95, 1-58062-496-0

Everything® **Wedding Book, 2nd Edition**
$12.95, 1-58062-190-2

Everything® **Wedding Checklist**
$7.95, 1-58062-456-1

Everything® **Wedding Etiquette Book**
$7.95, 1-58062-454-5

Everything® **Wedding Organizer**
$15.00, 1-55850-828-7

Everything® **Wedding Shower Book**
$7.95, 1-58062-188-0

Everything® **Wedding Vows Book**
$7.95, 1-58062-455-3

Everything® **Wine Book**
$12.95, 1-55850-808-2

Everything® **World War II Book**
$12.95, 1-58062-572-X

Everything® is a registered trademark of Adams Media Corporation.

For more information, or to order, call 800-872-5627
or visit everything.com
Adams Media Corporation, 57 Littlefield Street, Avon, MA 02322

OTHER EVERYTHING® BOOKS BY ADAMS MEDIA CORPORATION

EVERYTHING®

Trade paperback, $12.95
1-58062-338-7, 336 pages

The Everything® Online Investing Book

by Harry Domash

Buy, sell, trade, research, and make money investing online! The Internet gives you the tools to be your own stock market expert. From finding stocks and mutual funds to placing trades, keeping up with the news, and tracking your investments, you can uncover all kinds of investing information with just the click of a mouse. This one resource is not only a map of the world of Internet finance, it also tells you the specific how-to information you need to make profitable investments.

The Everything® Golf Book

by Rich Mintzer & Peter Grossman

Packed with information about the game of golf, its rich history, the great players and outstanding personalities, tours and tournaments, proper etiquette, as well as anecdotes, trivia and jokes, *The Everything® Golf Book* really does have it all! Whether you are an avid player or an enthusiastic spectator, you'll find something new for you, from helpful hints and techniques to lists of public and private golf courses in the United States. From bunker shots to golfing buddy movies, this one volume highlights everything you need to know to thoroughly enjoy the game of golf.

Trade paperback, $12.95
1-55850-814-7, 336 pages

See the entire Everything® series at everything.com

Available Wherever Books Are Sold

For more information, or to order, call 800-872-5627
or visit adamsmedia.com

Adams Media Corporation, 57 Littlefield Street, Avon, MA 02322. U.S.A.